D0844777

WITHDRAWN

Alexander of Aphrodisias
Ethical Problems

VILLA JULIE COLLEGE LIBRARY
STEVENSON, MD 21153

Alexander of Aphrodisias

Ethical Problems

Translated by

R. W. Sharples

Cornell University Press

Ithaca, New York

© 1990 by R.W. Sharples

All rights reserved. Except for brief
quotations in a review, this book, or parts
thereof, must not be reproduced in any form
without permission in writing from the publisher.
For information address Cornell University Press.
124 Roberts Place, Ithaca, New York 14850.

First published 1990 Cornell University Press.

Library of Congress Cataloging-in-Publication Data

Alexander, of Aphrodisias.
  [Essays. English. Selections]
  Ethical problems / Alexander of Aphrodisias : translated by
R.W. Sharples.
     p. cm. — (Ancient commentators on Aristotle)
  Includes bibliographical references.
  ISBN 0-8014-2267-1
  III. Series.
  B491.E7A44 1989 1990
  171'.3—dc20   89-39043

33.25

Printed in Great Britain

61719

Contents

In memoriam
William Arthur Sharples
13 June 1917 – 27 September 1988

Introduction

Alexander and the *Ethical Problems*

These *Ethical Problems* attributed to Alexander of Aphrodisias have never before, to my knowledge, been translated into English or into any other modern language. They deserve our attention for a number of reasons. Like the other minor works attributed to Alexander, they have their apparent origin in discussion and debate of Aristotle's works and thought by Alexander himself and his associates or pupils. They thus throw light, even if a dimmer and more fitful light than we might wish, on the functioning of a philosophical 'school' in the early years of the third century AD;[1] and, in their concern to remove apparent contradictions and anomalies, they exemplify an aspect of the process by which Aristotle's thought was, over the centuries, organised and formulated into the doctrine of Aristotelianism. The issues with which these *Problems* deal derive from Aristotle's *Nicomachean Ethics*, perhaps the work of ancient philosophy most widely studied today, at least in Anglo-Saxon countries, among those whose concern with philosophy is not primarily historical;[2] and some of these issues are not without direct relevance to public life and the conduct of politics in the last decades of the twentieth century – such as the attack on the demand for usefulness in everything in *Problem* 20, or the assertion of the importance of political community (*koinônia*) at the end of *Problem* 24.

The extant Greek commentaries on Aristotle's *Nicomachean Ethics* that can be reliably dated are either very early (second century AD) or very late (twelfth to fourteenth centuries). There is no commentary by any of the greatest commentators from the period 200 to 600 AD. But the present collection is the next nearest thing. The problems it contains reflect the work of the greatest exponent of Aristotelianism, and they address themselves closely to some

---

[1] I have endeavoured to say more about the evidence the minor works attributed to Alexander can give us for the functioning of his 'school' in Sharples (1989). (For works cited by author's name and date only, see the Bibliography, p. 89.)

[2] It is not indeed possible to study the history of philosophy without engaging with philosophical issues, consciously or unconsciously; and, conversely, philosophising is likely to be better philosophising if it takes account of earlier discussions of the same and similar problems. But there can still be a difference of emphasis between an approach that is primarily historical and one that is not.

portions of Aristotle's text, although in a problematic rather than an expository style.

Despite their focus on Aristotle, these *Problems* are often couched in the language of the Hellenistic philosophy that had intervened since his time.[3] This is not something that is peculiar to Alexander and his associates; by the Imperial period many terms that originally had a technical sense in the usage of a particular school of philosophy had come to be used in a more general way by members of many different schools. The *Ethical Problems* also show how a master of the Aristotelian school, or his pupils, would answer various theses of Stoic or Epicurean moral philosophy. They *may* also provide a glimpse of the arguments used by the Stoics or Epicureans for these theses (cf., for example, *Problem* 3, on the Stoic thesis that there is no intermediate state between virtue and vice); but it is important to remember that the discussion is carried on in the context of *Aristotelian* philosophy, and that arguments raising difficulties for Aristotelian positions might well be devised in the context of such discussions by Alexander himself, by his pupils, or by earlier Peripatetic tradition. Even where such difficulties are formulated in consciousness of Stoic or Epicurean positions, it does not follow that the *arguments* themselves represent Stoic or Epicurean ones, or that they would have been accepted by members of those schools.[4]

Alexander of Aphrodisias, known by later generations as *the* commentator on Aristotle,[5] was appointed by the emperors as a public teacher of Aristotelian philosophy at some time between 198 and 209 AD.[6] As a public teacher it is likely that he had, in some sense, a school; and among the works attributed to him there survive a considerable number of short texts, some of which seem to be related in various ways to his teaching activities.[7]

Some of these texts survive in collections apparently made in antiquity. Three books of these collected discussions are entitled *phusikai skholikai aporiai kai luseis*, 'School-discussion problems and solutions on nature' (often cited in modern literature as Alexander's *Quaestiones*); a fourth is titled 'Problems on Ethics' but

---

[3] cf. Todd (1976) 27-8; and below, n. 49 to *P. Eth.* 5; n. 100 to *P. Eth.* 9; n. 162 to *P. Eth.* 18; n. 170 to *P. Eth.* 19; n. 220 to *P. Eth.* 25; n. 253 to *P. Eth.* 27; n. 282 to *P. Eth.* 29.

[4] On Alexander's developing in purely Aristotelian contexts of controversies connected with the doctrines of other schools cf. Todd (1976) 75-88; and on his constructing of objections purely in order to argue against them cf. R.W. Sharples, *Alexander of Aphrodisias On Fate*, London 1983, 159-60 and 176-7. Cf. also n. 138 to *P. Eth.* 14; n. 162 to *P. Eth.* 18; n. 240 to *P. Eth.* 27.

[5] cf. Simplicius *in Phys.* 707,33; 1170,2; 1176,32; Philoponus *in An. Pr.* 136,20.

[6] cf. Todd (1976) 1 n. 3.

[7] Surveys of these may be found at Bruns (1982) v-xiv; Moraux (1942) 19-28; Sharples (1987) 1189-95.

sub-titled, no doubt in imitation of the preceding three books when it was united with them,[8] *skholikai êthikai aporiai kai luseis*, 'School-discussion problems and solutions on ethics'. A further collection was transmitted as the second book of Alexander's treatise *On the Soul*, and labelled *mantissa* or 'makeweight' by the Berlin editor Bruns. Other texts essentially similar to those in these collections survive, some in Greek[9] and some only in Arabic;[10] and there is evidence that there were other collections now lost.[11] The circumstances in which these collections were put together are unclear; it was not always expertly done, and while some of the titles attached to particular pieces seem to preserve valuable additional information, others are inept or unhelpful.[12] (In the *Ethical Problems* themselves the compiler failed to realise that *Problem* 26 was simply a repetition of the latter part of *Problem* 23; it is not therefore translated here.) Nor is it clear at what date the collections were assembled.[13] Sometimes the views expressed in a particular text are so different from those in other works by Alexander that it is difficult to believe that they are those of Alexander himself (though as it happens there are no very clear examples of this in the *Ethical Problems*); more often there are no very clear reasons to suppose a text is not by Alexander himself, but equally no way of proving conclusively that it is. In the notes I have sometimes for the sake of convenience referred to the author of a particular text as 'Alexander', without thereby intending to express a definite view as to its authenticity.

In addition to (i) 'problems' in the strict sense with their solutions, these minor works include[14] (ii) expositions (*exêgêseis*) of

[8] So Bruns (1892) v. The *Ethical Problems* are thus sometimes cited as '*Quaestiones* book 4', a title that has no MSS authority. The *Ethical Problems* should be distinguished from the (spurious) *Medical Puzzles and Physical Problems* also attributed to Alexander and edited by J.L. Ideler, *Physici et Medici Graeci Minores*, Berlin 1841, and H. Usener, *Alexandri Aphrodisiensis quae feruntur Problematorum libri 3 et 4*, Berlin 1859. Cf. Sharples (1987) 1198.

[9] Notably the two edited by G. Vitelli, 'Due Frammenti di Alessandro di Afrodisia', in *Festschrift Theodor Gomperz*, Vienna 1902, 90-3. It is hoped to include these as an appendix to *Quaestiones* book 2 in the present series of translations.

[10] cf. Sharples (1987) 1192-4, and the modern secondary literature referred to, 1187.

[11] 'Scholia logica' are referred to in what may be a gloss at Alexander *in An. Pr.* 250,2; and an 'Explanation and summary of certain passages from (Aristotle's) *de Sensu*', which Moraux suggests may have been a similar collection, is referred to by a scholion on *Quaestio* 1.2. Cf. Moraux (1942) 24; Sharples (1987) 1196.

[12] cf. the discussion at Bruns (1892) xi.

[13] Alexander's commentary on the *de Sensu* cites not only the lost *de Anima* commentary (167,21) but also a section of the *mantissa* (*in Sens.* 31,29, citing *mantissa* 127-30; cf. P. Wendland, preface to *CAG* 3.1, v; P. Moraux in G.E.R. Lloyd and G.E.L. Owen (eds.), *Aristotle on Mind and the Senses*, Cambridge 1978, 297 n. 71.

[14] The following summary account (which is not exhaustive) of the various types of texts to be found among the minor works may be supplemented by the discussions in n. 5 above.

particularly problematic Aristotelian texts, (iii) short expositions of Aristotelian doctrine on a particular topic, and (iv) straightforward and sometimes tedious paraphrases of passages in Aristotle's writings; both (iii) and (iv) alike seem to be described as *epidromai* or 'summaries'. There are also (v) collections, one might almost say batteries, of arguments for a particular Aristotelian position.[15] It seems likely that (iii), (iv) and (v), in particular, reflect teaching activity; it is difficult in some cases to see why else they might have been written. Some of these texts may be Alexander's own expositions of particular topics, while some may be more in the nature of exercises by his students.[16]

Some of the short texts attributed to Alexander are clearly related either to his monographs[17] or to Aristotelian works on which he wrote full-scale commentaries. The *quaestiones* include a number of discussions of passages in Aristotle's *de Anima*, and Moraux pointed out that these actually follow the sequence of Aristotle's own treatise, though interspersed with other material in the collections as they now exist.[18] Where the *Ethical Problems* are concerned, however, the matter is less clear. Many of these texts are related explicitly or implicitly to particular sections of Aristotle's *Nicomachean Ethics*; but they do not follow the sequence of topics in that work[19] – indeed, there is no very clear principle of arrangement that can be discerned. Nor is it clear whether Alexander himself wrote a full-scale commentary on the *Ethics*.[20]

---

[15] As Bruns (1892) xii-xiii notes, these are characteristic of the *Mantissa* rather than of the *Quaestiones*; they also occur in the *Ethical Problems*. (*Quaestio* 2.28, however, approaches close to the type.)

[16] cf. Bruns (1892) ix. Different discussions of the same topic (*Problems* 2, 9 and 13; 7 and 16; 8 and 28) sometimes read 'almost like (answers to) exam questions set in successive years' (Professor Sorabji's description). In terms of modern analogies, though, one might also think of a philosopher writing an article in a learned journal to set forth what he thought was a better solution to a particular problem than that in some earlier article, without particularly wanting to engage in direct controversy with his predecessor; true though it is that *modern* conventions make this less common in an article than in a book. Cf. my discussion cited in n. 1 above, and n. 94 to *P. Eth.* 8 below.

[17] For example, the last four sections of the *Mantissa* (pp. 169-86) are linked by subject matter with Alexander's treatise *On Fate*. Cf. Moraux (1942) 24; and on the exact nature of the relation in the case of two of these sections cf. R.W. Sharples, 'Responsibility, chance and not-being (Alexander of Aphrodisias *mantissa* 169-72)', *Bulletin of the Institute of Classical Studies* 22 (1975) 37-63; id., 'Alexander of Aphrodisias' second treatment of fate? (*De anima libri mantissa* pp. 179-86 Bruns)', ibid. 27 (1980) 76-94.

[18] Moraux (1942) 23.

[19] cf. the Index of Passages Cited.

[20] That he did so is suggested by a reference to '*hupomnêmata* on the *Ethics*' at Alexander *in Top.* 187,9-10; but this is the only evidence. The reference might rather be to these *Problems* and especially to *Problem* 11 (q.v.); it must be admitted, though, that the term *hupomnêmata* is elsewhere applied by Alexander to commentaries. Cf.

The chief interests of the *Ethical Problems* are in the solution of difficulties in the application of logical distinctions to ethical subject-matter (for example, the way in which pleasure and distress are opposites) and in topics (such as responsibility for actions) which Alexander dealt with in independent treatises. Concern with logical distinctions in ethical contexts is not indeed foreign to Aristotle himself.[21] Madigan has drawn attention to the way in which these *Problems* go beyond Aristotle in introducing themes from Aristotelian physics into ethical contexts.[22] That they do so is in accordance with Alexander's concern to interpret one part of Aristotle's writings by another, the consequence of which is a tendency to establish, as far as possible, a unified Aristotelian system.[23]

Whether or not Alexander himself wrote anything on Aristotle's *Ethics* beyond these *Problems*, they do have a place in the series of ancient Greek and Byzantine works on Aristotelian ethics, and a brief comparison with some other works may be useful. The earliest works after the revival of interest in Aristotelianism in the first century BC, the summary of Aristotelian ethics by Arius Didymus – himself a Stoic[24] –, the treatise *On Virtues and Vices* falsely attributed to Aristotle, and the work *On Emotions* wrongly attributed to Andronicus[25] are essentially doxographical in nature,

---

R.W. Sharples, 'Ambiguity and opposition: Alexander of Aphrodisias, *Ethical Problems* 11', *Bulletin of the Institute of Classical Studies* 32 (1985) 109-16, at 113.

[21] cf. Sharples (cited in previous note) 113 n. 1.

[22] Madigan (1987) 1279: his examples include the pervasive use made of the theory of contrariety (on which cf. the Subject Index to the present translation); the use of the physical notion of mixture in *Problem* 28 to illustrate a point about the virtues, and the appeal to the order of the universe to argue that activity is superior to pleasure (*P. Eth.* 23 144,17ff.)

[23] cf. Sharples (1987) 1179-80.

[24] Arius' work is preserved in Stobaeus *Ecl.* 2.7 pp. 37-152 Wachsmuth; 116-52 is the specifically Aristotelian section, but there are also references to Aristotle's views in the thematically arranged introductory section at pp. 37-57. Giusta has argued not only that Arius' work has not been preserved in its original form, but also that it was as a whole arranged by arguments rather than by schools. Cf. H. von Arnim, *Arius von Didymus' Abriss der peripatetischen Ethik*, Sitzb. Wien 204 (1926) no. 3; M. Giusta, *I dossografi di etica*, Turin 1964-67, *passim* but especially vol. 1 pp. 58-62, and id., 'Ario Didimo e la diairesis dell'etica di Eudoro di Alessandria', *Atti dell' Accademia delle Scienze di Torino*, cl. di Scienze Morali etc., 120 (1986) 97-132; P. Moraux, *Der Aristotelismus bei den Griechen* 1, Berlin 1973, 305-418; W.W. Fortenbaugh (ed.), *On Stoic and Peripatetic Ethics: the Work of Arius Didymus*, New Brunswick 1983 (*Rutgers University Studies in Classical Humanities*, 1), especially 1-37 and 121-236; H.B. Gottschalk, 'Aristotelian philosophy in the Roman world', *Aufstieg und Niedergang der römischen Welt*, Part II 'Principat', vol. 36.2 'Philosophie und Wissenschaften', Berlin 1987, 1079-174, at 1125-29.

[25] cf. Moraux, cited in the previous note, at 138-41; Gottschalk, ibid., 1129-31. [Andronicus] *On Emotions* (or *On Passions*) is edited by A. Glibert-Thirry in *Corpus Latinum Commentariorum in Aristotelem Graecorum*, Suppl. 2, Leiden 1977. Gottschalk points out that the *last* chapter of this work does show a desire to relate

concerned to set out doctrine in a systematic way, rather than to
consider problems in the interpretation of Aristotle's own writings.
In this respect they may seem not unlike the first type of
Alexander's *epidromai* mentioned above: but Alexander's *epidro-
mai* show more concern to elucidate the *arguments* by which an
Aristotelian position is reached, and to do so by drawing on
Aristotelian texts. Nor do they show the overriding concern for
division and classification that is characteristic of Arius.[26]

The earliest surviving full-scale commentary on an Aristotelian
ethical treatise, and indeed the earliest surviving full-scale
commentary on *any* Aristotelian text, is the commentary on the
Nicomachean Ethics by Aspasius, from the first half of the second
century AD.[27] Later in the second century AD Adrastus of
Aphrodisias wrote a work on Theophrastus and on Aristotle's
Nicomachean Ethics which seems to have been not a full-scale
commentary, but rather an explanation of the historical and literary
allusions in Aristotle's treatise. Adrastus' work itself is now lost, but
material from it was incorporated into scholia on *Nicomachean
Ethics* 2-5; the material from Adrastus is more valuable than the
rest of the scholia.[28] These scholia were later incorporated into the

---

the lists of virtues and vices explicitly to Aristotle's principles as expressed in the
Aristotelian text.

[26] cf. A.A. Long, 'The diaeretic method and the purpose of Arius' doxography', in
Fortenbaugh (ed.), *On Stoic and Peripatetic Ethics* (above, n. 24) 15-37.

[27] Aspasius' commentary is published in *CAG* vol. 19 part 1. Cf. P. Mercken, *The
Greek Commentaries on the Nicomachean Ethics of Aristotle*, Leiden 1973 (*Corp. Lat.
Comm. in Arist. Graec.* 6.1) 28*-29*; P. Moraux, *Der Aristotelismus bei den Griechen*
2, Berlin 1984, 249-93; Gottschalk, cited in n. 24, 1156-8. Aspasius includes the
'common books' (*Nicomachean Ethics* 5-7 = *Eudemian Ethics* 4-6) in his treatment of
the *Nicomachean Ethics*, but seems to regard them as Eudemian, the original
Nicomachean books having been lost. A. Kenny, *The Aristotelian Ethics*, Oxford 1978,
29ff., argues that it was none the less Aspasius himself who was responsible both for
the placing of the common books in the *Nicomachean Ethics* and for the subsequent
tradition of treating the *Nicomachean Ethics* rather than the *Eudemian Ethics* as the
definitive Aristotelian work; but on the first point at least his conclusions have been
called into question (cf. Gottschalk, 1101 n. 112 and 1158 with n. 375). The *Ethical
Problems* follow the standard post-Aspasius pattern of concentrating on the
Nicomachean Ethics, including the 'common books'. (It is notable that there is
apparently no reference in the *Ethical Problems* to *EN* 8 and 9; friendship, the theme
of those books, is perhaps a somewhat self-contained topic.) Alexander was aware of
Aspasius' work in another area, noting the similarity between an aspect of Aspasius'
views on the motion of the heavens and those of his own teacher Herminus;
Simplicius *in Cael.* 430,32-431,11; cf. Moraux, op. cit., 240ff. and 361 n. 5.

[28] cf. Athenaeus, 15.673e; Mercken, cited in n. 27, 14*-22*, and also in ch. 18 of R.
Sorabji (ed.), *Aristotle Transformed: the ancient commentators and their influence*,
London 1989; Moraux, cited in n. 27, 324-30, and also in his *d'Aristote à Bessarion*,
Laval 1970, 24f.; and Gottschalk, cited in n. 24, at 1155 and n. 363. The date of
compilation of the scholia themselves is uncertain (Moraux, 324 and n. 115). Both
Mercken (in Sorabji, cited above) and Moraux (p. 327) favour a date late in the second
century AD, but Professor Sten Ebbesen has indicated doubts about so early a date.
Kenny, cited in n. 27, suggested (37 n. 3) that the scholia were themselves the work of

composite commentary on the *Nicomachean Ethics*, most of which now appears as volume 20 of *Commentaria in Aristotelem Graeca*; in addition to these the composite commentary contains the commentary of Aspasius on book 8 (in *CAG* vol. 19.1), commentaries by Michael of Ephesus (first half of the eleventh century) on books 5 (in addition to the scholia mentioned above; Michael's commentary is in *CAG* 22.3), 9, and 10, commentaries by Eustratius (*c.* 1100) on books 1 and 6, and anonymous scholia on book 7 which seem still later.[29] A paraphrase of the *Nicomachean Ethics* of little value is attributed, probably falsely, to an otherwise unknown Heliodorus of Prusa; it was composed at some time before the fourteenth century (the date of the earliest surviving manuscript).[30] The *Ethical Problems* would in any case be of interest as evidence for the thought of Alexander and his associates; the relative paucity of ancient commentary material on the *Ethics* increases their interest further.

The present translation

Something should be said here about the procedures followed in the present translation. I have endeavoured – with what success, the reader must judge – to produce a translation that is close to the original Greek while still being readable. One immediate difficulty is the length and complexity of sentences that is characteristic both of Alexander's own writings and of those attributed to him. The long periods found in these texts have here been broken up into more manageable units.

A second and greater difficulty is consistency in the translation of particular Greek words. The range of meanings of a word in one language does not correspond exactly to that of any one word in any other language. It is desirable to translate the same Greek word by the same English word as far as possible, in order to indicate – especially to the Greekless reader – that there is a single Greek word in question; and this applies especially in the case of texts like those with which we are here concerned, replete with technical terminology in the original language. But there is also something to be said for deliberately varying the English rendering of a single Greek term in a single context just in order to give a sense of its range of meanings, where an author is exploiting this range.

Adrastus, but the arguments against this of Gottschalk and of Ebbesen (in Sorabji, op. cit.) seem decisive.

[29] On the composite commentary, and in particular on the question of the identity of the compiler, cf. Mercken, cited in n. 27, 3*-14* and 22*-28*; also the discussions by Mercken and Ebbesen in chs 18 and 19 of Sorabji, cited in n. 28 above.

[30] On the question of authorship cf. Moraux, cited in n. 24, 136-8. This commentary is published in *CAG* vol. 19.2.

Translation of a single word in one language by a single word in another seems increasingly common as familiarity with the ancient languages declines; it may reflect the need for those who do not know the original language not to be misled, but it may have the effect of insulating us from even that degree of access to the thought-world of the *original* language that is still possible even through the medium of translation.[31] Comparison with the techniques adopted in Arabic translations from ancient Greek, or medieval and Renaissance translations of Greek or Arabic into Latin, is not irrelevant here.

Two examples may illustrate the point. *Aretê* in Greek means the 'excellence' of any thing or creature, but, at least from Aristotle onwards, it has a particular application to the moral *virtues* as the particular *excellences* of man. How then is one to translate the word in texts, like *Problems* 25 and 27 here – or Aristotle, *Nicomachean Ethics* 1 – that argue *from* excellence in general to virtue in particular? What I have in fact done here is to compromise – to use 'excellence' or 'virtue' as seems most appropriate in the context, and 'excellence or virtue' – which does *not* represent a double expression in the original – sufficiently often to bring out the connection in the argument between the two. Again, in rendering Alexander's discussions of voluntary and involuntary action, based on *Nicomachean Ethics* 3.1, I have generally used 'compulsion' rather than 'force' to render *bia*, coupled with ignorance as the two possible grounds for regarding an action as involuntary, for this generally gives more natural English and makes the argument easier to follow. But I have not for that reason felt obliged to translate *biazomenos* at *Problem* 12 133,5 by 'compelled' rather than by 'forced', even though – or perhaps *because* – the noun *bia* is translated by 'compulsion' in the immediate context; the use of both renderings in the *same* context, I would contend, far from misleading the reader, helps to make it clear what sort of compulsion is meant. All occurrences of key terms like *aretê* or *bia* and its cognate expressions have been listed in the Greek-English index, which should resolve any doubts over what Greek term is

---

[31] It is because of considerations like these that, in *Plato: Meno*, Warminster 1985, I translated *aporein* and *aporia* at one point by 'be perplexed' but at another by 'at a loss' in rendering 80A, and similarly in 84A. This has puzzled at least one reviewer; but 'at a loss' serves to bring out the connotations of poverty and powerlessness in the word, which are important (cf. the uses of *aporia* and *porizesthai* at 78c-e). Guthrie in *his* translation (*Plato: Protagoras and Meno*, Harmondsworth 1956) used both 'perplexed' and 'helplessness' in his translation of 80A. It might be thought that the wordplay characteristic of Plato is far removed from the prosaic and pedantic style of Alexander, but similar issues can in fact arise.

being translated at any particular point, and assist the reader who wishes to consider all the passages in which a particular Greek term is used.

A further difficulty arises from the different syntactical range of Greek and English forms. The Greek *haireton can* be translated just by 'to be chosen', the opposite of 'to be avoided'. Sometimes, however, 'worthy to be chosen' or 'deserving to be chosen' may seem to make the sense clearer and produce more natural English. However, while 'worthiness to be chosen' is more natural as a *noun* than 'deservedness to be chosen', for verbal expressions, 'deserves to be chosen' often seems more natural English than 'is worthy to be chosen'. Since the latter does not seem intolerable, I have indeed generally opted for 'worthiness' and 'is worthy' rather than 'deservedness' and 'deserves'; but this may still serve as an example of the type of difficulty that can arise. 'Choiceworthy' and 'choiceworthiness' I have avoided as philosophical jargon; it could be argued that Alexander's philosophical jargon in Greek should be translated by philosophical jargon in English, but it seems preferable to make his meaning as clear as possible.

In general, I have sought consistency within a given problem rather than between different problems with different subject-matter. Thus in *Problem* 1, where the question is whether life in itself is good or *haireton*, I have translated *haireton* by 'valuable', following a suggestion from Dr Kenny, and similarly in *Problem* 20; but in *Problems* 2, 6 and 7, where what is at issue is a distinction between pleasures that are *hairetai* and those that are to be avoided, 'to be chosen' seems the more appropriate rendering. To discuss whether life in itself is a thing 'to be chosen', or whether certain pleasures are 'valuable' or not, does not seem to fall naturally on the English ear. 'Choiceworthy' as a rendering for *haireton* might meet the need for a single translation in both contexts, but at the cost of not writing natural English in *either*. In *Problem* 1, *kakos* has been rendered by 'bad' rather than 'evil', for it is more natural to say that having a bad sea-voyage is bad than that having an evil voyage is evil;[32] but in *Problems* 5, 6, 7 and 16 'evil' has been used for *kakos* and 'bad' for *mokhthêros*, since this makes possible a less stilted rendering of discussion whether something is 'a good' or 'an evil'. For similar reasons, *einai* and *ousia* have been translated sometimes by 'being' and sometimes by 'essence'. The Index may help to clarify these and similar points. I have also sometimes translated the optative with *an* by a present or future indicative; the tentativeness of the potential form sometimes seems

---

[32] 'Bad' has also been used for *kakon* in *Problem* 9, where the question of whether or not people are aware that bad things are bad for them is at issue.

to be little more than a mannerism which it would be misleading to reproduce literally in English.[33]

The present translation is rather more heavily annotated than some other volumes in this series. This seemed desirable, since we are here concerned not with the continuous exposition of a single Aristotelian text, but with relatively short and self-contained sections of argument which stand in need of some indication of their context in ancient, and especially Aristotelian, ethical discussion generally. It should however be emphasised that a good acquaintance with Aristotle's *Nicomachean Ethics* will be a considerable help to the reader of many of these texts. Many points of contact between the *Ethical Problems* and the text of Aristotle have been indicated in the notes, but it would have overburdened them too much if every connection that could be made were explicitly spelled out; I hope though that the notes will provide sufficient pointers to enable comparisons to be pursued further.

The Notes on the Text list places where I have diverged from Bruns' text (see below, in the Bibliography); these places are indicated by an asterisk (*) in the translation. Where I have followed Bruns' text I have not generally noted the foundations on which it rests even where these are themselves conjectural, except in major cases where the interpretation is substantially affected or where there is real doubt. Since there has been relatively little discussion of the text of these *Problems* since Bruns' edition appeared, I have taken the opportunity to record in the Notes on the Text all subsequent conjectures known to me, even those I have not adopted; the resultant increase in length of the Notes is minimal.

Conclusion

In *Ethical Problem* 20 the author makes the comment 'The person who in every action and every [type of] learning requires what is useful, and does not think anything worth doing or learning which is not useful, removes the existence of anything which is good and valuable on its own account.' What is characteristic of human beings, as *Problem* 24 states, is speech, the power to communicate. But speech is of no use unless there are people who listen. Human nature itself, if it is to be fully realised, thus requires that we listen to what others are saying. Past generations, too, can speak to us through the written word; and we should listen to them too, not because it can give them pleasure (Aristotle disposes of that point in *Nicomachean Ethics* 1.11), and not because what they have to say may be useful to us (though it would be foolish to assume it cannot

---

[33] cf. M. Giusta, 'Ario Didimo e la Diairesis dell'Etica di Eudoro di Alessandria', above n. 24, at 98-9, with the references there.

be), but simply because to speak and to listen are important parts of what it is to be human. An enterprise like the present volume of translations, however, *does* need to be judged on the grounds of its usefulness – of the extent to which it makes it easier for us to listen to people who lived long ago, but were reading and reacting to the same works of Aristotle that we can still read now. Whether these translations will in fact be useful as an instrument to assist in further study of Aristotelian ethics and the history of Aristotelianism – which is a not inconsiderable part of the history of human thought – is for others to judge; I hope they will be found so.

I am particularly grateful to Dr Anthony Kenny, who read through a draft of the whole of the present translation and made many valuable suggestions, and to Professor Richard Sorabji, who made suggestions for material in the Introduction and for additional footnotes. My thanks go also to Professor Sorabji and his editorial assistants for their work on this volume, and to Professor Sorabji, my other colleagues and the Institute of Classical Studies for making the University of London such a congenial and helpful place in which to discuss and study the philosophy of the later periods of the ancient world. The responsibility for remaining errors in the present work is, of course, my own. And, as ever, my warmest thanks are due to my wife Grace and daughter Elizabeth for their support and tolerance.

University College London   R.W.S.
May 1989

Alexander of Aphrodisias
Ethical Problems
Translation

Alexander of Aphrodisias, *Ethical Problems* Book I 117,1
Summary of Alexander's ethical school-puzzles and solutions[1]

---

[1] Bruns suggests (p. v) that this subtitle was added for the sake of uniformity when this collection was united with the preceding *Quaestiones*. This seems likely enough, though his further inference that there was originally more than one book is at best uncertain; *biblion A* could mean 'one book' as well as 'Book One'. Some of the titles in this list of contents, as preserved in the manuscripts, differ slightly from those at the head of the actual chapters; I have preserved these differences in the translation at each place, without generally drawing attention to them in the notes.

[2] Added by Victorius; 'neither good nor bad', B[2]. Cf. n. 4 below.

[3] Added from the chapter title below.

is and what is not to be done.

118,1   16. How, if all distress is an evil, it is not also the case that all pleasure is a good.

17. Under which [class] of goods pleasure will fall, the honourable or the praiseworthy or the beneficial.

18. Why Aristotle said in the first [book] of the *Nicomachean Ethics* that those who locate the end in pleasure are most vulgar.

5

19. That pleasures are not the same in kind.

20. That one should not require usefulness in every action and every [type of] learning.

21. On shame.

10 22. That the virtues imply one another.

23. If, according to Aristotle, pleasure is unimpeded activity of a natural state, how will happiness too not be pleasure according to him?

24. How the virtues are worthy to be chosen on their own account.

25. Summary account of the discovery and establishment of the virtues.

15 26. That what is noble is not for the sake of pleasure, but pleasure for the sake of what is noble.

27. Why the moral virtues are means.

28. About whether virtue is a genus or a totality.

29. That vices too are in our control no less than virtues, which is shown through a passage from the third book of Aristotle's *Nicomachean Ethics*.

20 30. How justice will not come from injustice and injustice from justice, if opposites come to be from each other.

1. Difficulties [raised] against those who say that life is <not>[4] a good.[5]

If making a good voyage is good, and [making] a bad one bad, making a voyage [in itself] is neither good nor bad; and if living a good life is good, and living a bad one bad, [simply] living a life is

25 neither good nor bad.

– Or rather: it is not true that potentialities for opposites are [themselves] indifferent and intermediate. Every potentiality like

[4] 'is not a good' Spengel, 'is neither good nor bad' B[2], 'is a good' V. The first sentence does indeed present an argument for life being neutral rather than a good, countered in what follows, and the title *could* have been carelessly given – or carelessly 'emended' – by reference to the first sentence only.

[5] i.e. the Stoics. 118,23-6 and 119,23-6 form no. 3.165 of H. von Arnim, *Stoicorum Veterum Fragmenta*. The Stoics would not indeed regard life as *good*, for virtue alone was good for them; but they would regard it as *to be preferred*, *proêgmenon*, provided it was not bought at the expense of virtue. Cf. Diogenes Laertius 7.106 (*SVF* 3.127).

this is good and valuable[6] because it has as its goal the *better* of the things for which it is a potentiality; where there is potentiality, the worse [outcome] comes about through some mischance. All things like this that are brought about by art are brought about with a view to the better of the potential outcomes, and similarly with those that come about by nature. Voyaging was contrived by the art of navigation with a view to voyaging *well*, and sawing by carpentry with a view to sawing finely; and for this reason voyaging is valuable for the one and sawing for the other, because without them these [crafts] are not able to achieve the end set before them. For they judge the things subject [to them] not on the basis of what comes about in something by mischance, but on that of the things towards which their being and coming to be is primarily directed.[7]

And as it is with the things that are brought about by art, so it is in the case of those that come about by nature. For in these cases too, [that is] those where there is a potentiality for both [the better and the worse], nature's goal is what is better, and it is with a view to this that nature provides [the potentiality]. For to all the things which are not able to possess their proper perfection as soon as they are produced by nature, to these nature gives the potentiality for becoming perfect;[8] but it is impossible for something to have the potentiality for something if it does not also have that of its opposite. For this is how potentiality is different from actuality. For this reason potentialities are primarily for better things, but it is a necessary concomitant that they are also for the opposites of these.

Let us take it, then, that [the value of] each thing is judged on the basis of what is primary and that <with a view to*> which it exists. The potentiality for walking is not directed towards not walking, even if that which has the potentiality for [walking] is sometimes characterised by the privation of this;[9] and if walking is a thing that may be valued, so too in its own nature is having the potentiality for walking, even if it also involves having the potentiality for not

30

119,1

5

10

15

---

[6] Literally 'choiceworthy', *haireton*.

[7] More literally, 'but on that of the things with a view to which, primarily, they are and come to be.' That is, for example: sawing is one of the things subject to the craft of carpentry, and the carpenter judges its value (and judges whether to use a saw or a chisel in a particular case, one might add) in terms of its intended end, not on the basis that it might go wrong.

[8] Cf. below, 119,19-21; also *P. Eth.* 29 161,14-29, and *Fat.* 27 197,30-198,26.

[9] Presumably the case envisaged is that of a man who can (usually) walk but is temporarily lame (whereas a bush doesn't suffer the disadvantage of being lame since it was never meant to walk in the first place). If the reference was to the fact that some men are permanently lame while men in general can walk, it is not clear in what sense the lame man in question has the possibility of not walking; if on the other hand the reference was to a man who simply chose not to walk at a particular time, it would not be appropriate to speak of *privation*. On privation cf. Aristotle *Metaph.* 5.22.

walking. If however [walking] is not a thing that may be valued, neither is having the potentiality for walking.

Life, too, has in itself the potentiality for living either well or badly, and is given to us by nature with a view to [our] living *well*. For it is not possible for us to possess [the actuality of] living well as soon as

20   we come into existence; there is nothing perfect in what is incomplete, and everything is incomplete immediately after it comes into existence. [It follows, then, that life too] will be a thing to be valued with a view to the *best* of the things that can come about in us. For what is best, and the end [at which we aim], is living well, and this cannot come about without life [itself].

How is it not inconsistent to say that [life] is something to which we are endeared[10] by nature, and that we do everything with a view to

25   our own preservation, and simultaneously to deny that nature endears us to it as a *good*? That we are endeared to life as a good is clear both from [our] being very concerned about producing children, on the grounds that we will in a way exist in future through them, and also through [our] fearing everything we fear [all] the more because[11] we are apprehensive that it will cause our death.

30   That things which are intermediate are judged on the basis of potentiality for what is better is also clear from its being agreed that man is superior to the other living creatures, and this is because none of the others has the capacity for virtue.[12] The better thing that man has the capacity for is better than the valuable things that the other living creatures possess,[13] and this is why man is better. For if

35   intermediates were judged on the basis of what is worse as well, nothing would prevent us from saying that man was the worst of living creatures, because he has the capacity for the worst of [all] things, [namely] wickedness, or [at least] that he was no better than any of the other living creatures, since in all matters of choice and

120,1 avoidance he must follow the judgement of the good man*.[14]

---

[10] 'Endeared': *oikeiôsthai*, a technical term used in Stoicism in the context of the theory that we initially identify with our own physical constitution and its preservation, and thus with 'things according to nature' that eventually become the material for virtue in the wise man. On this and on the other principal application of the term, to identification with progressively widening social circles, cf. S.G. Pembroke, 'Oikeiosis', in A.A. Long (ed.), *Problems in Stoicism*, London 1971, 112-49, and discussions cited there.

[11] For *dioti* 'because' Schwartz suggested *hote* 'when'.

[12] cf. *Fat.* 27 198,6-8.

[13] Literally 'that come to be in them'; if the connection of *ginesthai* with birth were pressed, the point could be that man's capacity for virtue is superior to the natural endowments of the other creatures *even though* those are present at birth and man's capacity for virtue has to develop.

[14] This interpretation, deleting *haireton*, was suggested by Dr Kenny: see Notes on

2. That pleasures are not the same in kind.[15]

<That pleasures are not the same in kind>[16] may be shown first of
all from desire (*epithumia*). If every desire is an appetition (*orexis*)   5
for what is pleasant, and it is in this that its being consists, and it is
agreed that some desires are to be chosen[17] and others avoided, it is
clear that this difference in them does not come from anything other
than the pleasures on account of which they exist, because of [the
fact] that some of these [pleasures] are to be chosen and others
avoided. So pleasures too will differ from each other in the same way
as desires, if it is from the former that the differences in the latter,   10
too, [arise]. And indeed it is not possible for things which differ in
their own nature to be the same in kind as one another.

Secondly, from activities (*energeiai*). For since every pleasure
supervenes (*epi… ginetai*) on some activity, and there is an affinity
(*oikeiotês*) between pleasures and the activities on which they
supervene – for they are in a way their ends – it is clear that in this
way [the pleasures] too themselves would be differentiated in [a
way] corresponding to the activities. But of the activities, on which
pleasures supervene, some are to be chosen and others to be   15
avoided; so the pleasures, too, will have the same difference from
one another.[18] But if so, they are not the same in kind.

Moreover, if what desires and wants something and does not yet
possess it is further removed [from it] than what possesses it and is
associated with it, desire will be further removed from pleasure
than is the activity on which the pleasure [supervenes]; for the
former is a wanting of pleasure, but pleasure accompanies activity   20
and attends upon it. So, if pleasures are differentiated in [a way]
that corresponds to desires, much more will they be differentiated in
[a way] that corresponds to activities. But it has been agreed that of
the activities, on which pleasures [supervene], some are to be chosen

---

the Text. It does seem slightly weak to say that man (in general) is no better than
other living creatures because he needs to follow the judgement of a good *man*. If with
Bruns in his apparatus we instead retain *haireton* and insert *to* before it, the sense
would seem to be 'For in every matter of choice and avoidance what is preferred must
follow the judgement of what is excellent'; this summarises the point of the chapter as
a whole, but seems out of place, for a *reason* for saying that man would be no better
than other living creatures is expected.

[15] cf. below, *P. Eth.* 19; Aristotle *EN* 10.5, 1175a21ff.

[16] Repeated from the title by B and Spengel.

[17] *hairetos*: cf. n. 6 above and Introduction, p. 9.

[18] For the claim that pleasures are differentiated in a way that corresponds to the
activities on which they supervene cf. Aristotle *EN* 10.5, 1175a21ff.; *P. Eth.* 16
173,2ff.; 17 137,35; 19 139,23ff.

and others to be avoided.

That pleasures are proper to the activities on which they
supervene, and that they too themselves differ from one another in
25   kind in a similar way to the activities, and that their difference from
one another is not just because they supervene on different
activities,[19] is clear from the fact that the pleasure which
[supervenes] on one activity cannot supervene on another. For the
temperate (*sôphrôn*) man the activities of the profligate are not just
to be avoided, but also without pleasure, because the pleasure
accompanying them* is proper to the activities and is differentiated
30   in [a way] that corresponds to them. If this were not so, nothing
would prevent the activities being [things] to be *avoided* by [the
temperate], but nevertheless bringing pleasure to them too.

121,1   Moreover, the pleasures [that supervene] on some activities
hinder those that supervene on others;[20] at any rate, those who
enjoy pleasure from piping are not able, while they are listening to
the pipe, to enjoy the pleasures that supervene on, for example,
story-telling. So pleasures can destroy [other] pleasures. But if
5   pleasures can destroy [other] pleasures, they will not be the same in
kind, [since] they have the relation to one another that opposites do.

Those who are treated in different ways for the same conditions
acquire the same state of health, and nothing prevents a person
from having the same state of health through being treated in
different ways at different times; but it is not the same in the case of
10   activities and the pleasures which [supervene] upon them. For it is
not possible for the pleasure which supervenes on one activity also
to supervene on another; it is not possible for the pleasures in
temperate activities ever to supervene on profligate ones*.[21]

3. That there is some state intermediate between justice and injustice, and in general between virtue and wickedness.

That there is some state intermediate between justice and injustice,
15   and in general between virtue (*aretê*) and wickedness, which we call
a middle state. – If justice and injustice are dispositions according to
them,[22] and dispositions cannot be lost, a man would not become

---

[19] That is: it is not just a purely accidental difference as far as the pleasures are
concerned.

[20] cf. Aristotle *EN* 10.5, 1175b3; below, *P. Eth.* 17 137,28, 19 139,16ff.

[21] See Notes on the Text; the MSS have 'ever to supervene in the case of profligate
persons'. But the point is presumably that the temperate person will not find his own
peculiar pleasures – the only ones that he can feel, it is implied – in profligate acts: to
say that *profligate* people cannot take pleasure in temperate activities seems to follow
less well from the preceding clause ('For it is not possible ...').

[22] 'They' are the Stoics; for their belief that all who were not virtuous were *ipso
facto* wicked cf. *SVF* 3.657-70, and for their denial of a state intermediate between

just after being unjust, or unjust after being just. But some people do become just or unjust, not having been so before; so this will[23] come about [starting] from some other condition. But everything that comes to be does so either from [its] opposite or from something intermediate between the opposites. So, then, the just and the unjust man too come to be [so] either from the opposite or from what is intermediate.[24] They do not do so from the opposite, so they do so from what is intermediate; and the condition from which just and unjust men come to be [so] will be intermediate between justice and injustice. And the same argument applies to all virtue and wickedness.

They[25] may indeed say that vices are not dispositions or things that cannot be lost, and that nothing prevents some people changing from [being] unjust to [being] just, and in general from wickedness to virtue. But from what [condition] do people change to [being] *wicked*? If indeed [they said that] wickedness was in man's nature and all were born wicked, wickedness would be natural for men. But that of which the opposite is natural for something, is itself [26] *unnatural* for that thing; so justice and virtue would be unnatural for men. If this is absurd, [the alternative is that] the unjust man must *come to be* unjust, in the same way as the just man, too, [comes to be] <just>.[27] And the state from which the change to injustice [takes place] will be the middle one.

20

25

30

---

virtue and wickedness cf. *SVF* 3.536 (parts of our text, 121,14-17 and 24-6, and 121,32-122,4, are *SVF* 3.537). For virtues as dispositions (*diatheseis*) cf. *SVF* 3.104 and B. Inwood, *Ethics and Human Action in Early Stoicism*, Oxford 1985, 39. Some Stoics did indeed hold that *virtue* could not be lost once achieved (cf. *SVF* 3.237-8, 1.569; J.M. Rist, *Stoic Philosophy*, Cambridge 1969, 16), but it is most improbable that any Stoic would have asserted this for *wickedness* in general, as he would thereby be excluding any possibility of moral progress for the vast majority of mankind. As elsewhere in the texts ascribed to Alexander, our author exaggerates his opponents' position for the sake of his own argument. Because of this unexplained 'they' Bruns xiv regards this text as a fragment; but it is not clear how far the term 'fragment' is justified in connection with these short texts whose original context in the activity of Alexander or his pupils is not always clear. Certainly our text is not a fragment in the same sense as *Quaestiones* 2.21 or 3.14.

[23] The Greek has '*would* come about'. The tentative expression can be explained on the grounds that our author is arguing on the basis of the assumptions he attributes to his opponents. However, the texts attributed to Alexander often use tentative optatives where an indicative is more natural in English in any case. Cf. Introduction, n. 27.

[24] This issue is discussed from a rather different point of view in *Ethical Problem* 30 below.

[25] The Stoics; cf. n. 22 above.

[26] The Greek has 'The opposite to that of which the opposite is natural ... is itself unnatural'; the fact that *both* items are opposites (to each other) has caused the case to be overstated.

[27] Added by Spengel.

They may say that children are not yet rational,[28] and that for this reason they are not just nor yet unjust, because these are states 122,1 of a rational being. (But if these are [states] of a rational being, so too is the middle one; and for this reason the child, being irrational, is neither in [a state of] virtue nor [in one of] wickedness *nor* yet in the intermediate [state] between these, just as nothing else irrational is either.[29]) When [children] change to being rational, however, [they would say,] they all at once *are* wicked, rather than *becoming* so. But through this they would be admitting that 5 injustice and wickedness are natural for what is rational, if the change to being rational and to these is simultaneous, and the change to being rational is equivalent to that to being wicked; so [again] virtue [would be] unnatural for what is rational.

Moreover, in general, if there is a change from wickedness to virtue, they [must][30] either say that wickedness is easy to change and get rid of, or that it is stable and hard to change. But if it is easy 10 to change, why is the change from wickedness to the virtues not easy? If however it is stable and hard to change, it is clear that in the change from [wickedness] to virtue one must first have got rid of the quality that wickedness has of being stable and hard to change, seeing that it changed to virtue through learning and practice and not suddenly. But if it becomes easy to change first, and its being wickedness depends on its being *hard* to change, then when it is 15 easy to change it will no longer *be* wickedness. But it is not virtue either. How then will the person in such a condition not* be in some middle state – especially as the change to virtue comes about from this disposition?

Moreover, even if children are not yet rational, and for this reason do not possess either virtue or wickedness, yet, from the [very] fact that it is from being irrational in this way that they came to be 20 either rational or[31] wicked, they will[32] be in a middle state. For they are not irrational in the same way as the other [creatures]; for then they would not even be capable [of being] wicked or virtuous themselves. But if, while they do not possess either [quality] yet,

---

[28] The connection of thought is: the Stoics, who hold that there is no intermediate state between virtue and vice and all but a minority of adults are wicked, may try to argue that wickedness does not come from an intermediate state by arguing that *no* moral evaluation is applicable to children, and that as soon as any moral term applies it is wickedness that does so in every case, some few adults later achieving virtue.

[29] From 'But if these are states' to 'just as nothing else irrational is either' is a digression by our author; the consequence he draws about the middle state would not be acceptable to the Stoics themselves, since they do not recognise the existence of a middle state between virtue and wickedness at all. What is said here is however contradicted, as a statement of our author's real view, by 122,17ff. below.

[30] The Greek has just 'they *will* say', but this is clearly the sense.

[31] Literally 'both rational and wicked'

[32] Literally 'they would'; but see above, n. 23.

they are able to admit either of them, [then] they are not irrational in [the same] way [as the other creatures]. What is irrational but capable of being rational is different from what is not capable of it, and will be irrational in a different way; and it is not in this way that what is irrational in the proper sense [is so]. And the condition of what is irrational in this way[33] will by this fact alone be a middle   25
state, since it is from this* that it changes to either of the opposites; and it is potentially either of the extremes,[34] since it is nothing[35] in actuality. For in the case of the child too there is a certain state and condition, from which change to wickedness or to virtue [takes place]; and this is not present in any of the things which are called irrational in the proper and unqualified sense.

4. Solution of the difficulty which states that an instrument   30
has no opposite, that poverty is opposite to wealth, and that
therefore wealth is not an instrument.

'An instrument (*organon*) has no opposite, but there is something opposite to wealth, [so] wealth is not an instrument.' – If he[36] supposes that *generally* no instrument has an opposite, [this] should   123,1
not be accepted, because wealth is an instrument but also seems to have an opposite. If however he supposes it as particular and indefinite,[37] one should show that he has not argued syllogistically. For both premises are particular.[38] He *would* necessarily have supposed that there is no opposite to an instrument *in general*, *if* it   5
was implied in the definition and essence of an instrument that it has nothing opposite to it; but if having no opposite is not included in the essence of an instrument, but is something accidental to it, there is nothing to prevent it from *not* applying to all [instruments]. For neither is it the case that, since many of the things that are limited are limited by something alongside them, therefore they all are.[39]
  If it is part of the essence of an instrument that an instrument is that through which something comes about, either only through it   10

---

[33] i.e. irrational, but capable of being rational.

[34] i.e. the opposites, virtue and wickedness.

[35] So the Greek; but 'none of them' or 'neither of them' would make better sense and is probably the sense intended.

[36] The (hypothetical?) proposer of the objection. Bruns xiv mentions this passage in connection with texts he regards as fragmentary, but if the reference is not purely hypothetical it may perhaps be in the context of a school-discussion. Cf. n. 22 above.

[37] That is, 'there is no opposite to what is an instrument' just applies to some, unspecified instrument, not to instruments in general.

[38] From 'some instrument has no opposite' and 'wealth has an opposite', two particular premises in the second figure, no conclusion follows.

[39] That the universe is limited and yet does not border on anything outside it is argued in *Quaest.* 3.12.

or best through it,[40] all the things with this property will be instruments, and this will apply to all instruments. Thus, if this is a property of wealth – for it is through this that the good man [performs] activities of liberality and magnificence – then [wealth] *will*[41] be an instrument for the good man; for it is on the basis of what is included in the essence of an instrument that we judge what

15   is an instrument, as in the case of all other things, and not on the basis of its accidents.

Someone might also show that neither of the premises is supposed rightly, neither that which supposes that there is nothing opposite to what is an instrument, nor that which says that wealth has an opposite. Suppose that there is nothing opposite to 'instrument' as a whole and a totality,[42] and that for this reason someone says there is nothing opposite to a saw[43] nor yet to a lyre;

20   then according to someone who speaks thus there will be no opposite to fire, nor yet to any other concrete[44] substance, because there is no opposite to matter, which underlies all things like this. But [this suggests that] opposition is [rather] a matter of affections (*pathê*) and qualities; for there are certain opposites to fire in respect of its hotness and its dryness, and if one takes the qualities of the adze

25   which determine its being, one will find some opposite to it in respect of these – for bluntness is opposite to sharpness, and lightness to heaviness, and it needs both heaviness and sharpness.

---

[40] cf. Plato *Republic* 353A.

[41] cf. Introduction, n. 27 and n. 23 above.

[42] *tôi holôi kai sunamphoterôi organôi. sunamphoteros* here seems to have *not* its usual sense of 'concrete', 'compounded of matter and form' (cf. e.g. *Quaest.* 1.5 13,25, 1.26 42,12, 2.24 75,27, and 123,20-1 below), but rather that of 'unified' or 'taken as a sum', the particular types of instrument being considered together (cf. LSJ s.v., 3). (Could there be an allusion to the idea that particular types of instrument are compounds of the genus 'instrument' as matter, and the species as form?) The thought is 'if one can infer from the fact that there is no opposite to "instrument" in general that no particular instruments have opposites, one might as well infer from the fact that there is no opposite to "matter" as such that no particular material things have opposites'.

[43] In what sense, indeed, *does* a saw have an opposite? Bluntness may be opposed to *sharpness*, but – if a saw is a substance – it is Aristotelian doctrine that *substances* do not have opposites (cf. *Categories* 5, 3b25ff.). One may compare the remarks below, in which the adze seems to be regarded as in some sense *consisting in* the qualities that chiefly define it. Alexander is cited by Elias *in Cat.* 179,36ff. as arguing that the four 'elements' are opposed in quality, not in 'body'. That fire and water are opposed to each other in respect of 'a species-creating differentia' is argued by Dexippus *in Cat.* 52,5ff. and Simplicius *in Cat.* 107,26ff. and 108,9, while Philoponus *in Cat.* 74,17 argues that the heat *in fire* is not strictly speaking opposite to the coldness *in water* at all, since opposites must have a common substrate; similarly too Syrianus, cited by Elias, loc. cit. Elias' citation from Alexander presumably comes from Alexander's own *Categories* commentary, now lost; and the present *Problem* may reflect discussion there.

[44] Here *sunamphoteros does* seem to have the sense of 'composed of matter and form'; contrast n. 42 above.

And the same argument will apply to the other instruments too.

<It is not right, then, to say that there is no opposite to *any* instrument>;[45] but neither was it rightly supposed that wealth has an opposite. For poverty is not opposite to wealth, but is rather the absence and privation (*sterêsis*) of wealth; and health is not good as an instrument, but as the excellence (*aretê*) of the body, of which,   30 together with the soul, man consists.[46] If however someone were to say that the sort of privation from which possession (*hexis*) can come about again is an opposite, [then] this man would say that *all* things subject to coming-to-be have an opposite, and not just instruments; for this sort of privation occurs in them all.

5. Difficulty, that pleasure in general,[47] interpreted as a genus,   124,1
is neither a good nor an evil nor [something] indifferent.[48,49]

[I] [The question is] whether pleasure in general, interpreted as a genus, is neither a good nor an evil, because some of it is a good and some an evil – and what is general is not some *one* thing of those   5

[45] This is my supplement, suggested *exempli gratia*, to fill the lacuna posited by Bruns. There are two considerations suggesting that something has fallen out of the text: (i) in the Greek 'for there are certain opposites to fire – the other instruments too' is a parenthesis, and 'if' at 123,22 (translated for clarity by 'But this suggests that...') is left with no apodosis; hence 'then' in my restoration. An anacoluthon, however, is not impossible. (ii) 'but neither' (*oute*) in 123,27 follows more naturally if another negative clause has preceded it. It must be admitted, though, that making the restored clause the apodosis to 'if' in 123,22 and simultaneously linking it by 'neither ... nor' to what follows does not give a very smooth transition between the two paragraphs.

[46] Health and wealth are standard examples of two of the three classes of goods, those of the body and those which are external; and sickness, one might think, is opposite to health in the way, and *only* in the way, in which poverty is opposite to wealth. But since health is explicitly not an *instrumental* good, it is difficult to see what part the reference to it plays in the present context.

[47] Literally 'common pleasure' (*koinê hêdonê*). But it does not appear that there is a systematic distinction in Alexander between 'common' and 'general' or 'universal' (*katholou*, at 125,34 below); cf. Sharples (1987) 1202 n. 72, and references there.

[48] The title is most appropriate to the first section of this *Problem*. Bruns xiv, followed by Madigan (1987) 1275 and n. 17, distinguishes three separate problems in this text: [I] (124,3ff.) how pleasure as a genus can yet include both good and bad pleasures; [II] (124,18ff.) how distress can be opposed to pleasure given that some pleasures are good and others bad; [III] (125,5ff.) an explanation of indifferent pleasures based on the distinction between pleasures that are natural and those that are not. The last section, from 125,32, is formally part of the third problem, but is in effect a coda [IV] contrasting physical pain with distress generally, and summing up the conclusions of [III] in relation to [I] and [II]. With [II] and [III] one may compare *P. Eth.* 7 and 16; with [III] and [IV], *P. Eth.* 6.

[49] The terminology, though not the doctrine, is Stoic; for the Stoics virtue alone is good, wickedness bad, and all else 'indifferent', *adiaphoron*, though 'indifferent' things are further subdivided into those that are to be preferred (*proêgmena*), those that are not to be preferred, and those that are truly indifferent. Cf. above, *Problem* 1 118,23-6, and n. 5 there.

[that fall] under it – and yet will not be indifferent either (if at least there are also some pleasures which are indifferent, just as some too are good and others bad). Someone might ask these questions also in the case of activities, of which pleasures are in a way the ends (*telê*) – which is why they are differentiated in [a way] that corresponds to them.[50] For if some activities are good, others bad, and others
10   indifferent, activity in general and taken as a genus will be neither a good nor an evil nor an [something] indifferent. But, everything that there is must necessarily be either a good or an evil or [something] indifferent.

Or rather: [this applies to] everything that is in real existence[51] and which is capable of being in its own right;[52] but if there is[53] something general, under which all these things [fall], [then] that is no longer able to be any one of these things because it has all of them subordinate to itself. Every living creature that is in real existence
15   is either rational or irrational; but [living creature] in general, which is predicated of those in real existence as their genus, does not for this reason also [fall] within either of these [classes]. So neither pleasure in general nor activity in general will be either goods or evils or indifferent, [though] every pleasure and every activity in real existence has some one of these [characteristics].

[II] Since pleasures are differentiated in [a way] that corresponds to the activities on which they supervene, and those which supervene
20   on and accompany good activities are good, those which [accompany] bad ones bad and those which [accompany] indifferent ones indifferent, someone might enquire how one should speak about distress (*lupê*), since this is opposite to pleasure. For even if someone were to say that this too is differentiated in [a way] that corresponds to the activities on which it supervenes, firstly, how will the differentiation be made? Shall we say that [instances of distress]
25   that supervene on good activities are evil, that those that supervene on bad [activities] are good, and that those that supervene on indifferent ones are indifferent? Or is it absurd to say that what is distressed at the bad activities that it performs is in a good [state]? For the person who is like this is in an evil [state]; how is he not in an evil [state] when he is [engaged] in such activities [i.e. bad ones]? And then, it seemed reasonable for pleasure to be differentiated in [a way] that corresponds to the activities that come about before it.[54]

[50] See above, *P. Eth.* 2, 120,11ff.; 120,23ff.
[51] *en hupostasei.*
[52] *kath' hauto*: 'capable of being *per se*'.
[53] Literally 'if there were to be'; but our author continues in the indicative, 'under which all these things fall' (literally: 'are'). Cf. n. 23 above.
[54] 'before' presumably in the sense of logical, not temporal priority; the pleasure supervenes on the activities.

For it comes about by its affinity to them, as being a sort of end for them; but distress is a sign of alienation[55] from the things on which it supervenes. 30

Or rather: [distress] which supervenes on good activities is evil because it is [a sign of] alienation[56] from what is good. Because of this* it is reasonable that [distress] which supervenes on evil [activities] should be good, because it is some alienation from what is evil, and because the person who says that such distress is good is not supposing that it is the activities on which it supervenes that are 35 good, but that [what is good is] the alienation from such activities or circumstances and chances.

Or rather: it is altogether absurd to differentiate distress in this 125,1 way. For distress seems by its own nature to be an evil for those that have it. But if distress is an evil, and the opposite of what is evil is [either] good or evil,[57] it will be necessary for pleasure, which is opposite to distress, to be a good or an evil. But it was found that it was neither all a good nor all an evil, and there was also some that was indifferent. So will that [pleasure] which is good be opposite to 5 distress in the way that a good is opposite to an evil, and [will pleasure] which is bad [be opposite to distress] in the way that an evil [is opposite to] an evil?

[III] But if so, what should one say about the [pleasure] that is indifferent? It supervened on activities that were indifferent; and if* *this* is opposite to distress, not only good and evil but also what is indifferent will be opposed to evil, which does not seem right.

Or rather: it is necessary, in making a division of pleasures, to 10 take into account that some of them are in accordance with nature for those who take pleasure in them, and some of them contrary to nature. In accordance with nature are those that supervene on activities that take place in accordance with nature*, contrary to nature are those of which[58] the activities, too, are like this. For every living creature there are certain activities which are appropriate and in accordance with its nature. There are certain activities of a man which take place in accordance with the nature of man, and of a horse in accordance with that of horse, and of a dog 15 and of other living creatures similarly. The pleasures of these

---

[55] 'alienation', *allotriotês*; in effect the opposite of Stoic 'endearment' or 'affinity' (*oikeiôsis*). Cf. n. 10 above.

[56] Literally 'it is alienated from'.

[57] This sounds odd, but the thought is that cowardice (for example) has as its opposites both courage, which is good, and foolhardiness, which is bad. Cf. n. 74 below, and the final paragraph of the present *Problem*.

[58] Or conceivably 'those of the people of whom'; but a distinction between pleasures in terms of the different groups of people who enjoy them does not seem particularly to the point here (contrast 125,24 below).

[activities]⁵⁹ too should themselves be said to be in accordance with nature for those [creatures], while the pleasures that supervene on the activities which some undertake not in accordance with their own proper nature [should be called] contrary to nature – for which reason they are, moreover, [called pleasures] [only] through an ambiguity.⁶⁰ Those [pleasures] which are in accordance with nature for each [creature] should be called pleasures in the proper sense;

20   those which are contrary to nature for them are pleasures for those that take pleasure in them, but are not pleasures in the proper and unqualified sense, just as some things are healthy without qualification, others [healthy] for certain [people]. And one should say that those that are really and in the proper sense pleasures are good for those that take pleasure in them, while those that some experience contrary to nature, not being pleasures without qualification, are bad and evil.

If then it is the good man above all who is a human being and in a
25   condition in accordance with nature, it will be the pleasures that seem [pleasurable] to him that will be most in accordance with nature for a human being, and the things which he enjoys will be pleasant; while the things which are disagreeable to him are contrary to nature and not pleasant without qualification, even if some people take pleasure in them. And there will also be a difference in the pleasures which *are* in accordance with nature for each [creature], in that some of them are more appropriate and others less.

In this way distress, which is an evil, will have as its opposite
30   pleasure in the proper and unqualified sense, which is all a good, even if not in the same way; and the [pleasures] which are contrary to nature [will be] neither pleasures without qualification nor good.⁶¹ And there will be [pleasures] like this supervening on things that are indifferent, too, for indifferent things also are not among those in accordance with nature.

[IV] It is distress (*lupê*), not pain (*ponos*) that is opposite to pleasure; for pain indicates a bodily affliction⁶² and a [particular sort] of distress, but not distress without qualification. Distress, in the general
35   sense, means a certain disposition of the soul, whether it supervenes on an affliction of the body or some disposition of the soul;⁶³ just as

---

⁵⁹ Or 'of these creatures'; but this is less to the point, and for pleasures *of* activities cf. *P. Eth.* 17 137,35-6.

⁶⁰ That is, the name applies, but not the proper definition. Cf. Aristotle *Cat.* 1, 1a1-5.

⁶¹ Bruns supposes a lacuna after these words, but this does not seem necessary. Madigan (1987) 1276 and n. 18 adds 'and so are not opposed to pain as good to evil'.

⁶² *thlipsis*. Cf. n. 67 below.

⁶³ The awkward repetition of 'disposition of the soul' is present in the Greek.

pleasure is not just bodily [pleasure] but also [pleasure] of the soul. So distress in general is opposite to pleasure in general; but pleasure in [activities] contrary to nature destroys pleasure in the 126,1 [things][64] in accordance with nature, which is a good, in a way similar to [that in which] the distress which is proper [to each][65] does so, too; [and so this unnatural pleasure], too, will itself be an evil. For that which supervenes on things on which it should not is like an excess*. So, while all distress is an evil, those among pleasures which are in accordance with nature, and pleasures in the proper sense, are opposite to distress as being goods, while those that are contrary to nature are [opposite to distress] as [one] evil to 5 another.

6. That it is distress, and not pain, that is the opposite of pleasure.[66]

Pain (*ponos*) indicates some affliction of the body, but distress (*lupê*) a contraction of the soul.[67] If all pleasure consisted in bodily relaxation, pain would be opposite to it; but since pleasure is a certain relaxation of the soul which does not occur through the body 10 or in respect of the body alone, it will not be pain that is the opposite

[64] The discrepancy between '[*activities*] contrary to nature' (*tais*, feminine) and '[things] in accordance with nature' (*tois*, masculine) is present in the MSS; Bruns in his apparatus (but not his text) suggests emendation of the former, while the Aldine edition and Spengel emended the latter.

[65] The sense is probably 'proper [to each pleasure]' – i.e. each natural pleasure has its own particular opposed form of distress.

[66] This title really only applies to the section extending as far as 126,19, what follows being concerned with the goodness of some, but not all pleasures; cf. *P. Eth.* 5 124,3ff.; 125,9ff.; 7 127,20ff.; 16 137,10ff.

[67] For this contrast between *ponos* in the body and *lupê* in the soul cf. above, *P. Eth.* 5 125,32ff. It is made clear there that *lupê* includes distress in the soul occasioned by bodily pain; the position of the present *Problem* is the same, as is shown by 126,11-13. A different view of the relation between *ponos* and *lupê* is taken at *P. Eth.* 7 127,9-10 (below). The description of distress as a contraction (*sustolê*) of the soul – not found in *P. Eth.* 5 – is Stoic (*SVF* 3.386, 394; cf. 3.391 and Posidonius fr. 34 Edelstein-Kidd), as is that of a type of pleasure as relaxation or *diakhusis* (*SVF* 3.400; cf. Posidonius loc. cit. I am grateful to Professor Sorabji for drawing my attention to these points). The term *thlipsis*, used both here and in *P. Eth.* 5 in connection with bodily pain, is more problematic. It literally means 'pressure' or 'crushing', but is common metaphorically in the sense of 'affliction' (Aristotle has the related verb *thlibesthai* in this sense at *EN* 1.10, 1100b28; it is quite common in Epictetus, very frequent in the Septuagint). The verb and noun are used quite frequently in the physical sense by Epicurus (e.g. at Diogenes Laertius 10.53, 56, 101, 107, 109), but there is as far as I know no extant text in which Epicurus or any other philosophical writer before Alexander uses it in an account of physical pain in general. At Plutarch *Amatorius* 765c, the Epicurean context in which the term is used is a pleasurable one. There is a reference to pressure causing pain (*ponos*) at Theophrastus *de Lassitudine* 9 (cf. ibid. 3 and 8; [Aristotle], *Probl.* 2.15, 867b2; 5.11, 881b31); but this is different from the use of the term in a general theory of pain.

to this sort of pleasure, but distress. For, as with pleasure, there is both distress at the afflictions of the body and [distress] of the soul itself occasioned by itself; but pain is in respect of the body only. And for this reason it will be distress that is opposite to pleasure without qualification, [while] the [distress] that is [in the form of] pain [is opposed to] a certain [type of] pleasure. For the opposite of bodily

15 relaxation and a sound condition of the body, and the pleasure in respect of these, will be affliction and pain of the body.

So-called 'pain'[68] in regard to the soul, in the way that some people are called 'painstaking', is not even opposed to pleasure in the first place; at any rate, its occurrence is accompanied by pleasure. And if someone is distressed by taking pains, then it is the distress, not the pain[s], that will be the opposite to the pleasure.

Distress being opposed to pleasure, it would be reasonable to say

20 that all distress is an evil; for it is by its own nature [something] to be avoided. But not all pleasure is a good. Some of the activities on which pleasure supervenes admit of excess, and the pleasures that supervene on these will also admit of excess; and these are the bodily ones. And for this reason* among these those that are proportionate are to be chosen, and of this sort are those concerned with the things necessary for the body (for necessary things, too, are to be chosen[69]);

25 but those that are excessive are to be avoided, and of this sort are those of the profligate (*akolastoi*). And in respect of [bodily pleasures[70]] distress will be an evil, as being a certain lack, and so too will excessive pleasure, as being a certain excess; but proportionate [pleasure] is a good, being in a way in the mean [between] the aforementioned. But there are some pleasures that admit of no excess; e.g. those that supervene on all the activities that will become

30 *more* deserving to be chosen as they progress and are added to.[71] Of this sort are [pleasures] in respect of the virtues. And in the case of these there will not be any excess of the pleasures either;[72] and for

---

[68] *ponos* can mean 'toil' or 'labour' as well as 'pain'; hence 'painstaking'.

[69] That 'necessary things, too, are to be chosen' is spelled out to guard against the thought that necessary things are not to be counted as deserving of choice since in their case the question whether to choose them or not simply does not arise.

[70] That 'these' in the text refers to bodily pleasures in general, and not just the excessive ones, is made clear by the sequel.

[71] Professor Sorabji contrasts this with the Stoic view that virtue cannot be increased. Aristotle in *EN* 7.14 draws a contrast between bodily pleasures that admit of excess and natural ones that do not, though he does not also say that the natural pleasures admit of *increase* without excess. Cf. below, *P. Eth.* 7 127,26-8.

[72] It is clearer in the Greek text than in my translation, where I have simplified the sentence structure, that 'in the case of these' picks up the earlier 'But there are some pleasures that admit of no excess'. No doubt our author *intended* 'in the case of these *activities*', but his way of expressing himself has been careless. The position of *oude* is

this reason all such [pleasures] are to be chosen and are good by their own proper nature.

7. Why, if all distress is an evil by its own nature, it will not   127,1
also be the case that all pleasure is a good by its own nature.[73]

It was necessary[74] either for every pleasure too to be an evil, being opposed to distress (*lupê*) as one evil to another, or, if pleasure was opposed to what is evil not as a thing to be avoided or an evil, but as   5
a good, for all [pleasure] to be a good. For if some pleasure were an evil, [then], [since] all cases of distress are evil, and pleasure is opposed to distress, some [pleasure] would be opposed [to distress] as one evil to another, and some as a good to an evil, which needs explanation.[75]

– Or rather: not even all distress is an evil, if at any rate in these [cases] too virtue aims at the mean, and there are certain [types of] distress and pain that are proper to the good man. And pain (*ponos*) will be wider[76] than distress (*lupê*); for distress is a [type of] pain.   10
Pleasure accompanies activities and is in a way a part or the end of them, and it is from them that it has its [worthiness] to be chosen or avoided; for [it is] the [pleasures] that [supervene] on activities that are to be chosen that are [themselves] to be chosen, and those that [supervene] on those that are not like this[77] that are to be avoided. Similarly it is reasonable to suppose that distresses, too, supervening on certain activities, themselves derive from these   15
their worthiness to be chosen or avoided, in the opposite way to the pleasures. For those that supervene on noble activities are to be avoided, those that [supervene] on shameful [activities] are to be

---

against Spengel's attempt to improve the sense by emendation, 'in the case of these <activities> there will not be any excess of the pleasures', which in any case supposes an anacoluthon.

[73] cf. below, *P. Eth.* 16; also *P. Eth.* 5 124,18ff.; 125,29ff. and 36ff.; 6 126,19ff. This was used by Eudoxus as an argument for pleasure being the good (Aristotle *EN* 10.2, 1172b18-20; Madigan (1987) 1276 and n. 21.)

[74] The past tense *may* indicate the report of a discussion: see below, n. 80; *P. Eth.* 17 137,23; *Mant.* 169,34; 170,3. For the thought that things can be opposed as evil to evil or as evil to good cf. above, *P. Eth.* 5 125,2; our author starts with the more paradoxical of the two alternatives.

[75] Or perhaps 'which is lacking in reason', 'is inexplicable'. B[2] marks the phrase, and has in the margin 'the solution however is not exact'.

[76] Literally 'more common', *koinoteron*. Contrast above, *P. Eth.* 5 125,32ff.; 6 126,11; Madigan (1987) 1276 and n. 23. Perhaps the thought is that a virtuous action may involve the pain of physical effort without occasioning *distress*.

[77] A euphemism: 'not like this' is equivalent to 'are to be avoided'.

chosen.[78] And if some cases of distress and some pains are to be chosen, the pleasures that are opposed to such cases of distress, too, will be [of a type] to be avoided; and the pleasures that are opposed to distress [of a certain type] are those that supervene on activities of such a type.[79] And the reason why not all pleasure is a good is that
20 not all distress is an evil either.

Something like the following was also said.[80] Even for those who suppose that all distress is an evil, it does not necessarily follow either that all pleasure is a good or that it is all an evil, [even] accepting that pleasure is opposed to distress. For in the case of those pleasures where there are certain excesses, there are some pleasures that are to be chosen and some that are to be avoided. The moderate[81] ones are to be chosen, but those corresponding to the
25 excesses are base. And the pleasures that have this [characteristic][82] are the bodily ones.

For [there are] some [pleasures] in the case of which there are no excesses, because even those of them that are intensified remain in the [class] of what is to be chosen. These are all to be chosen; and of this type are those that [supervene] on activities relating to speculative thought. There are also certain unnatural pleasures; of this sort are the bestial and the diseased ones, which have been
30 discussed in the seventh book of the *Ethics*.[83] These would not be called the pleasures of a man in the proper sense, because they are not in accordance with nature, nor [would they be said to be deserving] to be chosen.

Pleasures being like this, distress will be opposed to all of them as an evil, because it is accepted that all distress is an evil. All the pleasures that are contrary to nature will be opposed to distress as one evil to another – if indeed one were to reckon these too among

[78] The thought is *not* of course that one should avoid noble but painful actions and pursue base painful actions; rather, it is the rather abstract and schematic point that one should seek to be in a condition where noble actions are not painful but base ones are. (Hence the pleasures that are opposed to pains that should be chosen are themselves to be avoided, 127,17-18; the pains and pleasures in question both alike supervene on shameful actions.) Cf. above, *P. Eth.* 5 124,24ff.; cf. also Aristotle, *EN* 10.2, 1173a5-13 and 7.13, 1153b4-6. Madigan (1978) 1276 and n. 74.

[79] That is, to pain felt at (e.g.) betraying a friend, which is desirable – one *should* feel pain at such an act – there is opposed pleasure in betraying a friend, which is undesirable.

[80] This may indicate the record of an actual discussion; cf. above, n. 74. It seems to refer not just to 170,20-3 but to the whole subsequent development of the argument, and the recording of that development is a large part of the reason for this *Problem* in its present form existing at all; it is indeed in a way just a restatement of what was found difficult at the beginning of the text (127,5-7), but now stated in terms of distinctions between different types of pleasures.

[81] Literally 'middle', *mesai*.

[82] That is, the characteristic of admitting of excess. Cf. *P. Eth.* 6 126,21-3.

[83] Aristotle *EN* 7.1, 1145a15ff.

pleasures [at all]; while in the case of all those that admit of excess,   35
some will be opposed to distress as goods, [namely] those which are
in the mean and are defined by right reasoning, while those
corresponding to excess, among which are those of the profligate,   128,1
these [will be opposed to distress] as one evil to another. And those
of which there is no excess will all be opposed to distress as a good to
an evil.

8. That virtue is neither a genus nor a totality.[84]

[It is] not a genus, because a genus is not removed if one of the
species is removed, but virtue is removed along with one [of the   5
particular virtues].[85] For if [i] the virtues accompany each other
reciprocally, [then] when any [virtue] whatsoever is removed virtue
too is removed; and* in this case one of the species will remove the
other species along with [itself], which does not even seem sound [in]
itself.[86] [But] if [on the other hand] they do not [all] accompany each
other reciprocally, [still] if *wisdom* were removed virtue would be
removed, because for* all [the virtues] their essence is [to be] in
accordance with right reasoning, and right reasoning comes from   10
wisdom.

Virtue will not [however] be a totality. For among things that do
not have parts similar to one another[87] the part does not admit of
the definition of the totality; but the virtues differ from one another
and yet admit of the definition of virtue.[88]

[Solution I] – Or rather: [there are] cases where one [thing] is
first, another second, so that when the first is removed so are both
that which is common *and* the other things that follow [the first
one]. And these are those of the things that are said in many ways   15

---

[84] 'A totality'; that is, a whole of parts (*holon*) which requires the presence of every
part if it is to be complete. See below, *P. Eth.* 28; and for the discussion of
genus-species and part-whole relations in this *Problem* compare *Quaest.* 1.11, and P.
Moraux, *Der Aristotelismus* vol. 1, p. 126 and nn. 36-7, with parallels in Boethius. The
statements of the dilemma in *P. Eth.* 8 and in *P. Eth.* 28 are very similar, but the
solutions are different, as is pointed out by Madigan (1987) 1263. Cf. also *P. Eth.* 22
and *Mantissa* 153-6, especially 155,13ff.

[85] The virtues are interdependent; one cannot possess one without possessing all,
so removing one means removing all. Cf. Aristotle *EN* 6.13, 1144b32-1145a2, and R.
Sorabji, 'Aristotle on the role of intellect in virtue', *Proc. Arist. Soc.* 74 (1973-4)
107-29, at 114-15, reprinted in A.O. Rorty (ed.), *Essays on Aristotle's Ethics*, Berkeley
1980, 201-19, at 207. Cf. also below, *P. Eth.* 22.

[86] Removing or doing away with the genus will, quite generally, mean removing the
species that fall under it; but it is not in general the case that removing one *species*
means removing all the others.

[87] i.e. anhomoiomerous things; a face or a table, as opposed to flesh or wood.

[88] i.e. virtue cannot be a totality of parts. For the individual virtues are different
from one another and yet seem to admit of a single definition which is also that of the
totality; and this is not the case with a totality made up of dissimilar parts.

that are said [starting] from one thing or in relation to one thing.[89] So, if virtue was removed when some one [virtue] was removed, [virtue] too would be one of the things spoken of in this way.[90]

[Solution II] – Or rather: one should rather say that the definition of virtue, which seems to be predicated of the virtues synonymously, is [in fact] more general,[91] and not peculiar to the virtue which is the totality of which these [virtues] are parts. The definition of *that* will
20   be 'the best state of the whole rational soul', and this definition does not fit the individual virtues.[92] And Aristotle, too, seems to say that perfect virtue is a totality and not a genus.[93]

Something has been said about this difficulty also in what follows.[94]

9. That not all those who act wrongly do so through ignorance that what they are doing is bad and harmful.[95]

---

[89] *aph' henos* or *pros hen*. Cf. Aristotle *Metaph*. 4.2, 1003a33ff.; G.E.L. Owen, 'Logic and Metaphysics in some earlier works of Aristotle', in I. Düring and G.E.L. Owen (eds), *Aristotle and Plato in the mid-fourth century*, Göteborg 1960, 163-90, reprinted in G.E.L. Owen, *Logic, Science and Dialectic*, London 1986, 180-99. Professor Sorabji observes: 'To put the point in a more linguistic way than Aristotle himself does, when an expression is ambiguous (the thing spoken of is "said in many ways"), one of the different uses of the expression may be a primary one on which the other uses depend (the things spoken of start from or relate to the primary thing, *pros hen* or *aph' henos*), in ways that Owen brings out. One of the uses of the word "virtue" (or one of the virtues: wisdom) might be primary in this way, according to Solution [I].'

[90] Wisdom (*phronêsis*) is the first virtue in the series, so that removing it involves *both* removing all the other particular virtues that come after it *and* removing it as a genus. – On the question whether there can, as this solution implies, be a genus in cases where there is something prior and something posterior, cf. *Quaest*. 1.11b 23,9ff; Alexander *de Anima* 16,18-17,8; 40,4-10; *in Metaph*. 152,6ff.; 208,31ff.; and Philoponus *in GC* 309,17ff.; Moraux (1942) 51-2. But as Moraux (1942) 57-8 points out, Alexander does argue that there can be a hierarchy within a genus, and gives the example of different types of creature, at *in Metaph*. 210,6-8, against Platonists who deny the existence of a generic idea of number.

[91] Literally 'more common'. See n. 47 above.

[92] The problem indicated in n. 88 above is here resolved by a distinction between virtue as the sum of the individual virtues, on the one hand, and virtue as a generic term on the other, virtue as a genus presumably covering both the totality and the parts. The definition of virtue as a genus will apply to both complete virtue *and* to the individual virtues; that of complete virtue, 'the best state of the *whole* rational soul', will not apply to the individual virtues.

[93] cf. Aristotle *EN* 6.12, 1144a5, and also 5.1, 1130a9; Madigan (1987) 1263.

[94] i.e. in *P. Eth*. 28 below. This sentence is bracketed as an editorial addition by Bruns. Different solutions to a single problem are found in the *Problems* attributed to Aristotle (cf. e.g. [Aristotle] *Probl*. 10.18 with 10.54; 10.48 with 34.1; 11.20 with 11.47; 38.1 with 38.11).

[95] In fact this *Problem* is concerned with excluding, as the cause of all wrongdoing,

<That not all those who act wrongly do so through ignorance that   25
what they are doing is bad and harmful>[96] is clear from those who
are convinced that they are acting wrongly, but do not hold out
against themselves because of softness and lack of discipline.
Among these are also those who are diseased and do things that
harm themselves, not being ignorant of what sort of things these
are; for because they are not ignorant, they reproach themselves,
summon the help[97] of those who do not act wrongly in the same way,   30
and pray to the gods that they may be in a better state of mind. And
among these are also those who are in love; if falling in love   129,1
<and>*[98] ceasing to be in love are in their control (*ep' autois*), they
will do[99] the things in accordance with their love voluntarily
(*hekousiôs*).

[The point] is also clear from those who are beginning to act
wrongly. For none of them embarks upon bad things in the
beginning without knowing that they *are* bad; at any rate all [of
them], when they begin, are ashamed and are eager not to be   5
observed, and embark* upon these things on the basis that they will
not do them a second time, being convinced that they will be harmed
by them to some extent, but yielding to pleasure, not through
conviction that it is preferable for them, but through not wishing to
make a small effort in resisting it. The reason why they do have this
conception of bad things, and understand what they are like, is first
of all nature; for those who have not yet been completely corrupted,   10
but retain the common and natural notions, do not lack

---

not just ignorance but also compulsion (*bia*); cf. 129,19ff. Ignorance and compulsion
are the two reasons for an action being non-voluntary in Aristotle *EN* 3.1, with which
this *Problem* should be compared; cf. also *EN* 3.5, on responsibility for the way in
which one's character develops (129,24ff., 130,19ff.) and *P. Eth*. 11, 12 and 29 below.

This *Problem* is discussed by K.A. Neuhausen, *De voluntarii notione Platonica et
Aristotelica*, Wiesbaden 1967 (*Klass. Philol. Stud.* 34; in Latin), 172f. n. 86.

[96] Added by B, the Aldine edition and Spengel.

[97] Apelt proposed 'praise'; cf. 129,13ff. below, and Notes on the Text.

[98] So Apelt. Bruns has rather 'if falling in love is in their control <as> ceasing to be
in love is'. See Notes on the Text.

[99] The Greek has 'they *would* do'; but see n. 23 above. Since the verb in 129,1 is
omitted, 'if falling in love *were* in their control... they would' is grammatically
possible; but Alexander presumably holds that they *do* 'do the things in accordance
with their love' voluntarily; cf. Aristotle *EN* 3.1, 1111a24ff. A normal Greek view
would have been that the impulse to love is involuntary, but that it is up to us
whether we try to resist it; cf. K.J. Dover, *Greek Popular Morality in the Time of Plato
and Aristotle*, Oxford (Blackwell) 1974, 208. Apelt proposed 'they will voluntarily
cease from doing the things in accordance with their love'; see Notes on the Text.

understanding of better things.[100] That the nature of each person inclines towards what is better is clear from the fact that even those who are already [involved] in wrong actions continue to praise those who are not acting wrongly, and that those who do act wrongly do not lead their own children in the same direction. The common

15   utterance and conception of mankind, too, is sufficient to teach how bad things are inappropriate. The laws, too, proclaiming these things, are sufficient to teach what is better; and in addition to these all teachers and tutors, generally advising [the young] to avoid what is bad, do not allow the young to lack understanding of better things.

Well, that wrong actions do not [come about] through ignorance of what is bad is clear from these things and things like them. That [those who do] base things do not do them under compulsion (*bia*)[101]

20   is clear from the fact that they themselves are the people who do these things,[102] and that they move their bodily parts to perform such actions in accordance with an impulse from themselves, deliberating about them and choosing them. For if [even] those who choose [act] under compulsion, who will those be who do not [act] under compulsion?

25   If, [once] they have developed the habit of acting wrongly, they are neither ashamed <nor> think <about bad things as being> bad <for themselves>*, this in no way shows that [their deeds] are involuntary (*akousia*). For they themselves are responsible (*aitioi*) for their having got into such a state that they do not suppose that bad things are bad for themselves too; [they are responsible for having done so] at the time when it was still in their power (*ep'*

---

[100] cf. *Mant.* 175,12ff.; *P. Eth.* 18 139,9 and 29 160,34. 'common and natural notions' (*koinai kai phusikai ennoiai*) is Stoic terminology; 'conception' (*prolêpsis*) in 129,9 is also Stoic, though the term is apparently one the Stoics themselves had borrowed from the Epicureans. Cf. F.H. Sandbach, 'Ennoia and prolepsis', in A.A. Long (ed.), *Problems in Stoicism*, London 1971, 22-37; R.B. Todd, 'The Stoic common notions: a re-examination and re-interpretation', *Symbolae Osloenses* 48 (1973) 43-76. *prolêpseis* are for the Stoics those *ennoiai* that develop naturally, sometimes therefore translated 'preconceptions' as opposed to 'conceptions' for *ennoiai*; whether Alexander intends the term to have that strict sense here is debatable, but in any case '*pre*conception' does not seem a very clear way of conveying the point in the present context. As elsewhere, Alexander uses Stoic terminology to express a non-Stoic point. Cf. R.W. Sharples, *Alexander of Aphrodisias On Fate*, London 1983, 18 and n. 113, and above, Introduction n. 3. The hybrid expression *koinê prolêpsis* at 129,15 (noted by Professor Sorabji) is one that is found also in other philosophical writers of the imperial period; whether it is one that the Stoics themselves would have used is debated (cf. Sandbach, op. cit., 22-4, and, *contra*, Todd, op. cit., 73 and n. 79).

[101] *bia*, compulsion, is defined by Aristotle as a completely external cause, such as a wind which blows someone off course (*EN* 3.1, 1110a1-4). An internal desire will not therefore qualify as *bia*; actions which are the result of deliberation and choice (*bouleuesthai, proaireisthai*) will not be involuntary even if they are a response to a difficult situation (Aristotle *EN* 3.1, 1110a4-19). Cf. below, *P. Eth.* 12.

[102] Diels added *aitious*; 'from the fact that those who do these things are themselves <the causes>' or 'are themselves <responsible>'.

autois)[103] not to do the things on account of which they came to be like this, through not having taken precautions. At the beginning of their wrongdoing, bad things did not seem to them beneficial and to 30 be chosen; but when they have persevered in [their wrong actions] and through neglect of themselves got into a bad state, [things] do seem like this to them. [It follows that] they themselves will be 130,1 responsible for their having such impressions, as a result of [their wrong actions]; for they are themselves responsible for their being in such a state, and it is on account of this that they have such [false] impressions about bad things.

Witness is borne to these things by the fact that people who act wrongly in this way are hated and punished, on the grounds that [they act] voluntarily and are responsible[104] for their performing such deeds; while those, who do something like this involuntarily, 5 receive pardon. If all [such deeds] are involuntary, why are some of them pardoned and others not? If, when it was in their power to learn what [these things] are like and to refrain from them, they knew this but neglected [to do] it, then they themselves are again[105] responsible, and they are in [their present condition] voluntarily. But if they did not even know *that,* how are they not also themselves deserving of pardon?[106]

---

[103] *ep' autois*, translated 'in their control' above; but 'in their power' seems more natural here.

[104] Or 'are responsible for themselves performing', 'are causes for themselves performing'.

[105] There are two ways in which people might be responsible; first by knowing what they were doing at the time in question, and second, as here, by having failed to acquire moral knowledge when they could have done. Hence 'again' here.

[106] Professor Sorabji points out that this, like 130,25 below, goes beyond Aristotle, for whom an agent's not knowing what is right is not a reason for pardoning, though his not knowing the particular circumstances of an action is. (Cf. Aristotle *EN* 3.1, 1110b28-1111a2; 3.5, 1114a9-10, 1114a31-b25). It may be doubted though whether there is any real divergence from Aristotle here. What is suggested in the present passage is that we should pardon people who did not even know that it was in their power to refrain from bad actions and thus cause their character to develop for the better rather than for the worse; Aristotle describes a person who does not know that actions influence character as 'altogether lacking in perception' (*EN* 3.5, 1114a9-10), and it may be doubted whether either he or Alexander think that there are many such people in reality. (Even those who profess a belief in determinism show by their actions that they have a better understanding than their theories would suggest; Alexander, *Fat.* 18 188,19-189,8). That exceptions to the human norm cannot be brought within general moral theories without qualification is suggested by *EN* 7.5, 1149a16. As for 130,25 below, the case envisaged there is that of people to whom bad things always gave the impression of being good. This forms part of a dialectical counter-argument which our author does not indeed answer directly, but which could only be applied to people in general at the cost of making virtue as involuntary as wickedness. The reference to people to whom bad things have always seemed good comes between two references to people who *are* responsible for their wrongdoing, and again it is not clear that our author thinks that there are many, or any, people who can be excused because bad things always gave them the impression of being good. Aristotle too is prepared to concede for the sake of argument that people may

There is sufficient evidence that some of those who act wrongly do
10   not act wrongly either under compulsion or through ignorance of
what is better, in the fact that they are neither distressed at their
wrong actions nor regret [them]. For things that are done involuntarily cause distress and are objects of regret.

That, if wrong actions were involuntary (*akousia*), they would not
be in our control (*eph' hêmin*) either[107] is clear from the fact that it is
things that come about under compulsion or through ignorance that
are involuntary, and that neither the things <we do> under
compulsion <nor those which> we do <on account of ignorance>*
are in our control not to do – for it is the things that are not in our
15   control to do or not to do that are done under compulsion. Now they
say that wrong actions on account of anger or desire are committed by
the doers under compulsion; so wrong actions on account of anger or
desire [would not be] in our control. If then punishments apply to
things that are in our control, it would not be reasonable to punish
those who act wrongly on account of anger or desire.

As for wrong actions on account of ignorance, if those who act
20   wrongly are responsible for their own ignorance, these [wrong
actions] will be their responsibility;[108] and they will be responsible
for their own ignorance if, when it was possible for them to turn to
better things and not come to be in such a state that they will be
ignorant of good things, they neglected [to do] this. – But surely, it
was not possible for them to turn to better things, if they did not ever
25   suppose that good things *were* [good]. If bad things always gave the
impression of good things to them, it was not in their power *not* to
choose these.[109] – However, those who suppose that good things are
good and *then* do not choose them do act wrongly voluntarily. For they
did not pass over the choice of better things on account of compulsion
or ignorance, and therefore, just as their acting wrongly was in their
control, so it was also voluntary. If they were not responsible for their
30   own ignorance, acting wrongly on account of ignorance would not be
in their control; and then it would not be reasonable to punish any of
those who act wrongly, since punishments apply to things that are in
our control, but no wrong action is in our control if it is involuntary,
and all that is involuntary is a result either of ignorance or of
compulsion.

---

not be responsible for how the end appears to them, while insisting that in that case
virtue is no more voluntary than wickedness (Aristotle *EN* 3.5, 1114a31-b25; cf.
W.F.R. Hardie, *Aristotle's Ethical Theory*, Oxford 1968, 176-9).

[107] In Alexander's *de Fato* it is suggested that 'in our control' is a narrower category
than 'voluntary' (cf. *de Fato* 14 183,26-7, and pp. 145-6 of my commentary, London
1983); but there seems no suggestion in the present passage of a real distinction
between the application of the two terms. Cf. also 130,28-9 and 32-3 below.

[108] Literally 'be in their control', *ep' autois*. Cf. n. 281 below.

[109] cf. n. 106 above.

10. That man is for the sake of the virtues, and not vice versa.

If there is, in the things that come to be by nature, something for the   35
sake of which things that come to be in this way do so; and if that,
for the sake of which certain things come to be, is the end (*telos*) of   131,1
those things: then there is some end in the things that come to be by
nature. But the end is better than the things that come to be for the
sake of the end; so of things that come to be by nature, too, the ends
are better than the things that come to be for their sake.

Man too is [one] of the things that come to be by nature; so for him
too there is some end, and this is better than the things to which it   5
applies. The end of man is to become a good man; man is for the sake
of this. And to become good is to possess the virtues of a man. But it ✔
would not be possible for a man to possess the virtues, if he were not
first of all a *man*; so man is for the sake of the acquisition of the
virtues, not the virtues [for the sake of] man. It is for this reason,   10
too, that the man who has acquired the virtues is better than the one ⟋
who is without them.

For the virtues do not come to be <separately>*.[110] For we do not
acquire them like a piece of land or a slave or a house [*sc.* that exists
already], but each [man's] virtues come to be in the [very]
acquisition of them. But if their coming-to-be is in the acquisition of
them, and their being consists in this, and the acquisition of them is
our end, then the virtues too will be be our ends and we will be for   15
their sake. And it is for this reason that the virtues are better than
us; for indeed our end consists in the presence and acquisition of the
virtues.

11. That 'involuntary' does not have several senses [just]
because it covers the results both of compulsion and of
ignorance.[111]

'Living creature' does not have several senses[112] because it includes

---

[110] So Bruns. Dr Kenny suggests keeping the MSS text and interpreting 'the
virtues do not [strictly speaking] come to be'; but this would seem to indicate a
contrast between things that go through a process of coming to be and those that just
are not and then are (cf. Aristotle *Metaph.* 8.3, 1043b15; 8.5, 1044b22, and W.D.
Ross's note on *Metaph.* 6.2, 1026b23 in his *Aristotle: Metaphysics*, Oxford 1924, vol. 1,
p. 360), and it is not clear from the sequel how this is to the point. Neither,
admittedly, is it clear from the sequel why the fact that virtues do not exist
independently of their possessors should be put in terms of their not *coming to be*
independently.

[111] As often, the title relates to the opening section of the *Problem* rather than to

20 both the rational and the irrational; and 'wickedness' does not do so
    because some is by excess and some by deficiency. So too
    'involuntary' *(akousion)* does not have several [senses] because it
    covers both what is due to compulsion *(bia)* and what is due to
    ignorance. For these are parts or species of the involuntary.

    But if 'involuntary' does not have several senses, this can no
    longer be used to impugn the commonplace[113] which asserts 'if one
    of the opposites has several senses, so does the other', [by claiming
25 that] the voluntary does not have several senses, while the
    involuntary, which is its opposite, does. For neither does
    'wickedness' have several senses [just] because some of it is in excess
    and some in deficiency. For wickedness is a genus covering excess
    and deficiency as its species; *each* is wickedness, both that in excess
    and that in deficiency. It is not possible for the bad man to be bad in
30 both respects simultaneously; yet virtue is not also double,[114] with a
    particular virtue being opposed to each of the [sorts of] wickedness.
    For it is not sufficient for [having] virtue not to be in excess, or again
    not to be deficient, but, if there is to be virtue, one must be in *neither*
    of these. And similarly the voluntary *(hekousion)* too has its essence
    in the antithesis of *both* the things in which the essence of the
    involuntary consists. For the person who does something

---

the text as a whole. Discussion of whether 'involuntary' is ambiguous leads on to that
of the general thesis that, in so far as two terms are truly opposites, it is not possible
for one to be ambiguous and the other not; and it is this that is the real theme of our
text, the last section from 132,7 being concerned with this issue rather than with the
specific example of the involuntary at all. – On this text cf. R.W. Sharples, 'Ambiguity
and opposition: Alexander of Aphrodisias, *Ethical Problems* 11', *Bulletin of the
Institute of Classical Studies* 32 (1985) 109-16. The position adopted here is similar to
that of Aspasius, *in EN* 59,2-11, and to be contrasted with that in Anon. *in EN, CAG*
20 141,10-20 (cf. Introduction, n. 28). Cf. also Alexander, *in Top.* 99,2-20; and below,
n. 116.

[112] 'does not have several senses' translates *ou pollakhôs legetai*. Another form of
the same phrase was rendered 'said in many ways' at *P. Eth.* 8 128,14 above; there
the emphasis was on the things to which a term applied in virtue of its meaning, here
it is rather on the meaning in virtue of which the term applies. No one rendering will
capture the appropriate nuance and be equally helpful to the reader in every context.
The Greek-English index will assist in locating this and other cases where more than
one rendering has been used for a single English expression.

[113] 'The commonplace' is 'if one of the opposites has several senses, so does the
other', only; what follows, from 'the voluntary does not' to 'its opposite, does' is not
part of the commonplace under attack, as Bruns' punctuation might suggest, but a
statement of the way in which the alleged multiplicity of senses of 'involuntary' might
be used to impugn the commonplace. See below, n. 115. Similarly Madigan (1987)
1268 and n. 10.

[114] 'Also' may suggest that wickedness, unlike virtue, *is* 'double'. It may be so
without for that reason having several senses; but the point hardly helps to clarify
the general argument that is being put forward.

voluntarily must both have within himself the origin of the things　132,1
that are done, and also know the particular [facts]; the former
excludes compulsion, the latter ignorance.

And this is why the voluntary is simultaneously opposed to both
the parts of the involuntary, which are quite unable even to exist
together. For it is not possible for the person who does or suffers
something under compulsion *also* to do the wrong thing　5
(*hamartanein*) in ignorance of the particular [facts]. For ignorance
or knowledge of the particular [facts] does not at all contribute to
involuntary action on the part of those who are compelled by
someone.

And the commonplace[115] is not done away with, either, by the fact
that 'to love' (*philein*) has several senses,[116] while 'to hate' (*misein*),
which is opposite to it, does not also have several senses. If 'hate'
were opposite to 'love' as a whole, and did not have several senses,
the commonplace *would* be done away with; but if 'hate' is only　10
opposite to 'love' as a disposition (*philein kata diathesin*), and not
also to 'love' in the sense of 'to kiss', the commonplace is not
impugned.

It *would* [indeed] have been impugned, if the *whole* of what is
indicated by what has several senses did not have as its opposite
something which did itself have several senses. [In fact, though[117]],
'white', which has several senses, has 'black' as its opposite; and
['black'] has several senses, because it is opposed to all the things　15
indicated by 'white'. For black is opposite both to white-in-colour
and to white-in-voice,[118] since, if it were only opposed to one of them,
it would not itself have several senses.

12. The passage from the third [book] of the *Nicomachean
[Ethics]*.[119]

'It seems indeed that compulsion (*to biaion*) is where the origin
(*arkhê*) is external, the one who has been compelled contributing　20
nothing.'

---

[115] i.e., the commonplace 'if one of the opposites has several senses, so does the
other'; above, n. 113.

[116] *philein* in Greek has the senses both of 'to love' and, in a physical sense, 'to kiss'.
For the example compare Aristotle *Topics* 1.15, 106b1-4, and with the whole of this
paragraph compare Alexander *in Top.* 100,31-101,14.

[117] The *gar* in the Greek is elliptic; '[But in fact the whole of what is indicated by
what has several senses *does* have as its opposite something which itself has several
senses;] for, [for example]...'

[118] Greek speaks of 'white' and 'black' in voice where we would speak of 'clear' and
'indistinct'. For the example compare Aristotle *Topics* 1.15, 106b7-8.

[119] Aristotle *EN* 3.1, 1110b15. Cf. the List of Titles on p. 15.

In what preceded[120] [Aristotle] said 'in which the agent or the one who is acted upon contributes nothing' in place of 'the one who has been compelled [contributes nothing]'; this he shows[121] through what is now said, making a substitution and no longer saying 'the agent or the one who is acted upon contributing nothing', but instead of these saying 'the one who has been compelled'. Sometimes

25   we speak [of such a person] as acting, and sometimes as being acted upon; for we say both 'he did it under compulsion' and 'he suffered under compulsion'.

The origin that he says is external, in the case of those who are compelled, will be the efficient [cause]. For the final cause and that 'for the sake of which' is external in the case of *all* actions, if everyone who acts does what he does for the sake of something which is outside himself. Moreover, a final cause will not be present

30   in the case of those who do something or have something done to them under compulsion. For the person who is compelled by someone does not have some end set before *himself* for the sake of which he is compelled by the one who compels him. The person who compels someone and *acts** does have some end set before him, and it is on account of this that he <compels[122]> the one whom he does. But [the latter] has none.

133,1   Those who suffer compulsion are those who have the efficient principle outside themselves, the one who is acted upon contributing nothing to what happens and not co-operating at all. [Aristotle] shows[123] that this happens in the case of voyagers, when they are driven off course by some wind, and [that it applies to what is done] by those who have power and take those who have been conquered

5   in whatever direction they decide.

Someone who is forced by someone to move one of his bodily[124] parts, in a movement which contributes towards what happens by compulsion, will not just for *that* reason contribute through himself* to what happens by compulsion. For it is not the case that, if someone who had been pushed by someone fell on someone or knocked something down, moving his legs, he would just for that reason be said to contribute to what happened. Rather, if he did this

10   in accordance with his own impulse (*hormê*) and purpose, he would contribute; but if he moved his legs in a normal and natural way,[125] [this would] no longer [be the case]. Aristotle too says this, in 'for the origin of the movement of the bodily parts in such actions [i.e. those

---

[120] 3.1, 1110a2.

[121] The Greek has 'he showed', but the present tense seems more natural in English.

[122] Added by Bruns.

[123] Aristotle *EN* 3.1, 1110a3.

[124] Literally 'organic'; and so below at 133,12.

[125] That is, in the way in which anyone would naturally stumble when pushed.

in accordance with one's own impulse] is in [the agent] himself'.[126]
For the man who throws the cargo out of the ship into the sea with
his own hands[127] acts voluntarily not because he moves his arms,   15
but because he does it having chosen to do it.

Again, those who do something through pleasure do not [act[128]]
under compulsion, because they themselves do what they do on
account of the pleasure, and do not have the efficient [cause] outside
of themselves. For what is pleasant is a cause in the sense of an end
and goal, but not in the sense of an efficient cause.

13. Concerning pleasure.[129]

Pleasure is proper to the activity on which it supervenes. It is not   20
the case that all pleasure is the same in kind, one differing from
another only numerically, while the things that produce pleasure
differ; rather, pleasures differ from each other in a similar way to
the things that produce them. [All this] Aristotle clearly showed
through showing that the pleasures that are proper to activities
encourage[130] the activities on which they supervene.[131] Pleasure in   25
doing geometry encourages the activities of geometry, and that in
lyre-playing those of lyre-playing, since they have an affinity to
them and differ from each other in the same way as the activities on
which they supervene. For if pleasures were the same, it would not
be the case that this one encourages these activities, another others.

For those whose goal is amassing money perform the activities   30
through which they think it is possible that this will result for them,
and more those through which [they think that it will result for
them] the more, on the grounds that there is some one and identical   134,1
thing which results from the different* activities.[132] And for this
reason the same people acquire money through different [activities],
and no more through some than through others, [provided that] they

---

[126] Aristotle *EN* 3.1, 1110a15.

[127] For the example cf. Aristotle *EN* 3.1, 1110a8.

[128] The Greek *could* mean 'those who do something through pleasure under
compulsion [do not act voluntarily]', picking up 'voluntarily' as well as 'act' from what
has preceded, but this suits neither what follows nor Alexander's doctrine. Cf. *P. Eth.*
9 130,12-19, which is a statement of a view which Alexander rejects, and 29
159,26-28.

[129] cf. the List of Titles on p. 15. The subject matter of this *Problem* is to some
extent similar to that of *Problems* 2, 17 and 19, but the argument that we choose
between pleasures and activities in themselves, rather than as means to some further
end, is distinctive.

[130] Literally 'increase'.

[131] cf. Aristotle *EN* 10.5, 1175a30ff.

[132] That is, the activities are valued only in so far as they all contribute, to a greater
or lesser extent, to one and the same result, making money. For 'from the different
activities' one should *perhaps* read 'from the activities, whatever they may be'; see
Notes on the Text.

produce possessions and wealth. But in the case of pleasures it is not
5   so. [People] do not, as if the same pleasure resulted from all the things
that produce pleasure, seek what will bring this[133] about most of all;
rather, on the grounds that the [pleasures] which supervene on
different activities are different, they choose those that supervene on
certain (particular) [activities], and are distressed and annoyed by
the activities and pleasures that lead them away from these
activities. For these [distractions] hinder the pleasures that are these
10 people's goal, by hindering the activities on which they supervene.
Just as the activities on which pleasures supervene damage each
other, so do the pleasures which supervene on them.

And yet, if all pleasures were the same in kind, and we chose
activities for the sake of pleasures, the activities most deserving to be
chosen would be those most productive of pleasures. But if it is not
from the pleasure produced that we judge the activities that produce
15 it*, but conversely we judge the pleasures by the activities, activities
will not deserve to be chosen on account of the pleasures [they
produce], nor will they be the same in kind as each other.

Further, we do what we do in the case of the activities that cause us
distress – [namely], we stop performing them – [also] in the case of
[the activities that cause us pleasure[134]], when we experience
pleasure in some other activities. So it is clear that the pleasures that
supervene on activities are proper to them.

20 Further, if shameful activities bring distress (*lupê*) to the temperate (*sôphrones*), but temperate and noble ones bring pleasure, and
conversely to the profligate (*akolastoi*), [pleasures] from shameful
things will not be the same in kind as those from noble ones. It is not
the same in the case of money. For it is not the case that living off
immoral earnings is a cause of poverty for the prudent and temperate, but of affluence for the wicked; rather, it would cause the
25 same prosperity for the temperate too, if they could bear to perform
these [activities]. In the case of pleasures, however,[135] not only are
shameful activities to be avoided but, in addition to bringing no
pleasure to [the temperate[136]], they actually cause them distress.

---

[133] The Greek has 'these things'; perhaps because there are in actual fact different
sorts of pleasure, even if those whose view is being counterfactually hypothesised
suppose otherwise. But vagueness over pronouns in general and singular and plural
pronouns in particular is common in these texts.

[134] The Greek simply has 'them'. The sense is clear from the context, but our author
has hardly expressed himself clearly.

[135] 'For' in the Greek is elliptical: '[The case with pleasures is different, however,]
for...'

[136] Again, the Greek simply has 'to them'; the sense is clear, but the expression is
not.

14. How to maintain the existence of something intermediate between pleasure and distress.

If pleasure is an *unimpeded* activity of the natural state, as he [Aristotle] said in the seventh book of the *Nicomachean [Ethics]*,[137]   30 and [natural activities] that *are* impeded [cause] distress, how will it be possible for absence of distress (*alupia*) to be separated from pleasure?[138] For in what activities will it be located? Not in those   135,1 which are unimpeded, nor in those which we are impeded in performing.[139]

The same difficulty also follows from what he says about pleasure in the final [book], when he says:

'All sensation is active with reference to the object of sensation, and the perfect [action] is that of [sensation] that is well disposed, applied to the noblest of the objects of sensation. For perfect activity   5 seems to be most like this – let it make no difference whether we say that it [itself] is active or that that, in which it is, [is active]. In each particular case the best activity is that of that which has the best disposition, applied to the best of its objects. This will be most perfect and most pleasant. For there is pleasure in each of the senses, and similarly in thought (*dianoia*) and contemplation   10 (*theôria*);[140] that which is most perfect is most pleasant, and that which is most perfect is that which belongs to what is in a good condition, applied to the best of its objects.'[141]

For both from these [remarks] and from what is said after them the same difficulty is constructed, and persists. Yet they[142] think

---

[137] Aristotle *EN* 7.12, 1153a14.

[138] Epicurus held that the limit of pleasure is the removal of pain (*Kuriai Doxai* 3), and from this it would follow that there is no intermediate state between pleasure on the one hand and pain or distress on the other. On the other hand, Plato already refers to those who fail to distinguish between pleasure and absence of pain (*Philebus* 44A-C; cf. *Republic* 9 583B-584E. Cf. also Speusippus at Aristotle *EN* 7.13, 1153b4-7). Nor is pleasure for Epicurus to be interpreted merely negatively as the absence of pain; rather, it is related to a harmonious movement of the soul-atoms, as opposed to an unharmonious one. (Cf. J.C.B. Gosling and C.C.W. Taylor, *The Greeks on Pleasure*, Oxford 1982, 361 and 392-3; D.N. Sedley, 'Epicurean anti-reductionism' in J. Barnes and M. Mignucci (eds.), *Matter and Metaphysics*, Naples 1989, at 300.) Epicurus would not accept that an unconscious person was experiencing pleasure (cf. 135,14 below); Gosling and Taylor, op. cit., 361. It seems therefore that the present *Problem* is best interpreted not just as a polemic against Epicurus but also in the context of issues raised by Aristotle's own discussion in the *Ethics* and the rival views discussed there.

[139] As Madigan points out ((1987) 1279 and n. 26), this is only a problem if one supposes that absence of distress must be located in activity of some sort; it could be located in *absence* of activity. Our author indeed goes on to mention absence of activity, at 135,14ff.

[140] Or perhaps 'there is pleasure in each sensation, and similarly in [each] thought and [each act of] contemplation'.

[141] Aristotle *EN* 10.4, 1174b14-23.

[142] The identity of the proponents of this view, which our text itself goes on to

that there is some condition intermediate between pleasure and distress.

15   – Or rather: first, if pleasures and distress are [located] in the activities of the senses and of thought and of contemplation, it is clear that in the absence of [any] activities of these we will be in neither of these [states]. And sometimes we are not active either in respect of the senses or in respect of contemplation, as in sleep or in relaxation (*anapausis*) apart from sleep.

Next, if what is most pleasant is [located] in the best activities,
20   and the best activities are those of the best disposed states (*hexeis*), whenever they are concerned with the best of their objects, it is clear that, if both [the states and their objects] are not like this, the activities will no longer be the most pleasant. For if there occurs a small deviation from, or slackening (*anesis*) of, that which is best in each, they will still remain pleasant, even if not most pleasant. Suppose they were even more slackened – that is, clearly, in the direction of* being engaged in without pleasure or distress [at all];
25   like this are* acts of seeing and hearing and smelling and touching that take place for the sake of what is useful, for example avoiding or recognising something. [Then] they clearly would not possess [the quality] *either* of [causing] distress *or* of [being] pleasant. After all,[143] [Aristotle] himself said of what sort intermediate activities are, through what he added, saying:

'How then is it that no one is continuously pleased or wearied? All that is human is incapable of continuous activity. So pleasure, too,
30   is[144] not [continuous]; for it follows on activity. Some things give enjoyment when they are novel, but not in the same way afterwards; [and this is] for the same reason. For at first thought is attracted, and is eagerly active concerning these things, as with those who
136,1 gaze intently, in the case of sight. But subsequently the activity is not like this but is [carried on] negligently, and for this reason the pleasure, too, is weakened.'[145]

For in such slackenings and negligent activities and weakenings of pleasure it is possible to find absence of distress without pleasure.

5   That we perceive some things without pleasure or distress [Aristotle] also says in the second [book] *On the Soul*. For speaking in it about the sense of smell and the objects of smell he says: 'man has a poor sense of smell and does not perceive any of the objects of

---

defend (as Madigan (1987) 1278 and n. 28 points out), is not further indicated. The reference may be to Aristotelians and right-thinking people in general (whom Alexander at times identifies; cf. R.W. Sharples, *Alexander of Aphrodisias on Fate*, London 1983, 18, and references there). Cf. n. 22 above.

[143] Literally 'if ' (VS¹F Bruns; Schwartz suggested 'since' (*ei ge*)).

[144] Literally 'does not come to be'; and so at 136,1 below.

[145] Aristotle *EN* 10.4, 1175a3-10.

smell without distress or pleasure'.[146] But if [he has the sense of smell] poorly, because he perceives only things that are pleasant or cause distress, it is clear that with the other senses, with which we do *not* perceive poorly, we will perceive also things which are neither   10
pleasant nor cause distress.

Moreover, if with each sense we perceive also the absences (*sterêseis*) of the proper objects of that sense, it is clear that the sensation of these [absences] is accompanied neither by pleasure nor by distress.

15. That folly is ignorance of those things of which the understanding is wisdom.[147]   15

If wisdom (*phronêsis*) is the understanding (*epistêmê*) of what is and what is not to be done, folly (*aphrosunê*) will be ignorance of the same things, and the foolish will be those who do not know some of these things and are in error (*diapseudesthai*) concerning them. But if so, not all those who are in error concerning something, through having been deceived, will be foolish; for not all knowledge (*gnôsis*) or being deceived is concerned with what is or is not to be done. For   20
knowledge, or being deceived, about the world's being of a certain [particular] shape is not concerned with what is to be done; nor is that about its having come to be or not having come to be, or being limited or unlimited, or there being one or an unlimited [number of worlds], or whether the number of the stars is even or odd, or about part of the world being above and part below, or in general any of the things which contribute to knowledge and speculative thought (*theôria*) alone.[148] But if understanding of these things belongs to   25
another virtue and not to wisdom, [then] similarly being deceived about them is not folly, but some other defect.

16. How, if all distress is an evil, it is not also the case that all pleasure is a good.[149]

If all distress (*lupê*) is an evil, and pleasure is the opposite of   30
distress, how is it not the case that [pleasure] too itself is either all a

---

[146] Aristotle *DA* 2.9, 421a10-12.

[147] Bruns (1892) xiv regards this text as 'obviously a fragment', and Madigan (1987) 1262 interprets this as suggesting that it was intended for inclusion in a longer work. It seems possible though that it is a succinct attempt to argue a particular point in the context of class discussion; some of these texts should not perhaps be interpreted in terms of eventual intended publication at all.

[148] The foregoing examples may be compared with those of things about which we do not deliberate at Aristotle *EN* 3.3, 1112a21ff.; and a similar point is made in Aristotle's own discussion of wisdom (*phronêsis*) at *EN* 6.5, 1140a35. Cf. also below, *P. Eth.* 29 160,5ff.

[149] cf. *P. Eth.* 5 124,18ff.; 125,36ff.; 6 126,19ff.; 7 127,3ff., 31ff.

good or all an evil, if it is necessary for that which is opposite to what
137,1 is evil to be either a good or an evil?

– Or rather: if all pleasure were of a single kind, it would all be
either a good or an evil; but it is not so, and [pleasure] is
differentiated in [a way] that corresponds to the activities on which
it supervenes. For [pleasures] that supervene on good activities are
good, those [that supervene] on wicked [activities] evil, just as also
5 [in the case of] desires (*epithumiai*); for of desires, too, those that are
for good things are good, those for base things evil. And so nothing
will prevent distress, which is an evil, having opposite to it some
pleasures as good and some as evil; those which are in accordance
with reason and in respect of good things as good, those which occur
contrary to right reasoning and in respect of base things, as evil. For
10 the opposite of what is evil was[150] either good or evil. And pain
(*ponos*) is not all evil; for [pain] which comes about for the sake of
noble things deserves to be chosen.

– Or rather: one should say that pleasure is a good and distress an
evil in a similar way [to each other]. For someone might say that,
while all pleasure was a good, some [was so] both without
qualification (*haplôs*) and by its own proper nature, that is [the
pleasure] of good men – for the things that are good or evil for good
men are also like this by their own nature – while some [is] a good
15 for a particular man in a particular condition, but not a good without
qualification. The pleasures of wicked men are like this; for they are
good and [worthy] to be chosen for *those* men, but not [good and
worthy to be chosen] without qualification. And of cases of distress,
too, those which relate to things that are really evil will be evil
without qualification, while those which relate to things that are not
like this [will be] evil for *those* people,[151] but not also [evil] without
qualification. The good man too will sometimes be in this sort of evil
[situation],[152] as also in poverty and disease. For the things at which
20 the good man is distressed are evil.

---

[150] This might be supposed to refer back to *P. Eth.* 5 125,2ff., or 7 127,3ff. More
probably, however, the past tense indicates a reference to a generally accepted
principle.

[151] Not, presumably, 'those who are wicked', as what has preceded would imply, but
more generally 'those who judge wrongly'; for it would be rather hard to suggest that
all those who find things evil that are not really so are for that reason *wicked*. But our
author may have been careless.

[152] That is, presumably, in a situation which is only evil for certain people, not evil
without qualification (by contrast with poverty and disease; Madigan (1987) 1277
suggests that not even pain caused by *these* is evil without qualification for the good
man; but this may seem a Stoic rather than a Peripatetic view). Will the good man
then feel distress at what are only qualified evils? The final sentence suggests he will
not, as does also the parallel case of pleasure; for the good man will not presumably

17. Under which [class] of goods pleasure will fall.

Since of good things some are honourable, some praiseworthy, some are faculties (*dunameis*) and some are beneficial,[153] there was an enquiry[154] under which [class] of these pleasure should fall. If all pleasures are a good and all are the same in kind, it is necessary to enquire about [pleasure] as a whole and [to ask] under which among 25 goods all [pleasures] will come*. But [perhaps[155]] not all are a good, but [those that] follow on activities that are to be chosen – for pleasure does not exist in its own right, but supervenes on some activity, and comes about according to its affinity to the activity; pleasure from one activity is not the same as that from another. At any rate, pleasures from one set of activities frequently destroy those from others. For the man who greatly enjoys the pleasure from 30 pipe-playing, even if he happens to be performing some activity with pleasure, when he hears the pipes leaves the activity in hand and the pleasure that [supervenes] on it, and attends to the piper,[156] enjoying the pleasure from pipe-playing which is different from that in his previous activities.

If then the [pleasures] that supervene on different and varied activities are [themselves] different, and have an affinity to the activities on which they supervene, it is clear that they will be 35 differentiated in a corresponding [way] to them, so that the [pleasures] of [activities] that are to be chosen are [themselves] to be chosen, while those of [activities] that are to be avoided are [themselves] to be avoided. And, being differentiated in a corresponding [way] to them, it is clear that they will come under 138,1 that species of goods under which are also the activities to which

---

feel any pleasure at all in the things in which the wicked man does. Cf. *P. Eth.* 13 134,25ff.; 19 139,25ff.; and n. 21 above.

[153] For this classification of goods cf. [Aristotle], *MM* 1.2 1183b19; Arius Didymus (?) ap. Stobaeum *Ecl.* 2.7.19, p. 134,20 Wachsmuth-Hense; Aspasius *in EN, CAG* 19.1 p. 32,10; Alexander *in Top.* 242,4 (= Aristotle fr.114 Rose³); R.W. Sharples, 'The Peripatetic classification of goods', in W.W. Fortenbaugh etc. (eds.), *On Stoic and Peripatetic Ethics: the work of Arius Didymus (Rutgers Studies in Classical Humanities* 1, 1983), at 144-5.

[154] This may suggest a reference to a seminar discussion; cf. n. 74 above.

[155] Literally 'But if not all are a good'; however, there is an anacoluthon in the Greek. Our author starts as if intending to say 'if not all are a good, but following on activities that are to be chosen <they are a good, following on those that are not to be chosen they are not>'. However the parenthesis at 137,26-33 intervenes, and the 'if'-clause is subsequently resumed by 'If then the pleasures that supervene on different and varied activities are [themselves] different....'.

[156] cf. Aristotle *EN* 10.5, 1175b3, and compare *P. Eth.* 2 120,31ff.; 19 139,16ff.

they have an affinity. If the activities are among those that are praiseworthy – and among these are virtuous [activities] – [the pleasures] too will be like this; if [the activities] are those of things that are good as faculties, as are those concerned with nourishment
5   and sex, [the pleasures] too will fall in this region of good things.

18. Why [Aristotle] said, in the first [book] of the *Nicomachean Ethics*,[157] that those who locate the end (*telos*) in pleasure are most vulgar.

They are vulgar (*phortikoi*) either because they locate happiness in bodily enjoyments, as do also slaves and cattle, <or>[158] because,
10   according to those in whose view pleasure alone* is to be chosen and pain (*ponos*)[159] is to be avoided on its own account, what is noble is not to be chosen on its own account, nor is what is shameful to be avoided on its own account.

Moreover:[160] if only pleasure is to be chosen [sc. on its own account], all the things that produce pleasure <are to be chosen>,[161] so that those things too will be good. And if the things that produce pain are to be avoided, and noble things sometimes produce pain, some noble things will be [things] to be avoided; and [among those] like these are courageous activities.
15   Moreover, [consider] those[162] who [say] that nothing is noble or shameful in its own nature, but some things seem like this on

---

[157] Aristotle *EN* 1.3, 1095b16. Bruns xiv regards this *Problem* as akin to the collections of arguments found in the *Mantissa* and exemplified in the *Ethical Problems* by 19 and 22. Its structure is, however, noteworthy; three positive arguments are followed by replies to three possible counter-arguments. Cf. *P. Eth.* 27 below.

[158] Added by Bruns.

[159] Madigan (1987) 1272 and n. 12 points out that pain (*ponos*) seems to have a more general sense here than in *P. Eth.* 6 126,11-14, where it is distress (*lupê*) rather than pain that is contrasted with pleasure.

[160] The second argument in fact begins not here but at 'or' in the previous paragraph, as is indicated by the summary in Madigan (1987) 1272; the present paragraph is a development of the second part of the previous one.

[161] Added by Bruns; V²(?)BSGF Ald. and Spengel have 'so too are all the things that produce pleasure'.

[162] Although it is not explicitly indicated who is meant here, and although the reference to 'those who locate the end in pleasure' in the title is a general one, it *may* be that it is the Epicureans in particular whom our author has in mind in the present passage. Epicurus' position on what is right is not a purely conventionalist one, being based on real advantage to society, but it might well give that impression; cf. Epicurus *Principal Doctrines* 31-8. And while Epicurus did distinguish between natural and unnatural desires, and say that not all pleasures were to be chosen, while yet maintaining that pleasure was the end (cf. *Letter to Menoeceus* 127 and 129) there are problems over the internal consistency of this position. Cf. J.C.B. Gosling and C.C.W. Taylor, *The Greeks on Pleasure*, Oxford 1984, 407-12. The use of the term *prolêpsis* is not conclusive, even though it was probably Epicurean in origin; cf. n. 100 above.

account of men's preconceptions (*prolêpseis*), and that it is on account of these that we avoid the shameful as an evil, [though] it is not <shameful> in its own nature. [According to their view] we will suffer the greatest penalties in respect of pleasures, by refraining from them in avoiding what is shameful. None at all of the irrational creatures does this; so being rational would be a bad thing for us.[163]   20

[They] may say 'Not even we ourselves think it right to choose shameful pleasures'. If [1] they were to say this in this way and for this reason, that what is shameful is to be avoided on its own account, they would speak well, but would not however preserve [their claim] that only pain is to be avoided on its own account. [2] If however [they say this] not because of the shamefulness itself, but because certain penalties are laid down for such things by the lawgivers, then [2a] if [the penalties are laid down] well, shameful   25 things will again be bad in their own nature; but [2b] if [they are not laid down] well, this is to say that it is a penalty for men to be rational, if on account of reason they suppose that things that are not evil *are* evil, and on account of them are deprived of the things that are truly good.[164]

To say that we choose everything that we choose as [being] pleasant, and to use this to persuade [us] that pleasure is the greatest good, is not true, if we choose each thing that we choose   30 either as [being] noble or as [being] advantageous or as [being] pleasant.[165] It is false to say that what is advantageous, too, is   139,1 pleasant; for we often choose it when it is clearly unpleasant. And if it happens that what is noble is also pleasant in the respect in which it is noble, nevertheless it is not chosen *because* it is pleasant. At any rate, we often turn away from and avoid the shameful when it is pleasant; but if we avoid [the pleasant] because it is shameful, we will also choose the pleasant because of its nobility.   5

Furthermore, to say that nothing is noble or shameful in its own nature, but that these [terms] are applied in respect of personal preconceptions, and to require that their nobility should be shown through some argument, is like requiring an account of why something is white. For none of the things that are clear by their

---

[163] With this use in a *reductio ad absurdum* of the idea that being rational will be a disadvantage for men one may perhaps compare the use in *P. Eth.* 2 121,32ff. (in a very different context) of the idea that virtue will be unnatural for what is rational.

[164] The argument seems overstated; it is not necessary to suppose that men mistakenly think that pleasures forbidden by the laws are *evil*, only that they reckon that fear of the law's penalties makes them not worth pursuing. That is, men need not suppose that the shameful pleasures are not good in themselves, only that their goodness (i.e., on the hypothesis being entertained, their pleasantness) is outweighed by the painfulness of their consequences. The consequence that bad laws will deprive men of what is really good will still follow.

[165] cf. Aristotle *EN* 2.3, 1104b30; Alexander *Fat.* 15 185,24; *Mant.* 174,21.

own nature needs the support of argument, and for all who are not
10   corrupted[166] that eye of the soul is clear by which it is recognised
that there is such a thing as what is noble and what is shameful.
That we possess from nature [the power] of recognising shameful
things and noble things is clear from the fact that [people] blush at
shameful things not only when they happen but even when they are
spoken of, being affected in some way [by them];[167] and this can be
seen happening even in the case of small children. For these too
often blush as if at something shameful.

15   19. That pleasures are not the same in kind.[168]

Things that are the same in kind as each other do not destroy each
other. For white is not destroyed *qua* white by white, nor black by
black, nor hot by hot. But pleasure can destroy pleasure*; at any
rate, the pleasures from the [things] concerning which [people] are
very eager destroy those from the things about which [they] are less
20   eager. In the theatres, at any rate, the [pleasure] from hearing
someone performing well in a comedy destroys that from eating
sweetmeats.[169] But if pleasure from something else has the same
effect as the distress which is opposite to pleasure, it will not be the
same in kind and differ only numerically.
          Moreover: if pleasures are proper to the activities on which they
supervene, being the ends of those very activities which differ from
25   one another in kind, pleasures too will be different in kind from one
another.
          Moreover: if the temperate (*sôphrôn*) man cannot enjoy the
pleasure of the profligate (*akolastos*), or the profligate that of the
temperate, all pleasures will not be the same in kind as one another.
But the first; therefore the second.[170]

          20. That one should not seek usefulness everywhere.

30   The person who in every action and every [type of] learning requires
what is useful, and does not think anything worth doing or learning
140,1 which is not useful,[171] is removing the existence of anything which

---

[166] Literally 'mutilated', 'disabled'. Cf. Alexander, *Mant.* 175,12ff., especially
175,22; *P. Eth.* 9 129,10f., and 29 160,34.

[167] Madigan (1987) 1273 and n. 13 here compares *P. Eth.* 21, below.

[168] cf. above, *P. Eth.* 2. Bruns xiv regards this text as a fragment.

[169] cf. Aristotle *EN* 10.5, 1175b10 with 1175b1; above, *P. Eth.* 2 120,31; 17 137,28.

[170] The way in which the argument is expressed is drawn from Stoic logic.

[171] The attitude attacked in this *Problem* is not an unfamiliar one today; nor is the
suggestion that what is not 'useful' may have a place, but only as an amusement or
pastime (on which see the last two paragraphs here; and for the view that the goal of
life cannot be amusement cf. Aristotle *EN* 10.6, 1176b27). In antiquity a utilitarian

is good and valuable (*haireton*) on its own account; for what is useful comes about for the sake of something else for which it is useful, and that which comes about for the sake of something else, deriving [its own] value from it, also derives from it [the quality] of being a good, and everything is useful that produces some good and comes about because it produces it. But if what is good and valuable on its own 5
account is better than that which derives its goodness from something else, the person who requires usefulness in everything removes the existence of anything which is good in the proper sense and in its own right.

Moreover: the person who says that only what is useful is good and valuable removes the existence of anything *useful*. For what is useful is valuable because it produces [some] good, and derives its goodness from that which comes about because of it; but there is 10
nothing like this according to those for whom only what is useful is valuable. [So] <what is useful will be removed>*, through the removal of what is brought about by what is useful and is the reason for what is useful possessing value.

For if what is useful is useful because it produces some good thing which is *useful*, everything which is brought about by what is useful will be useful, and as being useful it will again be referred to 15
something else.[172] And this will go on to infinity, what is useful always being useful because it produces something, but everything which is brought about by what is useful being useful itself also. And if this is so, not even what is useful will still remain useful; for there is no ultimate thing which, by being valuable and good on its own account, causes the things which contribute to it and are useful for it 20
to be like this*. For if what comes about is not [itself] valuable, what is useful for it will not possess value either; and similarly, none of the things that are useful for something else that is useful will possess value either, since none of the things which are brought about by them is valuable on its own account.

If then it is absurd to remove the existence of anything good at all (and it *is* removed according to those who say that only what is useful should be taken seriously, as has been shown), and if it is also 25
absurd to say that nothing is useful (and [there being anything useful] also is removed by those who say that only what is useful

---

attitude to education is portrayed in the remarks of Echion at Petronius *Satyricon* 46; but the debate can be traced back further to Plato *Republic* 7 526D-527A, 527D-528A (cf. 525CD), and indeed to Protagoras' attack on Hippias at Plato *Protagoras* 318DE. With the last section of the present *Problem* one may compare Aristotle's assertion in *Politics* 1.2, 1252b29-30 that the city-state comes into existence for the sake of life, but exists for the sake of the *good* life.

[172] That is, if A is useful because it produces B, which is useful, there must in turn be something else produced by B which makes B useful, to which B can 'be referred'; and so *ad infinitum*.

[should] be taken seriously), this opinion will be absurd.

In addition to this, [even] if useful things give us assistance for the necessities and troubles and circumstances of life, the end [at which we aim] is not to be free from troubles, but [rather], being free from 30   all troubles, to perform certain activities, which are proper to men and are the activities of free men*. For it is the characteristic of 141,1 slaves to do everything with a view to freedom from trouble and to spend the rest of their lives in amusements, performing no activity worthy of being taken seriously.

It would be absurd, in the case of the gods, either to say that they perform their activities with a view to what is *useful*, when they are not in need of anything like this but are beyond all need and being 5   affected, or to locate their end in amusement. Similarly, it is absurd to say that the end of men's serious activities and of their whole life is amusement. For if we all differ from the other living creatures by having a capacity for understanding and by possessing a perception of the truth, it is clear that our end too will be in the activities according to these, those that take place insofar as we are human. 10   We are most of all human in the respects in which we differ from all other living creatures, and these are understanding and truth, which are not located in amusement or in things which are to be valued [just] on account of usefulness.

21. On shame (*aidôs*).

[Aristotle] has said in the second [book] of the *Nicomachean* 15   *[Ethics]*[173] that [shame] is a feeling (*pathos*), and not a state (*hexis*) or a virtue (*aretê*); he also says [this] in the fourth book,[174] and shows that it is a feeling, through the definition of shame and through the things that happen to those who are ashamed. But in the former place he said that it is a praiseworthy feeling; here however, while he says that it is desirable for the young, because [those of] that age easily go wrong, and shame prevents many 20   [wrong actions], for those who have advanced further in age he says that [shame] is thenceforth alien. For shame is fear of ill repute (*adoxia*), and fear of ill repute arises in respect either of shameful things that have already happened or of ones that are going to happen or of reputed ones;[175] and those that have advanced further in years and [now] possess the virtues no longer do [such things].[176] For it is easy for them to avoid even those things that are not [in

---

[173] Aristotle *EN* 2.7, 1108a30. The present text is in fact a 'problem' in the strict sense in its content (*pace* Bruns xiv), even if not in the form of its presentation.

[174] Aristotle *EN* 4.9, 1128b10.

[175] *dokousin*, cognate with 'ill repute' (*adoxia*).

[176] Or perhaps 'are no longer able to do [such things]'.

fact] shameful but are thought to be causes of ill repute [nevertheless]. 25

It is worth deciding about this matter, especially since we are conscious that we ourselves, [although] we have already reached this age, are ashamed at many things and frequently.[177] Well, if what was said was that one should think little of ill repute, we would not need any discussion. But it is not this that is being said; it is accepted that one should avoid ill repute, if reputation and honour are the greatest of external goods, and it is being said that those who 30 neither do nor have done anything shameful no longer become subject to ill repute. So we will say something about what has been mentioned already, the things about which we are conscious of being ashamed.

For it does not seem that ill repute comes about only in respect of 142,1 deeds that are [really] not noble, but also in respect of those that are objects of suspicion and which can be misrepresented, this having its greatest influence among the ignorant. But if ill repute some[times] comes about in respect of such things, the person who has done nothing shameful is not excluded from being able to become the subject of ill repute. If then one ought to fear this ill repute which comes from misrepresentations, no less than [that] 5 from [actual] deeds,[178] this feeling [sc. shame[179]] will not be alien to any* of those who are respectable and further advanced in years, not even according to [Aristotle], if one should avoid and fear ill repute, and this [fear] is shame.

Moreover: for those who have lived noble and respected [lives], because they are at variance with all shameful things in every way*, the fear of ill repute in respect of these is greater, and they avoid it 10 more. And so it comes about that those people for whom shameful things are very hateful feel the greatest shame. For shame does not seem to be fear of ill repute without qualification, but much rather alienation from shameful things, on account of which those who are in this condition fear ill repute in respect of them.

But if shame is like this, it will no longer be a feeling, without 15

---

[177] The author is presumably speaking for people of his age in general, not of a personal tendency of his own to excessive embarrassment. So too Madigan (1987) 1266.

[178] The text actually has 'one ought to fear this ill repute, which comes from misrepresentations no less than from [actual] deeds'; but the intended sense is as given in the translation.

[179] That the identification to be supplied is 'shame' rather than 'fear of ill repute' is clear from the fact that it is clear in the Greek that 'and this fear is shame' at the end of the paragraph is part of the argument, dependent on 'if', rather than a statement of the conclusion; accordingly a reference to 'shame' is needed at the present point. The reference to 'shame' is awkward to supply, and the text in fact has, after 'from [actual] deeds', 'and the fear of ill repute is shame'; but Bruns deletes this as a gloss, and it does make the end of the paragraph seem redundant.

15   qualification, either, but rather a state (*hexis*) and disposition (*diathe-sis*) on which the afore-mentioned feeling follows.[180] At any rate, among those who have advanced further in age one will not see those who do not avoid shameful things being ashamed at all; because of the familiarity of the things they do, they think little of ill repute in respect of them. But those who keep themselves pure from such things feel the more shame at that time [of life], to the extent that
20   they have persuaded themselves that ill repute in respect of shameful things is more shameful for those who have reached such an age than it is for the young.

        22. That the virtues imply one another.[181]

        That the moral virtues imply one another is to be shown also from choice (*proairesis*). For virtue is judged most by choice, and right
25   choice comes both from wisdom (*phronêsis*), if* deliberation is [the work] of wisdom, and from moral virtue, if it is necessary for the man who deliberates well to have the right goal set [before him], with a view to which he deliberates about the things that contribute to it, and [if] the goal is defined by moral virtue. For we deliberate about that which we desire, and the desire for things that are fitting
30   comes from moral virtue, as Aristotle said. So choice is not right in the absence of wisdom or of virtue. For one [makes us pursue] the end, the other makes [us] do the things that lead to the end.[182]
143,1   Moreover: it is[183] necessary for the person who possesses any moral virtue whatsoever to possess wisdom, if moral virtue performs the actions defined by wisdom and right reasoning. And it is also necessary for the person who possesses wisdom to possess moral virtue, if it is proper to wisdom to enquire how it is possible to
5   achieve the necessary goal, which it belongs to moral virtue to define. For this is the virtue of the appetitive faculty; for it is in this way that wisdom and cleverness differ, in that wisdom finds and enquires after the things that lead to the right goal, but cleverness those that [lead] to just *any* [goal].[184]

---

[180] 'state' (*hexis*) and 'disposition' (*diathesis*) may be distinguished in that the former is more permanent (Aristotle *Cat.* 8 8b27). For the distinction as drawn by the Stoics cf. *SVF* 2.393.

[181] The title of this piece is the same as that of *Mant.* 153,28-156,7, and the argument is broadly similar to the last two sections of that discussion, 155,38-156,25. That the present text is a fragment of a larger discussion is suggested by 'also' in the first sentence; cf. also n. 183 below.

[182] cf. Aristotle *EN* 6.13, 1145a4-6; R.-A. Gauthier and J.-Y. Jolif, *Aristote: l'Ethique à Nicomaque*, 1958, vol. 2, p. 560.

[183] The Greek has 'if it is necessary', but there is no apodosis unless one takes *de* in 143,2 ('it is also necessary for the person who possesses wisdom to possess moral virtue') as apodotic. At the end of this *Problem* MS G has a marginal note 'it seems to

23. If pleasure is unimpeded activity of a natural state according to Aristotle,[185] how will happiness too not be   10 pleasure according to him.

Well, if unimpeded natural activity is pleasure for each thing, and all desire it, pleasure and living like this is <not[186]> just for this reason also the end. For the cause of living like this is that from   15 which the absence of impediment comes. If then it was pleasure that was the cause of unimpeded virtuous activity,[187] the good in the strictest sense would be located in it; but if [it was] not pleasure but something else, that [other thing] would be <the cause*> of such a life. So, if it is virtue that is for the most part the cause for men having this sort of activity (for the results of chance will also appear   20 to contribute to some extent to the absence of impediment), it will be [virtue] that will most of all be the cause among men of such a life. And so, if happiness too for a man is supposed to consist in the activities that are natural for him and proper [to him] in that he is a man*, provided that they take place without impediment, [then] it is virtue most of all that will be the cause of happiness, being the cause both of a man's performing the activities proper to him and of his doing so without impediment.   25

Moreover: pleasure* is an activity because it accompanies activity which comes about in this way,[188] as [Aristotle] showed in the last book of the *Ethics*,[189] and pleasure, accompanying activity which comes about in this way, will be a sign that happiness is present for those who are active in this way, rather than [itself being] happiness. Pleasure is said to be an activity by Aristotle not as being an activity according to its own proper account, but as having its   30 being in relation to activity and not being able to occur without it. And for this reason, being happiness will apply to [pleasure] in the same way as does being an unimpeded activity. [Pleasure] is unimpeded activity because it accompanies such activity, and it is happiness because it accompanies happiness and is a sign of its   144,1 presence. The extent to which we fall short of unimpeded activity in respect of the virtues in accordance with which such activities

---

me incomplete'; similarly Bruns xiv. On the relation between wisdom and virtue cf. Aristotle, *EN* 6.13.

[184] cf. Aristotle *EN* 6.12, 1144a23ff.

[185] Aristotle *EN* 7.12, 1153a14; see n. 137 above.

[186] Added by Schwartz.

[187] Or 'activity in accordance with excellence (*aretê*)'; it is assumed that the supreme good for each thing consists in activity in accordance with its natural excellence, and for men moral virtue will be a major part of this. Cf. Aristotle *EN* 1.7, 1098a7-18.

[188] That is, naturally and without impediment.

[189] cf. Aristotle *EN* 10.4, 1174b14ff.

<ought[190]> to be performed, is the extent to which virtuous activity, too, fails to have perfection* in itself.[191]

5   That it is characteristic of a slave to locate happiness in bodily pleasures and the life of enjoyment was sufficiently shown by [Aristotle][192] through the fact that slaves and cattle esteem such a life, and also through [the example of] Sardanapalus. Even in the case of activities of the soul the activities are not for the sake of the pleasure, but the pleasure [for the sake of] the activities, [as] is clear. For even if virtuous activities are as pleasant as they can

10   possibly be, nevertheless [people] do not pursue them eagerly for the sake of pleasure, but vice versa. For we choose virtuous activities even if they sometimes become causes of distress and pain, as happens in the case of courageous activities;[193] but it is never reasonable to choose shameful pleasures. Accordingly, if virtuous activities are to be chosen even if they involve distress, which is

15   opposite to pleasure, while pleasures are never to be chosen if they involve the opposite to virtue and to what is noble, it is clear [both] that we choose the pleasures* that supervene on virtuous activities, [and that we do so] on account of such activities.

This matter could most easily be settled, if we follow nature and note and observe which of the two it is that nature gave to us, as soon as we were born, for the sake of the other, activity on account of

20   pleasure or pleasure on account of activity. It is well known that pleasure has been given to living creatures by nature on account of their activities, if they are going to survive. For [survival] is impossible for them if they are not nourished. And this is why* [nature] gives us pleasure in nourishment; on account of this pleasure we seek nourishment when it is not present and make use of it when it is present, excusing the distraction from better things

25   that sometimes comes about through this. For it would be altogether absurd to say that we take nourishment not because we will be preserved through it, but for the sake of the pleasure there is in it.

And if someone examines from the point of view of nature the pleasure that supervenes on sexual intercourse, too, he will find that it has not been introduced for the sake of anything other than the production of offspring, so that living creatures, being led on[194] by the pleasure, should not shrink from mating, which is the cause of

30   the eternity in species of living creatures, on account of which it

[190] added by S²B² Ald. Spengel.

[191] Madigan (1987) 1273 and n. 15 finds the relevance of this sentence problematic. The implication is presumably that activity that falls short of perfection will not be perfectly pleasurable.

[192] Aristotle *EN* 1.3, 1095b19ff. Cf. *P. Eth.* 18 138,8ff.

[193] cf. *P. Eth.* 18 138,12-14.

[194] The verb is the technical word for 'escorting', *inter alia* for 'escorting to the bridal chamber'.

comes about that the world itself, too, always remains alike.[195] But if in these cases living creatures clearly possess pleasures for the sake of their activities, it is reasonable [to suppose] that it is so also in the case of the other natural activities.[196]

That, in the cases where nobility (*to kalon*) and pleasure exist [151,19] together,[197] it is not what is noble that is to be chosen for the sake of pleasure, but pleasure [for the sake of] what is noble, is clear – as we 35[20] have mentioned already[198] – from the fact that, if what is noble deserved to be chosen for the sake of pleasure, [pleasure] being the 145,1 end and deserving to be chosen on its own account, and nobility deserving to be chosen [only] because it produces pleasure, [then] what is shameful would deserve to be chosen in the same way as what is noble, since [what is shameful] too produces pleasure. For the choice of the things which are to be chosen because they are productive is assessed in terms of what is brought about by them. 5 Either one must deny that certain pleasures supervene also on [25] shameful actions, [saying that they supervene] only on noble ones; or else what is shameful will truly[199] deserve to be chosen in the same way as what is noble, if it is the pleasure which they produce that is the cause of their being chosen. But if this is absurd, recommending every shameful action to us as no less deserving to be chosen than noble [action], <or even more[200]> if it provides 10 pleasures more and for more people, then what is noble will not [30] deserve to be chosen on account of pleasure on the grounds that it produces it. And if it is necessary either that what is noble is to be chosen on account of pleasure, or pleasure on account of what is noble, and what is noble is not [to be chosen] on account of pleasure, it is from nobility that pleasure will derive its worthiness to be chosen.

For it is not possible to say that nobility and pleasure are the [152,1] same thing in the cases where they co-exist and exist at the same 15 time as each other. For if their essence were the same, it would be necessary for them to be convertible with each other, so that everything that was noble would, in being noble, also possess the quality of being pleasant, and everything that was pleasant would simultaneously be both pleasant and noble. But if it is false to say [5] that every pleasure is noble, because we see pleasures supervening no less on shameful activities [than on noble ones], not even the

---

[195] cf. *Quaest*. 3.5 89,18ff.

[196] From here to the end of the chapter is repeated almost verbally as *P. Eth*. 26 below, as is noted in the margin of V. Cf. the two versions of *Quaest*. 1.11.

[197] *P. Eth*. 26 omits 'in the cases … exist together'.

[198] *P. Eth*. 26 omits 'as we have mentioned already'.

[199] *P. Eth*. 26 has 'or if this is not true, what is shameful will deserve'.

[200] Omitted by the MSS of *P. Eth*. 23, but added by B[2] and Bruns; present in *P. Eth*. 26. So too Madigan (1987) 1274 and n. 16.

20   pleasures that supervene on noble activities will be the *same* as the
      activities on which they supervene.
          [Someone might] say both [1] that only pleasures are to be chosen
      on their own account, and that each of the other things that are to be
      chosen [deserves to be chosen] to the extent that it contributes
[10] something to pleasure, and also [2] that, while what is noble is to be
      chosen because it produces pleasure, what is shameful is not also to
25   be chosen because of the pleasure brought about by it. [But this is not
      the sort of thing said] by those who are saying things that are
      [generally] agreed, but of those who unconvincingly deny the [very]
      things which they concede, through their principles,[201] to be so. For
      no one who had not adopted such a contrivance would defend so
      absurd an opinion.
[15]   [This person might indeed] say that the pleasures that supervene
      on noble activities are pure and free from mixture with the opposite
30   [forms of] distress, and that on this account the activities that
      produce them, too, are to be chosen; while those [pleasures] that
      [supervene] on shameful [activities] possess little that gives enjoy-
      ment and much and more that produces distress, for which reason
      such activities too are not to be chosen, being productive of distress
[20] rather than of pleasure. But how is [this] not the [position] of those
      who differentiate pleasures in [a way] that corresponds to the
      activities on which they supervene, and do not keep them the same in
146,1 kind? For if those that [supervene] on noble things are of one sort,
      those that [supervene] on shameful things of another, it is the noble
      and the shameful things that will be the causes of the difference in the
      pleasures.
          For the activities do not derive their worthiness to be chosen from
      the pleasures, but the pleasures from the activities, since it is on
      account of [the activities] that [the pleasures] possess even [the
[25] quality of] being of a certain sort.[202] And [pleasures] from noble
5   [activities] will be of one kind, those from shameful [activities] of
      another, if all those from the noble [activities] are pure and unmixed
      [with distress] and not causes of any regret or distress, being made of
      a [particular] kind by activities of this type, while all those from
      shameful [activities] are mixed and involve regret. This being the
[30] relation of pleasures to activities, it is quite clear that the activities do
      not derive their worthiness to be chosen from the pleasures, but the
10   pleasures derive from the activities, in some cases worthiness to be
      chosen, in others [worthiness] to be avoided, if those which have more
      [in them] that gives distress than that gives pleasure are to be
      avoided, and all those that [supervene] on shameful activities are like
      this.

----

[201] *haireseis*: 'choices', but also the technical term for a philosophical sect. Cf.
Alexander *Fat.* 14 182,27ff.

24. How the virtues are worthy to be chosen on their own account.

How indeed could someone say that the virtues, and [virtuous] activities, are worthy to be chosen on their own account, if they are   15
worthy to be chosen by us on account of [their] removal of immoderate feelings (*pathê*)?[203] For indeed we choose courage so that we may be able to moderate fears and boldness, and temperance [so that we may be able to moderate] distress and pleasures [that arise] through touch. And we choose each of the other virtues, too, either for the moderation of certain feelings or [for that] of actions: liberality and magnificence in order to be able to   20
moderate the actions which we perform through the giving and receiving of money, greatness of spirit and ambition for choice among honours which is proportionate and in accordance with [one's[204]] worth, mildness for due proportion in what concerns anger; and we also choose justice, because it preserves the community which is natural for us if we are by nature [inclined to   25
live] in a community and a city-state. The art of building is not worthy to be chosen on its own account just because the things that result from it are worthy to be chosen; neither is the art of wrestling worthy to be chosen on its own account [just] because it produces [the ability] to wrestle well. [So] too none of the virtues will be worthy to be chosen on its own account, if they derive their worthiness to be chosen from the things that are brought about through them.
Or rather – if there were a difference between [i] that on account of which we say that each of the virtues is worthy to be chosen and   30
[ii] the virtue itself, then it would be reasonable to rule out each of them deserving to be chosen on its own account. But if the essence of each of the virtues consists in that on account of which it is worthy to be chosen, it would be reasonable to say that the virtues are worthy to be chosen on their own account. If the art of   147,1
house-building were [itself] a house, on account of which it is worthy to be chosen, it would be worthy to be chosen on its own account. Just so each of the virtues, if it is the same as that on account of which it is worthy to be chosen, will be worthy to be chosen on its own account – and still more and more clearly [so] if each of the

[202] 'since it is ... of a certain sort' is the text of *P. Eth.* 26, missing from *P. Eth.* 23.

[203] cf. David Pears, 'Courage as a mean', in A.O. Rorty (ed.), *Essays on Arisotle's Ethics*, Berkeley 1980, 171-87, discussing the internal and external goals of courage (nobility in action and victory in battle respectively). I owe this reference to Professor Sorabji.

[204] cf. Aristotle *EN* 4.3, 1123b3, 17, 24.

things in accordance with [the virtues] possesses [its] worthiness to
5   be chosen in itself and not through reference to something else, [in
the same way] as the house. It is on account of [the house] that the
art of building possesses [its] worthiness to be chosen, on account of
the shelter from winter and summer that comes about from it.

That the virtues are the same as the things on account of which
we say they are worthy to be chosen is clear from the fact that they
are means in feelings and actions, courage [the mean between] fear
and boldness, temperance that between distress [through touch]
10   and pleasure through touch, liberality between giving and receiving
money; and the same account applies to the rest too. Accordingly, if
their essence consists in those things on account of which they are
worthy to be chosen, they will indeed* be worthy to be chosen on
their own account, and still more on their own account because the
means relating to fears and boldness are not worthy to be chosen by
us on account of anything else, but each on its own account. For that
15   which has worthiness to be chosen in itself and in its own nature is
worthy to be chosen on its own account, and such are the means
which are concerned with the actions that are natural for us.

These things being so, if the preservation of political and of
economic community (*koinônia*) are not worthy to be chosen by men
on their own account, but on account of something else, [then]
justice too, which is the mean in the things on which the
preservation of the aforementioned things depends, will not be
20   worthy to be chosen on its own account either, according to those for
whom this is what justice is. But if community and its preservation
are worthy to be chosen by men on their own account,[205] justice too
will be shown to be worthy to be chosen on its own account, in that it
is a mean and an equality of what is equal[206] both in distributions
and in contracts, on which the preservation of the primary, political
community depends.

25   Community *is* worthy to be chosen by men on its own account, as
can easily be recognised from the fact that community is natural for
them. The clearest sign of this is that man differs most from the
other living creatures in that respect that is only useful to him in
community with others. For speech (*logos*) is his peculiar
[possession],[207] and the use of this is for indication to one's
neighbours of one's personal thoughts and feelings. And this is also
30   clear from the fact that a man is not able to live even for a short time
if he becomes isolated. Man's essence is in community, and speech is
for the sake of this. The best and most perfect of the communities

---

[205] The Greek has 'on its own account', treating community and its preservation as
two aspects of a single thing.
[206] Or 'fair'.
[207] cf. Aristotle *Politics* 1.2, 1253a8-18 (I owe this reference to Professor Sorabji).

that come about in accordance with speech is political [community],   148,1
and each thing is naturally judged [starting] from the things that
are best. Therefore man will be capable of speech,[208] and also
political; and the preservation of [political] community will be[209]
most natural for him and worthy to be chosen on its own account.
And this is what justice is like.

25. Summary account of the discovery and establishment of the   5
virtues.[210]

Happiness is the goal for men, and we must do everything in order
to acquire it, as being the end and the greatest of our goods. It is
impossible to do things as contributing to something, or in general to
recognise the things through which it is possible to reach some goal,
if the goal itself is not known. For the knowledge (*gnôsis*) of the goal
is the beginning of the discovery of the things which contribute to
the goal and of the actions which come about for its sake, and for   10
this reason the beginning of moral philosophy is to know what is
happiness, that for the sake of which we must do everything.[211]
We therefore enquired what happiness is,[212] and found[213] that the
good of each being is in the proper[214] activity according to which it
possesses its being what it is, provided that[215] this [activity] comes
about well. For it is like this in the case of the things that are
constituted by nature, and also in the case of those according to art,   15
<if art>* imitates nature. For the good of a horse is like this, if its

[208] *logikon*: often most naturally rendered by 'rational', but here the connection
with speech (*logos*) needs to be brought out.

[209] Literally 'would be'; but cf. n. 23 above and Introduction n. 33.

[210] This *Problem* draws heavily on certain sections of Aristotle's *Nicomachean
Ethics*, especially books 1, 2 and 6, and summarises central ideas of that text. Some
particular parallels have been noted in what follows – I am grateful to Professor
Sorabji for pointing out the need to draw attention to them; but the reader is urged to
compare the whole section with the text of Aristotle.

[211] Through a printing error Bruns' line numbers from 10 onwards are one too low
both in the margin of the text and in the apparatus for the rest of this page. However,
for the reader's convenience I have followed his printed numbers rather than
substituting the correct ones.

[212] The reference may be, not to any previous discussion in Alexander's circle, but
rather to the author and his hearers and readers as students of Aristotle joining in
Aristotle's discussion in the *Ethics*; that is, the sense may be 'We readers of Aristotle
...'. That seems possible even if we do not suppose that there had been a formal course
of lectures on the *Ethics*, though it is plausible enough that there should have been. (I
am grateful to Professor Sorabji for drawing my attention to this point.) Cf. also
below, 149,2.

[213] Literally 'having found', but there is an anacoluthon, and no main verb follows.

[214] *oikeios*; cf. the Greek-English Index. Here, as Professor Sorabji points out, it is
what is distinctive of man that will be counted as proper to him. Cf. also n. 187 above.

[215] That is to say: the good of each of the things that are is in the proper functioning
of the activity in which its being consists.

proper work, in that it is a horse, is running, and its good is running well. The same argument also applies to a dog; whether the work of a dog is to guard or to hunt, or whether of some it is the former and
20 of some the latter, the good for them is in doing these things well. And for the builder, too, the good and the end are in building well, since his work is building. And since in the case of each thing the <end>[216] of its activity and work comes from its own proper excellence, the end of each thing [is] in performing its proper work excellently.[217]

But if this is so, the good and end of man, too, will be in
25 performing excellently the activities that are proper to him in that he is a man*.[218] Now, the proper activities of man are those that come about in accordance with his rational soul; for the essence of man consists in living and in acting in accordance with [one's] rational soul. If this is so, the end for [man] will be in acting in accordance with excellence of rational soul, so that happiness, since
30 it is the good and end of man, will be activity in accordance with excellence of rational soul,[219] it being added that [it should be] in a complete life (for there is nothing complete in what is incomplete), and further that [it should be] in prime[220] [circumstances], on

[216] Added by V²BS² Ald. Spengel and Bruns.

[217] Literally 'in accordance with excellence' or 'virtue' (*aretê*). The argument, like that of Aristotle *EN* 1.7, 1097b24ff. on which it is based, depends on seeing moral *virtues* as among the *excellences* of man analogous to excellences in other things; I have therefore translated *aretê* sometimes by 'excellence', sometimes by 'virtue' as in the title, sometimes by 'excellence, or virtue' explicitly.

[218] cf. Aristotle *EN* 1.7, 1098a16.

[219] Or perhaps 'activity of rational soul in accordance with virtue', but in the light of 148,28 above the rendering in the text is more likely, in spite of Aristotle *EN* 1.7, 1098a16-17.

[220] That is, 'favourable' circumstances. Apelt here proposed *khorêgoumenois*, 'that it should be [equipped with] resources' (literally 'should be among resources'), for *proêgoumenois* of Bruns and the MSS; cf. Aristotle *EN* 1.8, 1099a31ff., and Appendix. However, this is one of a whole series of passages in which Aristotle's definition of *eudaimonia* is expanded *either* by the addition of a reference to activity that is *proêgoumenê*, as in the following clause here (Arius Didymus ap. Stobaeum, *Ecl.* 2.7.3 51,10; 2.7.18 132,8; cf. 2.7.3 51,11, 12, 14; 2.7.14 126,20; 2.7.17 129,19-20; 2.7.18 130,19; MSS text in each case, see below) *or* by that of the phrase *en proêgoumenois* (Arius Didymus ap. Stobaeum, *Ecl.* 2.7.3 50,12 Wachsmuth (MSS text); Aspasius *in EN* 26,14ff.; 151,11). Cf. M. Giusta, 'Sul significato filosofico del termine *proêgoumenos*', *Atti dell' Accademia delle Scienze di Torino* 96 (1961-2) 229-71, at 229-30 (cf. 255 on the present passage); A. Grilli, 'Contributo alla storia di *proêgoumenos*', in *Studi linguistici in onore di V. Pisani*, Brescia 1969, 409-500, at 439-44; P.M. Huby, 'Peripatetic definitions of happiness', in W.W. Fortenbaugh etc. (eds.), *On Stoic and Peripatetic Ethics: the work of Arius Didymus* (*Rutgers Studies in Classical Humanities* 1, 1983), 121-34, at 125-6; M.D. Rohr, ibid. 135-8). Wachsmuth emended *proêgoumenos* in these passages to *khorêgoumenos*, but subsequent discussions have generally rejected this (Giusta, 230-1; Grilli, 440 n. 2; Huby, 125-6). These discussions cite the present passage with the MSS text, not referring to Apelt's emendation; Apelt does not refer to the passages in Stobaeus or to Wachsmuth's

account of the fact that the primary activities [of the virtuous man] and those that are wished for*[221] need instruments.

This being the goal, it is clear from the [way we] discovered and came to know it that, for the acquisition of happiness, there is need 149,1 of the excellences, or virtues,[222] of rational soul. And enquiring which these are, we reasonably came first to seeing what the rational soul is, since it is excellence, or virtue, in this that we are seeking. Now, the faculty of reason was found to be double;[223] one [sort is] irrational in itself but rational by being able to obey reason 5 and be ordered by reason, and this is what the appetitive soul in us is like. The other is rational by itself having reason in itself. Each of the aforementioned faculties has a certain proper activity, and an excellence, or virtue, in accordance with which goodness in its

---

emendation, but bases his case on Aristotelian parallels (notably *EN* 1.10, 1101a14) and on the argument that *proêgoumenois* resulted from a scribe's eye jumping to the following *proêgoumenas*.

'Primary activities' seem to be those that are characteristic of an agent just as an agent of a certain sort, as opposed to those called for in particular and special circumstances, especially those that are less than favourable (cf. Alexander *Mant.* 160,31ff.; Giusta 254; Grilli 460ff.; Huby 126). In the case of a human agent simply *qua* human they will be the activities characteristic of human virtue *as such*, or that are primarily conducive to or constitutive of virtue (cf. Anon. *in EN, CAG* vol. 20 230,27ff., and Arius Didymus ap. Stobaeum *Ecl.* 2.7.19 134,18, cited by Grilli 444 and 447). Grilli 459 well suggests that *proêgoumenos combines* Aristotle's two criteria of 'natural' and 'unhindered'. *en proêgoumenois* may then indicate the presence of favourable circumstances, or as Grilli argues (456, cf. 461), supplying *agathois*, of those goods that principally contribute to the human end or *telos*. (Cf. also Huby 126-7; Rohr, 136-8). Throughout this discussion it is important to distinguish between the *meanings* of terms like *proêgoumenos* (Rohr 136, cf. Grilli 462 n. 43 on 'circumstances') and the applications they have in particular contexts. It thus does not seem that Giusta is right in interpreting *proêgoumenos* in these contexts as *meaning* 'free', though *proêgoumenai* activities as defined above *will in fact* be those that an agent performs when he is free from restraint or hindrance.

The train of thought in our present passage will then be the following; *proêgoumenai* activities, which are by definition those required for complete happiness, require certain instruments (such as wealth); activity in the presence of these instruments is described as activity *en proêgoumenois*; therefore the definition of happiness must include a reference to activity *en proêgoumenois*. (Cf. Grilli 446.) *EN* 1.8, 1099a31ff. thus remains an apt parallel for the point Alexander is making, and indeed it is cited as such by Giusta 230 and Grilli 446-7. Once again, it may be noted, Alexander – following others – uses Hellenistic terminology to make an Aristotelian point.

[221] This is the MSS reading (*boulêtas*). Spengel, followed by Bruns, emended to *bouleutas*, 'objects of deliberation'; but a reference to ends rather than means is needed here. (For the end as the object of *boulêsis*, the means of *bouleusis*, cf. Aristotle *EN* 3.5, 1113b3.) So Giusta 229 n. 1 (where the reference to '*Quaestio* 3.4' is an error); Grilli 446 n. 15.

[222] The Greek simply has *aretê*; see n. 217 above.

[223] Cf. Aristotle *EN* 1.7, 1098a4; 1.13, 1103a2. (I am grateful to Professor Sorabji for these references.)

proper activity comes about. In the case of the appetitive (*orektikê*)
[faculty the activities[224] are] actions and movements in respect of
10   feelings, and the excellences, or virtues, those which we call 'moral'
from the fact that they come about in [us] through certain habits.[225]
In the case of the reasoning (*dianoêtikê*) [faculty] the activities are
knowledge (*gnôsis*) of the nature of things that have come to be and
in general of those that admit of being otherwise, and excellence in it
is what brings[226] knowledge of truth in these things. And of the
intellectual (*noêtikê*)[227] [faculty] the activity is knowledge of the
eternal substances, and excellence in it what brings true knowledge
of these things.
15   The virtues or excellences being divided in this way, what each is,
and what its work is and what its contribution to happiness, is
ascertained from the work and activity of each[228] of the rational
faculties. The work of the appetitive faculty, then, is actions
concerned with pleasures and distress,[229] choosing and pursuing the
former and rejecting the latter. Moreover, in all things of the kind in
20   which there is excess and deficiency, lack of due measure naturally
destroys the goodness in each of them – and excess and deficiency
are like this – while due measure both preserves and creates the
goodness.[230] This is clear in the cases of exercise and of
nourishment; for both excess and deficiency of exercise destroy good
bodily condition (*euexia*), which is excellence in the body, while due
25   measure and the mean in [exercises] both create and preserve it,
and this is goodness in these matters. And in the case of food, again,
too, both excesses and deficiencies destroy health, while due
measures create and preserve it.
It is like this also in the case of the feelings (*pathê*) and of actions
(*praxeis*) concerned with them. So excesses and deficiencies of

---

[224] 'the activities' is added explicitly by V[2].

[225] Deriving *êthikos* from *ethos*; cf. Aristotle *EN* 2.1, 1103a17-18. The whole
chapter in Aristotle is devoted to the role of habit in moral virtue. Cf. also below,
150,18, with *EN* 2.3, 1104b11-13.

[226] Literally 'is that in accordance with which there is knowledge of truth in these
things'.

[227] The distinction between the appetitive faculty and that which is rational in
itself is here elaborated by a further division of the latter into 'reasoning' and
'intellectual' faculties. The two are sometimes contrasted as discursive reason
progressing from point to point on the one hand, and a direct intuition of first
principles analogous to vision on the other; cf. R. Sorabji, *Time, Creation and the
Continuum*, London 1983, 137-56.

[228] *hekateras*, implying 'each of the two'; that is, the appetitive faculty and that
which is rational in itself, *not* the 'reasoning' and 'intellectual' faculties into which the
latter is further subdivided.

[229] Here and in what follows the Greek has 'pleasures and distresses', i.e. instances
of distress; but 'pleasures and distress' seems more natural English.

[230] cf. Aristotle *EN* 2.2, 1104a11ff.

[pleasures and distress[231]] destroy goodness in these things, while
due measures create and preserve it. And since goodness in all things   30
is their proper excellence or virtue and everything that comes about
in accordance with it, it turns out that virtues concerning [pleasures
and distress] are constituted by due measure of actions and feelings.

For temperance is destroyed by both excess and deficiency in those
pleasures concerning which virtue is temperance, vice profligacy and   150,1
insensitivity; it is preserved and constituted by the mean and due
measure in these same things. Courage, too, is constituted by the
mean and due measure concerning fears and boldness, but destroyed
by excess and deficiency in these same things. And as in these cases,   5
so it is also in the rest; so if goodness in these is [to be found] in the
mean in feelings and actions, and goodness in each is in accordance
with its proper virtue, the virtues too concerning these things will be
[found] in the mean in the aforementioned things – the mean in these
being understood not without qualification or just as it chances [to
be], but, as has been shown, having been defined in accordance with
reasoning which is right and proceeds from wisdom (*phronêsis*).[232]
And the part of happiness which is located in the appetitive (*orektikê*)   10
soul will consist in activities which come about well, concerning
feelings and actions, as a result of the virtues.

Moreover, virtue in man is that from which a man comes to be good
– for in the case of all other things too each is and comes to be good in
accordance with its own virtue or excellence. And the man who comes
to be and is good is the one who is not lacking in due measure either in   15
feelings or in the actions concerning them. So from this too it will be
shown that moral virtue is [to be found] in the mean in the
aforementioned things. For the activities concerned with feelings and
actions produce virtue when they have been educated through habit
in such a way that those who have developed the habits enjoy noble
activities and dislike the opposite; and this [enjoyment] comes about   20
in the choice and discovery of the mean in them. And for this reason
we do indeed say that the moral virtues are states (*hexeis*) [located] in
the mean in feelings and actions [and] defined by right reasoning.[233]

Such, and concerned with these things, is the constitution of moral
virtue. As for the soul which reasons, and is rational in this way,

---

[231] That the reference is to pleasure and distress, rather than to *all* the preceding
examples, is clear from the fact that in the Greek the whole of 'This is clear in the
cases of exercise and of nourishment' to 'actions concerned with them' is a
parenthesis.
[232] cf. Aristotle *EN* 2.6, 1106b36; 6.1, 1138b20; 6.2, 1139a22-4. The judgement of
the wise man is needed because the mean in actions and feelings cannot be laid down
by rules (cf. Aristotle *EN* 2.9, 1109b20ff.). At *EN* 6.13, 1144b23-4 Aristotle says
rather that right reasoning is *in accordance* with wisdom; but in fact the two are to be
identified (ibid. 1144b25-8).
[233] cf. n. 232 above.

25   [part] of it is concerned with the knowledge (*gnôsis*) of things which
     are eternal and always in the same state,[234] and [part] with those
     which admit also of being otherwise;[235] we call the first scientific
     (*epistêmonikon*), the second calculating and deliberative. [Accord-
     ingly] there will be something good and in accordance with
     excellence or virtue concerning each of the aforementioned
     activities. In knowledge, excellence is truth, and excellence in each
30   of the faculties of the rational soul will be concerned with knowledge
     of the truth of the things considered by it.
         [The excellence or virtue of the rational soul] concerned with
     things that are objects of deliberation and admit of being otherwise
     will accompany the right appetite, for the discovery and knowledge
     (*gnôsis*) of the things that contribute to the objects of right
     appetite is worthy to be chosen; this sort of state and virtue we call
     'wisdom' (*phronêsis*). For wisdom is able to discover the actions that
35   contribute to the right goal, and for this reason we call wisdom
     'practical virtue', since its knowledge is concerned with the things
     that contribute to rightness of action.
         [The faculty of the rational soul] of which the activity is concerned
     with the knowledge (*gnôsis*) of eternal things has its goodness in the
151,1 discovery and knowledge of the truths in these matters, [and] is
     theoretical, not practical. For none of the truths in these matters
     has reference to any action, and for this reason the end in [these
     matters] is the knowledge of the truths in eternal things, and what
     is good and goodness in them is what is true*, what is bad in them
5   what is false; and we call this virtue '[scientific] understanding'
     (*epistêmê*), being a state capable of giving proofs.
         [Scientific] proof (*apodeixis*) is through certain things which are
     primary [in relation to] what is shown, and proper [to it] and true;[236]
     and what is primary in [these things] does not go on to infinity, but
     there is also something which is primary in the proper sense in
     them. [Accordingly] the knowledge (*gnôsis*) and discovery of what is
     primary in this way is called 'intellect' (*nous*). 'Understanding'
     (*sophia*)[237] is [the name given] to what possesses both, both the
     discovery of the [first] principles and the discovery and showing,
10   through the principles, of the things that follow them.
         Accordingly, again, the virtues of reasoning, being such as to

---

[234] For example, the incommensurability of the diagonal and side of a square, or
(for an Aristotelian) the arrangement of the heavens. Cf. Aristotle *EN* 3.3, 1112a21-3,
also 6.3, 1139b22, and below, *P. Eth.* 29 160,5ff.

[235] That is, those where there is the possibility of production or action.

[236] cf. Aristotle *An. Post.* 1.2, 71b20. Scientific understanding consists in proving or
demonstrating the things that follow from the primary truths apprehended by
intuitive intellect (*nous*); n. 227 above.

[237] 'Understanding' (*sophia*) is distinct from 'scientific understanding' (*epistêmê*); in
fact it involves both *epistêmê* and *nous* (Aristotle *EN* 6.7, 1141a18-20).

discover and enquire after what is good in the aforementioned activities, will include the most important part of what contributes to happiness,[238] by virtue of the fact that the activities of the most important faculties of the rational soul derive their goodness from these. <So virtue*[239]> will take its start from its contribution to happiness, but have its being in the activities of each rational faculty of the soul, being such as to discover and prove what is good in these.

26. That what is noble is not to be chosen for the sake of pleasure, but pleasure for the sake of what is noble.

[This text is almost verbally identical to the latter part of *P. Eth.* 23, 144,33-145,12, q.v.]

27. Why the moral virtues are means.   152,34

[I] Well,[240] [it is] because every virtue or excellence (*aretê*)[241] both 35
brings to perfection the good condition of that of which it is the excellence, and causes its work (*ergon*)[242] to be performed well. For the excellence of the eye makes both the eye and its work good; for it 153,1

---

[238] Our author has argued that reason contributes both to theoretical enquiry (150,36-151,10) *and* to virtuous moral conduct (150,31-6). It seems natural to take the present passage as suggesting that *both* of these are parts of human happiness, especially as 150,28-151,1 is a single sentence in the Greek. Aristotle's discussion in *EN* 10.7-8 has often been taken as preferring theoretical enquiry above practical action; for a different view cf. A.O. Rorty, 'The place of contemplation in Aristotle's *Nicomachean Ethics*', in id. (ed.), *Essays on Aristotle's Ethics*, Berkeley 1980, 377-94 (citing statements of the traditional view at 393 n. 1).

[239] Added by S²B² and the Aldine edition. With the text of V, followed by Bruns, the reference would be to 'understanding' (151,8-10 above, what intervenes then being parenthetical in the Greek); but as Dr Kenny points out, understanding or *sophia* does *not* have its being in both rational faculties. Cf. Aristotle *EN* 6.7, 1141b2.

[240] Literally 'Or rather [it is] because', on the lines of the standard formula for introducing a solution in the *Quaestiones*, even though this is actually the *start* of the discussion. The first, positive part of this text (to 154,10) bears some similarity to *P. Eth.* 25. Cf. n. 157 above. Professor Sorabji points out that the topic may have become contentious because virtue is a mean in respect of feelings (*pathê*) and actions (cf. 153,26; Aristotle *EN* 2.6, 1106b16; *P. Eth.* 25 149,28ff., above), and the Stoics advocated the elimination, rather than the moderation, of *pathê* (better translated in Stoic contexts as 'passions' rather than 'affections'); cf. *SVF* 3.443-55. There does not however seem to be anything to link the actual objections to the doctrine of virtue as a mean in the present text with Stoic argumentation in particular. There *are* however striking parallels with the anonymous scholia on the *EN*; cf. Introduction, n. 28, and notes below. Aspasius' treatment of the topic is rather different (*in EN*, *CAG* 19 48,27ff.)

[241] *aretê*. See above, n. 217.

[242] Or 'function'; but 'function' implies subordination to some purpose higher than the individual agent, which applies in the case of an instrument but not in that of a living creature such as a human being, for Aristotle.

is by the excellence of the eye that we see well. And the same argument applies also to the other parts of the body. Moreover, the excellence of a horse, too, makes the horse both a good one, and good at running and carrying its rider and withstanding the enemy; and the same argument also applies to each of the other living creatures.

And it is the same in the case of the arts (*tekhnai*) and sciences (*epistêmai*) too; for it is by excellence in the gymnastic [art] that a man's body gets into good condition and performs its proper activities well. The same argument also applies to medicine; for it is through excellence in this that we are healthy in our bodies and perform healthy activities.[243] And a similar argument also applies to building and sculpture and carpentry and all the arts.

Since it is true that every excellence both brings to perfection the good condition of that of which it is the excellence, and also causes its work to be performed well, it is clear that excellence in man will be that as a result of which man will both be in a good condition himself and perform his proper work as well as possible. The next thing to consider, then, is what this is; for what is found will be excellence or virtue.

Well, we see that, in everything quantitative that admits of both addition and subtraction, excess and deficiency in these [quantitative things] are to be avoided and equality and due measure and the mean are to be chosen and comprise the proper excellence in [the thing in question]*. For, in the case of good bodily condition and excellence of the body, excessive exercises and lack of exercise prevent good condition from coming about and also destroy it when it has done so; while those that are in due measure and moderate both create and preserve [good condition]. Health, too, is destroyed by excessive food or lack of food, but is preserved if it exists, and created if it does not, by [food] which is moderate and in due measure. And in the case of sculpture, too, it is possible to see that what it produces excellently is a matter of guarding against excess and deficiency. And as it is in these cases, so it is in all others.

Moral virtue too is concerned with feelings (*pathê*) and actions (*praxeis*) which admit of addition and subtraction. So it is clear that, in the same way, virtue concerning [feelings and actions] too, will be [located] in the mean between these*. But, as in the other cases the mean is defined by the reason relating to the art, so in the case of feelings and actions the mean and due measure will be defined by wisdom and right reasoning. Being defined and enacted in accordance with this, [the feelings and actions] will reach the extreme of goodness. And for this reason we say that the definition

---

[243] That is, health is produced by virtue or excellence in medical skill – not ours, of course, but the doctor's.

of moral virtue is: a state which chooses[244] the mean in relation to
us, [the mean] concerned with feelings and actions and defined by
right reasoning, achieving the extreme in what is good and noble.[245]

That this is so is clear to those who examine each of the moral
virtues. For courage, by guarding against excesses both of boldness
and of fears, and also against deficiencies [in these],[246] arrives at
what is good in these; of the states (*hexeis*) concerned with excesses
and deficiencies in these, one is boldness and the other cowardice,
each of them being a vice. Temperance, too, arrives at the same
thing[247] in relation to pleasures and [cases of] distress which are
bodily and come about through touch, guarding against excesses
and deficiencies in them and choosing some mean in them in
accordance with right reasoning; of the states that [consist] in
excesses and deficiencies of these, that relating to excess is
profligacy, and that to relating to deficiency is insensitivity. And
similar to these states, but in connection with other actions and the
feelings in them, are the [other] virtues, which are means, and the
vices which relate to excesses and deficiencies.

[II] Some deny that the virtues *are* means, either through ignorance
of what has been said, or because [they are] ambitious [and want] to
appear [to have] something to say about this [matter] as well [as all
the others]. Of these some say[248] that virtue cannot be a mean,
because the mean must be defined in terms of the extremes and be
equally removed from these, while neither excesses nor deficiencies
are definite, either in feelings or in actions. For it is not definite up
to which point lack of due measure in boldness extends, nor [lack of
due measure] in being afraid. To these it may be replied that they
have not observed what is added to 'the mean' in the definition,
namely 'in relation to us', even though Aristotle clearly defined it,
and showed that, while the mean in relation to the *thing* needs the
extremes to be defined, if the mean in this [sense] is equally
removed from the extremes, the mean in relation to us is neither
single and the same for all, nor is it located in equal distance from
the extremes. On the contrary, the discovery of the mean in this

154,1

5

10

15

20

25

[244] So Vict., Bruns; 'that makes distinctions through' MSS, but cf. Aristotle cited in next note.

[245] cf. Aristotle *EN* 2.6, 1106b36ff.; and n. 232 above.

[246] This seems artificial, excesses of fear and deficiencies of boldness seeming to be the same thing. But perhaps 'boldness and fears' indicated not two different things but a single continuum.

[247] That is, what is good in relation to them; i.e. the mean.

[248] Literally 'some, saying'; there is an anacoluthon, no finite verb with the speakers as subject following, but the sense being picked up by 'to these'. The objection put forward in this paragraph to the doctrine of virtues as means also occurs in Anonymous *in EN, CAG* 20 133,28-35; so too does the reply (ibid. 133,35, 134,4).

[sense] makes known also the deviations from the mean in each direction. For in the case of the arts the mean and the due measure in each of the aforementioned cases, when it has been defined by the
30   reason in the art, indicates the deviations and transgressions to either side of the mean; and so it is also in the case of feelings and
155,1   actions. When the due measure in each has been defined for it by wisdom and by reason in accordance with this, it makes known all the transgressions from this, not standing in any need of an approach to their *limits*, but at once preventing them by resisting the first deviations that occur in them contrary to the mean and the
5   due measure.

[Someone may[249]] also say that virtue is not the mean of the two vices on either side of it; for [on this account] there is no opposite vice accompanying it, since the mean is not [the thing] furthest removed from either of the things at each extreme, while things which are opposite are those that are furthest apart from each other
10   in the same genus. But this man too will not alter any of the points laid down. For if virtue were the mean feelings and the mean actions *themselves,* [one who argues thus] would have a point; but in fact, virtue is not these things, though it is concerned with them. Its being virtue consists rather in its being defined by right reasoning and having its being in due measure; and the excesses and deficiencies derive their being vices from wrong reasoning and lack
15   of due measure, inasmuch as [virtue] does what it does in accordance with right reasoning, and is [located] in due measure, while [vice] is in accordance with wrong reasoning. And it is in lack of due measure that [the vices] are opposed [to each other]. For it is in respect of the feelings and actions themselves and their quantitative [aspect] that the deficiencies are said by [this man] to be opposite to the excesses.

[Someone may] also say that virtue is not a mean, for it will [then]
20   be necessary for the person who possesses virtue to pursue what is moderately good and not what is extremely so. But this man too speaks without taking notice of what has been said. For it has been said that [what is] the mean with regard to feelings and actions in the aforementioned way is an extreme of goodness.[250] For what comes about in [feelings and actions] moderately and in due measure is good in the extreme. For nothing prevents that which is in the mean between certain extremes from being the extreme of
25   certain [other] things. And for this reason that person too is absurd

[249] Literally 'The person, too, who says ... will not alter any of the points laid down, either'. Similarly also at 155,19 and 155,29 below. Reference is also made to virtue as a mean between two vices at Anonymous *in EN* 134,4-9 (cf. n. 248 above and n. 252 below), though the detailed argument is different.
[250] cf. Aristotle *EN* 2.6, 1107a7.

who says that if virtue is an extreme [state] of the rational soul it cannot be a mean because the same thing cannot simultaneously be an extreme and a mean. For if anyone were claiming that [it was a mean and an extreme] of the same thing, they[251] would have a point, but since it is not this that is being said, they will be finding fault where there is none.

[Someone may] also say that, if virtue is the mean of two vices, it will also be composed of these, on the grounds that means between 30 opposites are constituted from the mixture of the opposites, as [Aristotle] himself said concerning colours and odours and flavours in *On Sensation*.[252] But neither does this man affect any of the things that have been laid down. For it does not follow, just from the things that have already been said being so, that all means between opposites have their being as a result of the mixture of those [opposites]. For the mean in a certain quantity is not constituted 35 from the opposites; quite the reverse, their [the means'] being means 156,1 [consists] in their distance from the extremes. In the case of things that come to be by art the mean and due measure do not come from the *combination* of excess and deficiency, but [are rather found] in the avoidance of these. For good [bodily] condition does not come from a mixture of excessive and deficient exercises, although it is in the mean between them; nor does health come about in this way; nor 5 does sculpture combine excesses and deficiencies. The centre of a circle is not the result of a mixture of the [parts] from which it is furthest removed; nor are the things intermediate between good things and bad ones a mixture of them. And no one would say that a man who is on the way[253] to virtue is [characterised by] a combination of virtue and vice.

Nor yet is it sound to say that, if virtue is a mean, [the man who] 10 proceeds from deficiency to excess must first come to be in [a state of] virtue.[254] If the moderate feelings and the moderate actions were [themselves] the virtues, perhaps there would be something in what is said, but if virtue is in the fact that these are defined by right reasoning, the person who has come to be subject to some moderate feeling will not at all just for that reason come to be subject to it in such a way as to experience it in accordance with right reasoning or 15 to perform a moderate action in a similar way. Nor in other respects does this come about in this way in all cases; for that which changes from ugliness on account of the excess of some part to [ugliness] in

---

[251] The plural may refer to the *two* objectors mentioned in this paragraph; it may just be careless.

[252] Aristotle *Sens.* 4, 442a12. Again, the objection and reply in this paragraph also appear in Anonymous *in EN* 134,9-21.

[253] The term is Stoic: *prokoptôn*.

[254] That is, a coward who becomes over-bold (e.g.) must at some point in the process pass through the state of being courageous.

lack and deficiency does not first become beauty [*en route*].

20 It is also absurd to say that, for those for whom the virtues are means, virtue will actually be a part of vice, on the grounds that if the excessive [part] of boldness were to be removed, the part of it left behind would be courage, and if some part of courage, by which it surpasses cowardice, were removed the part of it left behind would become cowardice. For [Aristotle] himself too has spoken sufficiently about this, showing that every part of vice is vice, and every [part] of 25 virtue virtue. Or are these things not those resolved by the following passage?[255]

'Not every action or every feeling admits of a mean; for the names of some things immediately involve their combination with baseness, such as gloating, shamelessness and envy, and in the case of actions, adultery, theft and murder. All these things and those like them are 30 so called*[256] in virtue of being base, and not [just] the excesses, nor yet the deficiencies in them. For it is never possible to be right concerning them; [one must] always be wrong, and goodness or its absence concerning these things do not [consist] in committing adultery with the woman one should and when [one should] and in the way [one should], but to do any of these things at all is, without qualification, to do wrong. Similar too is the claim that there are a 35 mean and excess and deficiency in injustice or[257] cowardice or 157,1 profligacy; for in this way there will be a mean of excess and [of [258]] deficiency and an excess of excess and a deficiency of deficiency. But just as there is no excess or deficiency of temperance and courage because the mean is in a way an extreme,[259] just so there is no mean 5 or excess and deficiency of those things [i.e. cowardice, etc.], but however they are done they are done wrongly. For in general there is no mean of excess or of deficiency, nor an excess or deficiency of a mean.'

– Through this [Aristotle] has resolved not only the aforementioned difficulty, but also all difficulties that could be raised against [this] opinion.

10 **28.** Whether virtue is the genus or the totality (*holon*) of the [particular] virtues.[260]

Some may say that virtue is predicated of the [particular] virtues as

---

[255] Aristotle *EN* 2.6, 1107a8-27.

[256] So the MSS here; most but not all MSS of Aristotle's *Ethics* have 'are censured'. See Notes on the Text.

[257] Literally 'and', but as the examples are separate, 'or' is more natural English.

[258] The Greek could mean 'a mean between excess and deficiency', but *that* would not be problematic; clearly what is meant is that excess and deficiency, for example rashness and cowardice, would *each separately* admit of a mean and an excess and a deficiency.   [259] See n. 250 above.

a genus. But then it is odd that, if one is removed,[261] all are removed. For if wisdom is removed it is not possible to possess the rest of virtue; but this is not the relation of genus to species, that by the removal of one species both [the genus] and the other species are removed along with [it]. Others may say that [virtue] is a totality of parts; but then [there is the difficult[262]] consequence that, while a totality is not predicated in a single sense of the parts that are not uniform with it (for 'statue' and its definition are not [predicated] of the head of the statue*), the virtues are different [and yet] virtue is predicated of them all in the same sense. <So [virtue] ought not to be predicated [of the particular virtues] either as a genus or as a totality.[263]>

Or rather: if a *uniform* totality is predicated in the same sense of the parts, and all the virtues are similar to each other – if whichever you regard as complete is a mixture of all [the rest] in the same way – then it will be predicated of each [virtue] in the same sense, as a uniform totality. For the person who possesses complete virtue possesses all [the virtues] in the same way, but possessing them all in the same way he is sometimes said to perform acts of courage and sometimes of temperance, through the fact that he acts concerning the things with which temperance[264] is particularly concerned in a similar way to [that in which he acts concerning] all [the rest].[265] For, as in the case of bodies which are the products of mixture from certain different things what has been mixed becomes uniform in every way,[266] so it happens also in the case of dispositions (*hexeis*) and virtues.

For the virtues differ from each other by the fact that this one of

15

20

25

---

[260] cf. *P. Eth.* 8 and n. 84 above; also the List of Titles on p. 16, where this title is given in a different and shorter form.

[261] Not a general claim that the removal of *any* one involves the removal of all, but a specific point about wisdom, as the sequel shows. Cf. *P. Eth.* 8 128,8ff.

[262] Supplied by parity of reasoning with the first limb of the dilemma, above.

[263] I have translated Bruns' supplement (in his apparatus) *exempli gratia*. Similarly Madigan (1987) 1263.

[264] 'temperance' is the standard translation of *sôphrosunê*, but the word is etymologically related to 'wisdom' (*phronêsis*). This may explain why it is temperance, in particular, that is taken as an example here.

[265] That is, what makes action virtuous is the same in every case, but the specific virtue differs according to the context of the action.

[266] On mixture cf. Aristotle *GC* 1.10, 327a30ff., and (of blending, *krasis*) Alexander *Mixt.* 13, 228,34ff. with 228,25ff. However, these passages relate specifically to the mixing of opposites or intermediates between opposites, which act on each other (cf. Aristotle *GC* 1.10, 328a32; 2.7, 334b8, 30; Alexander op. cit. 229,10; 229,21ff.), and it is not clear how this could relate to the present example. Cf. R.B. Todd, *Alexander of Aphrodisias on Stoic Physics,* Leiden 1976, 232-3.

them is concerned with these particular things, another with others,
as we see in the case of the natural virtues. For in the completion,
30   that comes about in the mixture of each of them with the others,
these produce a whole which is uniform*.[267] Accordingly it seems
that activity is with each one of them [individually], when it is
concerned with the things with which the being of incomplete and
natural courage, say, is concerned. But [a man] does not act with
this [particular virtue] alone in respect of those [actions] of which
158,1 virtue is reasonably predicated in a single sense on account of such a
mixture of things which are similar to one another; and these indeed
we call virtues in the proper sense.

29. Interpretation of another passage in the third [book] of
Aristotle's *Nicomachean Ethics*, by which it is shown that vices
5   too are in our control (*eph' hêmin*) in a similar way to
virtues.[268]

'Suppose someone were to say that all desire the apparent good, but
are not in control of how things appear; rather, as each person is, so
the end [of action] appears to him to be. Then [i] if on the one hand
each person is in some way the cause of his own disposition (*hexis*),
10   he will also in some way be the cause of the appearance, but [ii] if no
one is the cause of his own evil-doing, but does these things
through ignorance of the end, thinking that through these he will
[achieve] the best [result]*,[269] the desire of the end is not something

---

[267] I take *hautai* as the subject of *poiousin* and *en teleiôsei* as adverbial, removing
Bruns' parenthesis and supposing an anacoluthon – the parenthesis in effect
beginning with 'as we see', in Bruns, but never being terminated. This is suggested by
Madigan's paraphrase ((1987) 1263): 'This is clear from the development of the
natural virtues into the developed virtues, which is due to the complete mixture of
each with the others.' The alternative would seem to be to render *hautai gar en
teleiôsei* as 'these (the *natural* virtues, presumably) [consist] in completeness': but
this seems odd both in logic (one would normally regard the being of a mixture as
deriving from that of the ingredients, not vice versa) and in terms of Aristotelian
doctrine. Natural virtue seems to be identified with *incomplete* virtue, below at
157,32. On the relation between natural virtues and virtues in the proper sense, and
its bearing on the unity of the virtues, cf. Aristotle *EN* 6.13, 1144b32-1145a2.

[268] This text is discussed by P.L. Donini, *Tre studi sull' Aristotelismo nel secondo
secolo d.c.*, Turin 1974, 170; and by R.W. Sharples, *Alexander of Aphrodisias: On
Fate*, London 1983, 160-1. The title obscures the fact that, in the context of a
discussion of *EN* 3.5, 1114a31-b12, the text in reality covers much of the ground
covered in the whole of 3.1-5. Cf. also above, *P. Eth.* 9, 11 and 12. The concerns of this
text correspond to some extent with those of Alexander's *de Fato* and the related
sections of the *Mantissa* (cf. especially 160,3-16 with *Fat.* 11 178,28-179,2; 161,14-29
with *Fat.* 27 198,3-26 and *Mant.* 175,12-15 and 21-32); but its relation to *EN* 3.1-5
means that it is not an exception to Moraux' observation that in general the
Quaestiones (and the *Ethical Problems*) are more closely linked with Aristotelian
texts, the *Mantissa* with Alexander's own treatises.

[269] Most MSS of Aristotle (but not Lb, Mb, Γ, which correspond to our text) have

we choose ourselves, but one must be born having sight, as it were, by which one may judge well and choose what is truly good. And that person is well endowed by nature who has this [faculty of moral sight] well formed by nature – for [this is] the most important and noblest thing, and what is not able to be got or learned from others;[270] but as he was born with it so shall each person have it, and for this to be well and nobly formed by nature would be good natural endowment of the most perfect and truest kind.'[271]

Or rather: that all desire the good [as it] appears to them is true, but it is not true that we are not in some way in control of how it appears. For as each person is, so the end appears to him to be; but we are ourselves contributory causes (*sunaitioi*) of the disposition in accordance with which each of us is as he is, if at least dispositions come from activities, and activities are in our control.

For the involuntary is that which comes about through compulsion (*bia*) and that which does so on account of ignorance of particular [circumstances].[272] It has been shown[273] that the things that people do, and do wrongly, in ignorance, as being themselves the causes of their ignorance, are neither involuntary, nor do they come about *on account of* ignorance in the first place. For this reason, at any rate, wrong actions resulting from drunkenness are not involuntary either, even though they are brought about by those who are in ignorance [of what they are doing]; but, since those who are drunk are themselves the causes of their own ignorance resulting from drunkenness, these are not placed among involuntary wrong actions – indeed Pittacus of Mytilene laid down

15

20

25

30

'but [ii] if not, no one is the cause... but does these things... the best [result]; and the desire...'. I have taken *de* in 158,12 as apodotic rather than as introducing a new sentence, as it does in Aristotle's text and in our text as punctuated by Bruns. If *all' ê* in 158,10 (where Aristotle just has *alla*) could not only be taken as 'but' after a preceding negative (cf. LSJ s.v.) but could also stand in apodosis, Bruns' punctuation could be retained with the sense 'but if no one is the cause of his own wrongdoing, he rather does these things... the best [results]; and the desire...'; but this gives a less good sense and is grammatically difficult.

[270] 'another' in Aristotle.

[271] Aristotle *EN* 3.5, 1114a31-b12.

[272] cf. Aristotle *EN* 3.1, 1110b33-1111a21; on 'compulsion' cf. n. 101 above. The Greek has an unanswered *men* at 'For what is involuntary'. Bruns suggests either that something has fallen out here (S²B² have in the margin 'perhaps it ought to say this: "For that which is on account of voluntary ignorance is neither due to compulsion nor involuntary" ') or that we should read *monon*: 'For the involuntary is only that which'. But there is a further problem, in that the Greek has 'For *if* what is involuntary'; the 'if' is unanswered. Bruns meets this difficulty by treating the whole of 158,24-159,1 ('It has been shown ... resulting from drunkenness') as a parenthesis, and 'those misdeeds ... in our control' (159,1-2) as the apodosis. But this involves the change of *ha gar* to *haper* in 159,1 (conjectured by Bruns, but not in his text) and, as elsewhere, Bruns' parenthesis seems in fact to obscure the natural connection of thought at its end (cf. Notes on the Text, on 27 153,18 and 28 157,17).

[273] Aristotle *EN* 3.5, 1113b30-1114a3; cf. 3.1, 1110b24-1111a2.

159,1 double penalties for wrong actions resulting from drunkenness.[274]
For those wrong actions that have a cause that is voluntary and in
our control[275] will themselves be voluntary and in our control.

But as those who are drunk are themselves the cause of the
ignorance that results from drunkenness, so are those who are
ignorant [themselves] the causes of those wrong actions that are due
5   to ignorance of what is noble and what is shameful, if at least
knowledge (*gnôsis*) of what is better and worse is in our control. For
those who through lack of concern are ignorant of the things that are
laid down by the laws, and how men who are praised behave, are
themselves the causes of their own ignorance, if lack of concern is in
our control. For ignorance of what is noble and fitting is in general
the cause not of what is involuntary, but of wickedness. The things
10   to which blame and punishment apply are voluntary; and people are
acquitted or punished for ignorance of such things.

So those things that have their origins in us, both among things
that are matters of ignorance and among those that are said to come
about by compulsion, are not involuntary. For the person who is
compelled and conquered by pleasure has within himself the origin
of his being moved towards the things that he does on account of
pleasure; he does not do [them] <having*> the cause of [his being]
compelled in this way from outside himself, [since] he has lived in a
15   dissolute manner and, through his activity in particular [matters],
developed the habit of being conquered by pleasure. [This] at any
rate [is so] if those things come about by compulsion of which the
origin   and   cause   is   from   outside   ourselves,   we   ourselves
contributing nothing to the things that come about on account of it;
while, in the case of the person who has in himself the origin of [his]
doing the things that he does, and has the power of deliberating
about them, the cause of his wrong actions [that come about] in this
way is not compulsion.

20   Well, the involuntary is, as was said, what has been stated
already; the voluntary is that of which the origin is in us, [when] we
know the particulars with which the action is concerned. For neither
does the person, who has in himself the origin and cause of the
things that he does, do these things through compulsion; nor does
the person who knows the particular [circumstances] with which his
action is concerned, and [the things] by means of which [it is
performed],[276] do [what he does] on account of ignorance. So, if it is
things that are through compulsion or on account of ignorance that
25   are involuntary, and those actions of which the origin is in us and [in

---

[274] cf. Aristotle *Pol.* 2.12, 1274b19; Diogenes Laertius 1.76.

[275] Spengel, followed by Bruns, deletes 'that is voluntary and in our control'.

[276] For example, that his spear is not one blunted for practice, or that a drug will in
fact be fatal; cf. Aristotle *EN* 3.1, 1111a12-14.

which] the particular [circumstances] are recognised are neither through compulsion nor on account of ignorance, they will not be involuntary either; and if not [involuntary, they will be] voluntary.

And for this reason actions on account of passion[277] and desire are voluntary;[278] for the origin of the things that come to be in this way is in us. Moreover, if the things that come to be on account of [passion and desire] were involuntary, neither irrational living creatures nor children would do anything voluntarily. For it is on   30 account of one of these that they bring about all the things that they bring about. – Moreover many noble things too come about on account of [passion and desire]. – Moreover, if it is absurd to say that those things that come to be rationally and reasonably are involuntary, and we have an appetite for certain things and are angry at certain things rationally, the things that come to be on account of [passion and desire] will not be involuntary.

All the things that come to be in this way, then, are voluntary (*hekousia*); [being] in our control (*eph' hêmin*) is present in those of   160,1 voluntary things that are objects of choice, and come to be by choice (*proairesis*). Everything that comes to be by choice does so accompanied by reason and choice; and for this reason choice seems to be that which is [both] voluntary [and] deliberated about beforehand.[279] For choice is concerned with things that are objects of deliberation, and those things are objects of deliberation with which deliberation and deliberating are concerned.

But no living creature deliberates besides man; and we deliberate   5 neither about the things that are eternal and always in the same state, nor about those which come to be always in the same way and according to a definite ordering, among which are risings and settings and turnings [of the heavenly bodies] and solstices, nor about things which are and come to be in different ways at different times, for example droughts and rainstorms, nor about things that come to be from chance, nor about *all* those that are brought about   10 by men. For none of those who are at Athens deliberates about how the Scythians might best govern themselves. For we deliberate about those things that can be brought about by us; deliberation is about those things that can be done by we who deliberate. Those who deliberate do so about the things that can be done by themselves, and the things that are like this are those which we are able to do in different ways at different times because the things in   15

---

[277] *thumos*, translated 'anger' at *P. Eth.* 9 130,15 above (and cf. 'we have an appetite for and are *angry* at' below). But it seems odd to say that all the actions of children are caused by *anger* or desire, and so it seems natural to give *thumos* its wider sense here.

[278] cf. Aristotle *EN* 3.1, 1111a24.

[279] cf. Aristotle *EN* 3.2, 1112a14-17. With 160,5ff. cf. Aristotle *EN* 3.3, 1112a21ff.; Alexander *Fat.* 11 178,28ff.

relation to which they come about are not definitely fixed. And such
are the things about which we hold opinions. Moreover, deliberation
is concerned not with ends, but with those things that lead to the
ends. Those things of which the ends are wished for, these being
things that can be done – it is the things leading to [these] that are
objects of deliberation. For we deliberate through what [means] we
can achieve them.

The things which are objects of deliberation, then, being like this,
20   that which is an object of choice is that which is preferred, among
the things that are objects of deliberation, as contributing to and
leading to the proposed end more than the others. And* the actions
that are brought about according to the things that have been
preferred among those that were objects of deliberation, are the
objects of choice, and they come about accompanied by desire for
what was preferred. For judgement is not in itself sufficient for the
doing of the things [in favour of which we have] judged, but
25   appetition too is needed. And for this reason choice is said to be
deliberative appetition.[280]

The things that come to be by choice are voluntary and in our
control; and it is established that dispositions (*hexeis*), concerned
with things that are able to be done, come to be as a result of the
activities concerning them which are performed by choice. [So] it
will also be established through these [premisses] that dispositions
concerned with things that can be done are voluntary and in our
control. For, as we acquire dispositions for skills (*tekhnai*) from
30   activities according to [these skills], so we acquire dispositions for
virtues; for it is by developing the habit of doing things that are
noble that we come to have the disposition for doing them, just as
those who are eager to become carpenters [acquire this disposition
by becoming accustomed to perform the actions] of a carpenter.

In the case of the skills one man is better endowed by nature than
another for acquiring the disposition for the skill in question, but
none of those who are in a natural condition has been disabled[281]
35   with regard to the obtaining and acquisition of it. This is much more
so in the case of the virtues, inasmuch as the acquisition of virtues is
more natural for man than that of skills. But if [this is true of the
acquisition] of virtues, it is clear that [it] also [applies to] that of
161,1   vices, if it is through opposed habits to [those through which] virtues
[are established] that vices are established, and that those who have
it in their power[282] to do* the one, also have it in their power [to do]

---

[280] *orexis bouleutikê*; cf. Aristotle *EN* 3.3, 1113a10; also 6.2 1139b4.

[281] cf. n. 166 above. It is not clear that there is any real conflict here with
Aristotelian principles of responsibility, for the point is that the unnatural condition
which makes it impossible to acquire virtue is an exceptional one. Cf. n.106 above.

[282] *eph' hautois*, the construction translated above by 'in their/our control'; but here

the opposites of these. So that, <if*> the conditional[283] is true that states 'if each man is in some way the cause of his own disposition, he will also in some way be the cause of how things appear', and [if] it *is* true that [each man] is himself* in some way the cause of his 5
own disposition, [then] it will also be true that each man is in some way the cause of how it appears to him concerning the things that are good and those that are evil. And if this is so it follows for the wicked too, [since] they [too] are in some way the causes of their [having] such a disposition, that in some way it is also in their control that good things appear evil to them.

For it is not the case that, if the wicked do evil things *in* ignorance 10
of (*agnoountes*) the end, they therefore do them *on account of* ignorance (*di' agnoian*).[284] For it was shown that the ignorance of those who are the causes of their own ignorance is voluntary. Their thinking that they will achieve the end even through doing base things [is something that] is in their hands, if it is in their control to know the things that are good and to do the things through which these come about.

The person who is going to acquire virtue or vice must indeed have 15
a certain natural [endowment], if not every living creature is able to acquire these, but only man. But it is not the case that, if the living creature that will possess these [needs] a certain type of nature, [therefore] he must also already possess by nature that eye by which he will judge well the things that he judges and choose that which is truly good, that is, virtue. For the senses are not natural in the same way as the virtues; [while] the senses are themselves natural, virtue 20
is not itself natural; the capacity to acquire it is natural, but it itself is not natural. And for this reason virtue is natural in a similar way to skills, rather than to the senses. For as with the skills our being able to acquire them is something which belongs to us by nature, but no one comes to be a craftsman (*tekhnitês*) by nature, in the same way it is also in the case of the virtues.[285] And for this reason, while no one would ever acquire the sight that is a matter of sense 25
perception if he did not possess it by nature, in the case of the 'sight' that goes with virtue one does not need to be born possessing this sight. But one does need to be born being able to acquire it, and to

---

'power' seems more natural. Cf. n. 103 above.

[283] *sunêmmenon*; both the term (*SVF* 2.212-217) and the argument form (*modus ponens*; *SVF* 2.241-2) are taken from Stoic logic, though less obviously than in *P. Eth.* 19; cf. n. 170.

[284] cf. Aristotle *EN* 3.1, 1110b25 and *EE* 2.9, 1225b10-11. I owe these references to Professor Sorabji, who points out that this contrast is not explicitly drawn in *P. Eth.* 9 above. On the other hand *P. Eth.* 9 too does have the contrast between ignorance that is one's own fault and that which is not (130,19ff.), so it has the substantial point even if not the verbal formulation.

[285] cf. Alexander *Fat.* 27 198,3ff.

try to get possession of it by our own efforts. And the person who is
well endowed by nature is not the person who already has virtue
and this [moral] eye, but the person who is able to acquire it more
easily than [someone] else, as was shown to apply also in the case of
skills.

30   **30. How, if opposites come from opposites, injustice will not
         come from justice and justice from injustice; and the same
         argument in the case of the other virtues and vices.**

Or rather:[286] these things happen in the following way. The man
162,1   who becomes just changes to justice either from injustice, which is
        the opposite state (*hexis*) to justice, or from the intermediate
        condition, and things which change from the intermediate to one of
        the extremes change from the intermediate as from an opposite. For
        it is because the intermediate in a way shares in both extremes*, but
        does not possess the [features] of either of them completely, that it is
        intermediate between these very things; and when it changes to one
    5   of them, it changes as from the opposite itself, through the fact that
        it changes from those things which, belonging to the intermedi-
        ates,[287] prevented it from already being in the [state] to which it
        changes.
          And if everything that changes to some state changes from the
        privation of that state, and such a privation is opposite to the state
   10   to which there is change, both justice and injustice will come from
        [their] opposites. For [they come] from [their] privations; for that
        which comes to be just [is previously characterised] by the privation
        of justice, and [that which comes to be] unjust similarly [by that] of
        injustice. If then the matter, from which coming-to-be in the proper
        sense [takes place] – and this is [the matter] of substances – existed
        in its own right without being accompanied by some form, [things]
        that come to be in an unqualified [sense] would come to be from
        matter and privation in the proper sense: [from] matter as
   15   something underlying that remained, from the privation as an
        opposite that did not remain. But it is impossible for matter to be in
        existence without some form; it is not possible for a certain matter to
        be without some form, for it is separable from the forms [only] in

---

[286] The standard expression introducing the solution to a problem; the statement of
the problem is implied in the title, and could be stated as, e.g., 'opposites come from
opposites; but in that case justice will come from injustice and vice versa, which does
not appear to be the case'. This text is concerned with logical and metaphysical issues
of coming-to-be, starting from an ethical example, rather than with ethical issues as
such; it may be compared with *Quaest.* 2.11. *P. Eth.* 3, while dealing with similar
material, is 'ethical' in a way in which the present text is not.

[287] Madigan (1987) 1266 rightly explains this as: 'from the properties of the
opposed contrary that persist in the intermediate.'

definition and through admitting the opposites in turn. Its existence is always with some one of those things into which it changes in turn when it changes into some form. So it is clear that it is [characterised] by the privation of [the form when it begins to] change into it. But since that, which is [characterised] by the privation of that into which it changes, [comes] from[288] some other form, it is clear that it possesses the opposite form from that into which it changes, and that it is also in this respect that this change comes about for it. For it is in respect of the [state] in which it is impossible for it to remain, when it changes into that into which it changes, that it changes and alters its form.

This is what the opposite forms are like, in which that which is [characterised] by the privation of certain things both is and is able to be; and for this reason coming-to-be in the proper sense is primarily from the privation, and from the opposite in the sense of the privation, but it is also from the opposite forms. Being in these [forms] before the change into their opposites, [the thing in question] is not able to change into the form, into which it changes, without changing from them.

So, when the states and the opposites are easily changed into each other, change comes about, for the things that change into something, also from the opposite forms, just as [it does] from the privation of that into which they change. But when the opposites are such as to be stable and not change easily, comings-to-be for such things take place from the privations and from the intermediate [states]. The things that come to be change from these as from things that are also themselves opposite to the forms into which the change takes place. The former [type of coming-to-be, that from opposites] is the coming-to-be of things that come to be in respect of* alteration and growth and diminution and by change in place; this is a type of coming-to-be, but it is not coming-to-be *in an unqualified sense (haplôs)* from opposites. [The latter type of coming-to-be], which is [coming-to-be] in respect of substance, is no longer from opposites, but from what is contrasted as a contradictory; for there is not even anything that *is* the opposite of substance.[289]

20

25

163,1

5

10

---

[288] 'is in some other form' B²S² Ald. Spengel. This is at first sight the more natural way to put the point, but our author may have expressed it in the more tortuous way because he is regarding the change from the point of view of its terminus rather than of its starting-point.

[289] For example, a horse comes to be from matter that was *not* a horse – was characterised by the negation and privation of 'horse' – but that does not mean that there is any specific thing that is the opposite of a horse. – In Bruns' edition the marginal number at 163,10 has been placed a line too early; as at *P. Eth.* 25 148,10 the printed numbers have been followed in the present translation, in spite of their inaccuracy.

Notes on the Text

The text of the *Ethical Problems*, as of most of the minor works attributed to Alexander, rests on a tenth-century MS, Venetus Marcianus 258 (Bruns' V). Bruns argued that all other extant MSS derive from this, their readings thus having the value of conjectures only. Particularly noteworthy are the suggestions of B², from the fifteenth century (cf. Bruns xxiii-xxiv). The *Quaestiones*, including the *Ethical Problems*, were first edited by Trincavelli (Venice 1536; cited by Bruns as 'a'); noteworthy too was the edition of Spengel (Munich 1842). For further details concerning the MSS Bruns' preface (xv-xxvii) should be consulted.

Sigla in the following notes are those of Bruns.

1 119,13. Read *hôn esti <kharin>* or *hôn estin <heneka>*, proposed by Spengel.

1 119,24. For *oikeiôsthai* ('we have been given an affinity') von Arnim, *SVF* 3.165, proposed the present *oikeiousthai*, 'we are given an affinity'. But it may be doubted whether an original present would have been changed to a perfect, in view of the present 'gives us an affinity' following. (For *oikeiôsthai* rather than *ôikeiôsthai* as the form of the perfect cf. *Mantissa* 152,8, 162,29.)

1 120,1-2. Delete *haireton*, as suggested by Dr Kenny.

2 120,28-9. Read *autais* with GFSa and Spengel. Bruns corrects V's *autês* to the singular *autêi*, but it is not clear to what this would refer. Admittedly, the texts attributed to Alexander do tend to be rather vague in their use of pronouns (cf. e.g. nn. 133, 134 and 136 to *P. Eth.* 13 and n. 151 to *P. Eth.* 16; also below on *P. Eth.* 13 134,14).

2 121,11. Read *tais akolastois* with Spengel; the MSS, followed by Bruns, have *tois akolastois*, which would have to mean 'in the case of the profligate *persons*', but seems less to the point. See note to the translation ad loc.

3 122,16. Read *ar' <ouk>* (conjectured by Spengel; not adopted by Bruns).

3 122,25. Read *ap' autou* (conjectured by Bruns in his apparatus, but not admitted into the text); the MSS *hapanta* cannot be construed grammatically.

5 124,31. Read *dia to,* suggested by Bruns in his apparatus but not incorporated into his text; *di' auto* MSS.

5 125,8. Read *ei estai,* suggested by Bruns in his apparatus; *ouk estai* MSS.

5 125,12. Reading (without much confidence) *ginomenais* with B²a; V and B¹ have *hêdomenas,* 'those (pleasures) that take pleasure in activities in accordance with nature', but apart from the awkwardness of expression *hêdomenas* is redundant with *ginomenas* just before. Bruns emends to *hêdomenois,* 'those that supervene on activities in accordance with nature for those that take pleasure' (sc. 'in them'), but this seems tortuous.

5 126,2. Read *mê dei* for *mêde* with Apelt (1894) 71. B², followed by a and Spengel, emended the whole passage to read '... will itself in a similar way be opposed to the pain which is proper (to each), as one bad (thing) to another; for (it is opposed to it) as an excess to a defect. So all pain ...'; cf. also Madigan (1987) 1276 and n. 20. Bruns printed the text of V and B¹ with an obelus.

6 126,14. *kai ho ponos* was proposed for *hê hôs ponos* by Usener (Bruns xlv, cf. xxxix).

6 126,23. Read *dio,* proposed by Spengel; *dioti* MSS Bruns.

8 128,6. Read *estai de houtôs*, suggested by Bruns in his apparatus.

8 128,9. Read *einai* for *en* with Spengel; approved by Bruns in his apparatus, but not in his text.

9 128,30. *epikalountai* is B²'s correction, followed by a, Spengel and Bruns, for *epikalousin* in V; Apelt (1894) 71 proposed instead *epainousin*, 'they praise' (cf. 129,13 below).

9 129,1. Read *autois <kai> to* with Apelt (1894) 71 (*autois <esti kai> to* B², a and Spengel), rather than *autois <hôs> to* with Bruns. See n. 98 to *P. Eth.* 9.

9 129,2. Apelt, loc. cit. proposes *an <an>eien*, 'they will voluntarily cease from doing the things in accordance with their love'.

9 129,6. Read *iasin* (Spengel's conjecture); *eisin* (with no accent) V.

9 129,25. Read *mête aidountai hautous <mête peri tôn kakôn hôs autois on>tôn kakôn phronousin* (Schwartz' conjecture, in Bruns' apparatus).

9 130,4. Read *oute de ha biazomenoi <poioumen oute ha di' agnoian> poioumen eph' hêmin mê poiein,* suggested by Bruns in his apparatus but not printed in his text. The two criteria of forcible compulsion and of ignorance are both mentioned in what precedes at 130,13-14, though it must be admitted that only forcible compulsion is mentioned in what follows at 130,14-15.

9 130,14-15. Read *ha gar [mê] eph' hêmin poiein ... tauta ou biâi.* V has both negatives; only one, clearly, is needed, and the *vetus corrector,* followed by Bruns, deleted *ou*. But 'what is in our control is not due to force' is both more to the point in view of what has preceded than 'what is not in our control is due to force', and also *true*; 'what is not in our control is due to force' is false, since ignorance as well as forcible compulsion renders an action both involuntary and not in our control (cf. 130,29ff. below).

10 131,11. Read *ou gar hai aretai <khôris> ginontai,* suggested by Diels (in Bruns' apparatus). Apelt (1906) 11 proposes *ou gar aphairetai ginontai,* 'for <the virtues> are not removable' (i.e. separable from the man who possesses them).

12 132,32. Read, with Apelt (1906) 11, following S and B, *kai touto prattonti,* for V's *kai touto pratton ê.* Bruns proposed *kai <tou> touto prattein,* 'the person who places someone under duress has some end in (literally 'of') doing this set before him'; but as Apelt argues this gives a weaker sense.

12 133,7. Read *di' hautou,* suggested by Diels (in Bruns' apparatus), for *hê tou* of the MSS, omitted by a, Spengel and Bruns.

13 134,1. Read *tou autou <tou apo> tôn diaphorôn,* with Bruns (suggested in his apparatus but not in the text). Dr Kenny suggests retaining *adiaphorôn* in the sense of 'without drawing distinctions', 'whatever they may be'; but this seems confusing where the activities *are* in fact different from one another and the question at issue is whether pleasures are so too.

13 134,14. Read, with Spengel, *autês* for *autôn* of the MSS and Bruns. These

texts are often careless about singular and plural pronouns, but Spengel's emendation is probably to be accepted.

14 135,24. Read, with Bruns (suggested in his apparatus; not in his text), *dêlonoti eis* for *dêlon hai eis* of VS¹B¹F.

14 135,25. Read *hoiai hai* with B²S²a and Spengel, for *aitiai* of VS¹BF. Bruns (in his apparatus; not in his text) proposes rather *hautai d' <hai>*.

17 137,25. Read *eien <an>*, suggested by Schwartz (in Bruns' apparatus). Cf. n. 23 to *P. Eth.* 3.

18 138,10. Reading *hê hêdonê monê* with B²; the MSS and Bruns have *hê monê hêdonê*, more naturally rendered as 'pleasure on its own'.

19 139,18. Delete *hupo* before *hêdonês* (or read *phthartê*, but this seems less likely).

20 140,11. Read *to khrêsimon, <anairethêsetai to khrêsimon> anairoumenou*, suggested by Bruns in his apparatus but not in his text.

20 140,20. Omit *tois* with SFa; including it with the MSS and Bruns would give the sense 'provides such things with their being', simply (taking *tois toioutois* as resumptive); but this seems too strong a statement.

20 140,30. Read *hai* (relative) for *hai* (article), taking *de* in 140,29 as apodotic, with Apelt (1906) 11-12. Bruns, reading *hai* (article), supposes a lacuna after 'free men', taking the whole of 'if useful things ... certain activities' as protasis and 'activities which are proper to men and are (the activities) of free men' as the start of an incomplete apodosis. Similarly Madigan (1987) 1270 and n. 11, except that he paraphrases 'which are proper to men' (reading *hai* (relative)?) and takes this clause as part of the protasis, supplying 'it is slavish not to (carry on these activities)' as the apodosis.

21 142,6. Read *oudeni* for *oude* (conjectured by Bruns in his apparatus; not in his text).

21 142,9. Read *panta aiskhra pantêi* with Apelt (1894) 71.

22 142,25. Read *ei ge to*, suggested by Bruns in his apparatus but not in his text, for *heipeto* of VB¹. Bruns actually proposed 'right choice comes both from wisdom <and from moral virtue>, if deliberation is (the work) of moral virtue and of practical wisdom, if it is necessary ...'; but cf. Apelt (1906) 12.

23 143,17. Read *<aition> tou*, conjectured by Bruns in his apparatus but not in his text.

23 143,22. Read *<kai> katho anthrôpos esti, oikeiais energeiais*, suggested by Bruns in his apparatus, but not in his text. So too Madigan (1987) 1273 and n. 14. Apelt (1894) 71 proposed *kath' hên eu anthrôpos esti*, 'according to which he is a man well', i.e. 'is a good example of man', comparing *Quaestio* 2.19 63,14; 63,16; 3.2 82,15, and Alexander *de Anima* 93,20; but this seems implausible.

23 143,25. 'If' is added here by B¹ (del. B²), Victorius and Spengel, followed by Bruns, giving the sense 'if pleasure is an activity ... last book of the *Ethics*, then pleasure, ...'. This involves taking *de* in 143,26 as apodotic, and seems an unnecessary addition; I have in any case adopted the simpler syntax in my translation.

23 144,4. Read *teleon*, suggested by Schwartz (in Bruns' apparatus) for *pleon* of the MSS.

23 144,16. Omit *dia tas* (at the beginning of the line) with a. The MSS text, followed by Bruns, gives *dia tas*: 'we choose pleasures on account of those

(pleasures) that supervene ...', but this seems at best tortuous and at worst inconsistent with our author's position.

23 144,22. Read *touto toi* for the *toutôi* of VB[1], which lacks a connective; this is suggested by Bruns in his apparatus, comparing Alexander *de An.* 8,25 and 97,1.

23 145,4. *ap' autôn* was proposed for *hup' autôn* by Usener (Bruns p. xlv, cf. p. xxxix).

24 147,12. Read *dân*, by crasis for *dê an*, as proposed by L. Rademacher, 'Griechische Sprachgebrauch', *Philologus* 59 (1900) 597; *d' an* MSS, *d'* deleted by B[2], Spengel and Bruns.

25 148,15. Read <*ei ge hê tekhnê*> *mimeitai* with S[2]B[2]a and Spengel; noted in Bruns' apparatus as 'perhaps correct' but not accepted into his text.

25, 148,24-25. Read *tas oikeias tas,* proposed by Diels (in Bruns' apparatus) for *kai* (del. V[2]) *oikeias tas* of the MSS. (Diels wished to delete the second *tas*, but this does not seem necessary.)

25 148,32. Read *boulêtas* of the MSS for *bouleutas*, Spengel's emendation also adopted by Bruns. Cf. n. 218 to *P. Eth.* 25.

25 151,4. Read *to alêthes to* with B[2] for *kai alêthes* of V and Bruns.

25 151,14. Read <*eiê an oun hê aretê*> *tên* with S[2]B[2]a. Cf. n. 229 to *P. Eth.* 25.

27 153,18. Read *autôi* with V[2] and Victorius. Spengel's *hautôi*, adopted by Bruns, gives the sense 'in itself ', taking 'equality and due measure and the mean' as a single thing; but this is awkward between two other references to them as grammatically plural.

27 153,18-27. Bruns punctuates this as a parenthesis, but this makes the reference of 'concerning them' in 153,28 obscure; by removing the parentheses 'concerning them' can refer back to 'affections and actions' in 153,26.

27 156,30. Read *legetai* with the MSS of the *Ethical Problems*; Bruns emended to *psegetai* which is found in most MSS of Aristotle himself. But it seems at least possible that our author may actually have written *legetai* here either by an error of his own or because he had a text of Aristotle which was already corrupt; contrast the following note in the translation, where it seems more likely that we are simply dealing with a later corruption of the text of the *Ethical Problems*.

28 157,17. End parenthesis in 157,17, not 157,19 with Bruns; *de* in 157,17 balances *men* in 175,15.

28 157,28-30. Remove Bruns' parentheses. Cf. n. 267 to *P. Eth.* 28.

29 158,12. Punctuate with comma rather than full stop after *esesthai*. See n. 269 to *P. Eth.* 29.

29 159,1-2. Retain the words deleted by Spengel and Bruns.

29, 159,14. Read *aitian* <*ekhôn*> (conjectured by Bruns but not in his text).

29 160,21. Read *kai* for *hai* (conjectured in Bruns' apparatus but not in his text).

29 161,2. Read *poiein* for *ti dein* (conjectured in Bruns' apparatus, but not in his text). Apelt (1906) 12 proposed *tisin* for *ti dein* ('on those on whom the opposites of certain things [depend], on them the opposites also of those things depend'), comparing *Quaest.* 1.15 59,31.

29 161,3. Add *ei* after *hôste* , rather than after *aitios* in 161.4. The argument then has the form of the Stoic first undemonstrated argument (*modus ponens*): 'if (if the first then the second) and the first, then the second.'

29 161,5. Read *auton* for the first *aition* (conjectured by Schwartz, in Bruns' apparatus).

30 162,3-4. Read *tôn amphoterôn* with the MSS. Bruns' *tôi amphoterôn* explains the infinitive *einai* where one would expect the indicative in 162,5, but the resulting structure seems unreasonably complex even for Alexander ('it is by the fact that {the intermediate, by the fact that [it shares in a way in both extremes but does not possess the features of either of them completely], is intermediate between these very things}, that, when it changes ...'). In 162,4-5 S^2B^2a and Spengel have instead '... either of them completely, that it is as it were the opposite of the things between which it is intermediate; and when it changes ...' B^2 prefaces 'that it is as it were' by 'the verb "leaves", or something like it, is left out'.

30 163,9. Read *ginomenôn* for *ginomenê*.

Bibliography

Alexander: general

Paul Moraux, the doyen of Alexander studies in the present century, intended to devote the third and final volume of his monumental work *Der Aristotelismus bei den Griechen* entirely to a study of Alexander, but was prevented from completing it by his untimely death. The work is now being completed by various hands. It would have superseded an earlier work,

P. Moraux, *Alexandre d'Aphrodise: exégète de la noétique d'Aristote*, Liège and Paris 1942 (cited here as Moraux (1942)), which includes some discussion of Alexander's work and writings in general. There is a general account of Alexander in the introduction of a recent work:

R.B. Todd, *Alexander of Aphrodisias on Stoic Physics*, Leiden 1976 (*Philosophia Antiqua*, 28), 1-20 (cited as Todd (1976))

and a general survey in Italian in:

P.L. Donini, *Le scuole, l'anima, l'impero: la filosofia antica da Antioco a Plotino*, Turin 1982, 220-48.

A full bibliography and survey of current research is given in:

R.W. Sharples, 'Alexander of Aphrodisias: scholasticism and innovation', *Aufstieg und Niedergang der römischen Welt*, Part II 'Principat', vol. 36.2 'Philosophie und Wissenschaften', Berlin 1987, 1176-243 (cited as Sharples (1987)).

The *Ethical Problems*

The standard edition, on which this translation is based, is by I. Bruns in *Supplementum Aristotelicum* 2.2, Berlin 1892, 117-63 (cited as Bruns (1892), or just Bruns when the context makes it clear that it is the edition that is meant). There are useful discussions of the minor texts attributed to Alexander in the Preface (v-xvii).

There has been little modern scholarly discussion of these texts. Two papers were devoted to the text of Alexander's *Quaestiones*, including the *Ethical Problems*, by O. Apelt:

'Die kleinen Schriften des Alexander von Aphrodisias', *Rheinisches Museum* 49 (1984) 59-71 (cited as Apelt (1894)); *Kritische Bemerkungen*, Jena 1906 (*Jahresbericht des Gymnasiums Carolo-Alexandrinum*: cited as Apelt (1906)).

Treatments of the content of particular *Problems*, often in the wider context of the philosophical issues to which they relate, have been cited in the notes to each text. There is a general discussion of the *Ethical Problems* in:

A. Madigan, 'Alexander of Aphrodisias: the book of *Ethical Problems*', *Aufstieg und Niedergang der römischen Welt*, Part II 'Principat', vol. 36.2 'Philosophie und Wissenschaften', Berlin 1987, 1260-79 (cited as Madigan (1987))

and a number of texts are discussed in relation to the light they throw on the activities of Alexander's school in:

R.W. Sharples, 'The School of Alexander', forthcoming in R. Sorabji (ed.), *Aristotle Transformed: the ancient commentators and their influence*, London 1989 (cited as Sharples (1989)).

Appendix
The Commentators*

The 15,000 pages of the Ancient Greek Commentaries on Aristotle are the largest corpus of Ancient Greek philosophy that has not been translated into English or other modern European languages. The standard edition (*Commentaria in Aristotelem Graeca*, or *CAG*) was produced by Hermann Diels as general editor under the auspices of the Prussian Academy in Berlin. Arrangements have now been made to translate at least a large proportion of this corpus, along with some other Greek and Latin commentaries not included in the Berlin edition, and some closely related non-commentary works by the commentators.

The works are not just commentaries on Aristotle, although they are invaluable in that capacity too. One of the ways of doing philosophy between A.D. 200 and 600, when the most important items were produced, was by writing commentaries. The works therefore represent the thought of the Peripatetic and Neoplatonist schools, as well as expounding Aristotle. Furthermore, they embed fragments from all periods of Ancient Greek philosophical thought: this is how many of the Presocratic fragments were assembled, for example. Thus they provide a panorama of every period of Ancient Greek philosophy.

The philosophy of the period from A.D. 200 to 600 has not yet been intensively explored by philosophers in English-speaking countries, yet it is full of interest for physics, metaphysics, logic, psychology, ethics and religion. The contrast with the study of the Presocratics is striking. Initially the incomplete Presocratic fragments might well have seemed less promising, but their interest is now widely known, thanks to the philological and philosophical effort that has been concentrated upon them. The incomparably vaster corpus which preserved so many of those fragments offers at least as much interest, but is still relatively little known.

The commentaries represent a missing link in the history of philosophy: the Latin-speaking Middle Ages obtained their

* Reprinted from the Editor's General Introduction to the series in Christian Wildberg, *Philoponus Against Aristotle on the Eternity of the World*, London and Ithaca N.Y., 1987.

knowledge of Aristotle at least partly through the medium of the commentaries. Without an appreciation of this, mediaeval interpretations of Aristotle will not be understood. Again, the ancient commentaries are the unsuspected source of ideas which have been thought, wrongly, to originate in the later mediaeval period. It has been supposed, for example, that Bonaventure in the thirteenth century invented the ingenious arguments based on the concept of infinity which attempt to prove the Christian view that the universe had a beginning. In fact, Bonaventure is merely repeating arguments devised by the commentator Philoponus 700 years earlier and preserved in the meantime by the Arabs. Bonaventure even uses Philoponus' original examples. Again, the introduction of impetus theory into dynamics, which has been called a scientific revolution, has been held to be an independent invention of the Latin West, even if it was earlier discovered by the Arabs or their predecessors. But recent work has traced a plausible route by which it could have passed from Philoponus, via the Arabs, to the West.

The new availability of the commentaries in the sixteenth century, thanks to printing and to fresh Latin translations, helped to fuel the Renaissance break from Aristotelian science. For the commentators record not only Aristotle's theories, but also rival ones, while Philoponus as a Christian devises rival theories of his own and accordingly is mentioned in Galileo's early works more frequently than Plato.[1]

It is not only for their philosophy that the works are of interest. Historians will find information about the history of schools, their methods of teaching and writing and the practices of an oral tradition.[2] Linguists will find the indexes and translations an aid for studying the development of word meanings, almost wholly

---

[1] See Fritz Zimmermann, 'Philoponus' impetus theory in the Arabic tradition'; Charles Schmitt, 'Philoponus' commentary on Aristotle's *Physics* in the sixteenth century', and Richard Sorabji, 'John Philoponus', in Richard Sorabji (ed.), *Philoponus and the Rejection of Aristotelian Science* (London and Ithaca, N.Y. 1987).

[2] See e.g. Karl Praechter, 'Die griechischen Aristoteleskommentare', *Byzantinische Zeitschrift* 18 (1909), 516-38; M. Plezia, *de Commentariis Isagogicis* (Cracow 1947); M. Richard, '*Apo Phônês*', *Byzantion* 20 (1950), 191-222; É. Evrard, *L'Ecole d'Olympiodore et la composition du commentaire à la physique de Jean Philopon*, Diss. (Liège 1957); L.G. Westerink, *Anonymous Prolegomena to Platonic Philosophy* (Amsterdam 1962) (new revised edition, translated into French, Collection Budé, forthcoming); A.-J. Festugière, 'Modes de composition des commentaires de Proclus', *Museum Helveticum* 20 (1963), 77-100, repr. in his *Études* (1971), 551-74; P. Hadot, 'Les divisions des parties de la philosophie dans l'antiquité', *Museum Helveticum* 36 (1979), 201-23; I. Hadot, 'La division néoplatonicienne des écrits d'Aristote', in J. Wiesner (ed.), *Aristoteles Werk und Wirkung* (Paul Moraux gewidmet), vol. 2 (Berlin 1986); I. Hadot, 'Les introductions aux commentaires exégétiques chez les auteurs néoplatoniciens et les auteurs chrétiens', in M. Tardieu (ed.), *Les règles de l'interprétation* (Paris 1987), 99-119. These topics will be treated, and a bibliography supplied, in a collection of articles on the commentators in general.

uncharted in Liddell and Scott's *Lexicon*, and for checking shifts in grammatical usage.

Given the wide range of interests to which the volumes will appeal, the aim is to produce readable translations, and to avoid so far as possible presupposing any knowledge of Greek. Footnotes will explain points of meaning, give cross-references to other works, and suggest alternative interpretations of the text where the translator does not have a clear preference. The introduction to each volume will include an explanation why the work was chosen for translation: none will be chosen simply because it is there. Two of the Greek texts are currently being re-edited – those of Simplicius *in Physica* and *in de Caelo* – and new readings will be exploited by translators as they become available. Each volume will also contain a list of proposed emendations to the standard text. Indexes will be of more uniform extent as between volumes than is the case with the Berlin edition, and there will be three of them: an English-Greek glossary, a Greek-English index, and a subject index.

The commentaries fall into three main groups. The first group is by authors in the Aristotelian tradition up to the fourth century A.D. This includes the earliest extant commentary, that by Aspasius in the first half of the second century A.D. on the *Nicomachean Ethics*. The anonymous commentary on Books 2, 3, 4 and 5 of the *Nichomachean Ethics*, in *CAG* vol. 20, is derived from Adrastus, a generation later.[3] The commentaries by Alexander of Aphrodisias (appointed to his chair between A.D. 198 and 209) represent the fullest flowering of the Aristotelian tradition. To his successors Alexander was The Commentator *par excellence*. To give but one example (not from a commentary) of his skill at defending and elaborating Aristotle's views, one might refer to his defence of Aristotle's claim that space is finite against the objection that an edge of space is conceptually problematic.[4] Themistius (*fl.* late 340s to 384 or 385) saw himself as the inventor of paraphrase, wrongly thinking that the job of commentary was completed.[5] In fact, the Neoplatonists were to introduce new dimensions into commentary. Themistius' own relation to the Neoplatonist as opposed to the Aristotelian tradition is a matter of controversy,[6] but it would be

[3] Anthony Kenny, *The Aristotelian Ethics* (Oxford 1978), 37, n.3; Paul Moraux, *Der Aristotelismus bei den Griechen*, vol. 2 (Berlin 1984), 323-30.

[4] Alexander, *Quaestiones* 3.12, discussed in my *Matter, Space and Motion* (London and Ithaca, N.Y. 1988). For Alexander see R.W. Sharples, 'Alexander of Aphrodisias: scholasticism and innovation', in W. Haase (ed.), *Aufstieg und Niedergang der römischen Welt*, part 2 *Principat*, vol. 36.2, *Philosophie und Wissenschaften* (1987).

[5] Themistius *in An. Post.* 1,2-12. See H.J. Blumenthal, 'Photius on Themistius (Cod.74): did Themistius write commentaries on Aristotle?', *Hermes* 107 (1979), 168-82.

[6] For different views, see H.J. Blumenthal, 'Themistius, the last Peripatetic commentator on Aristotle?', in Glen W. Bowersock, Walter Burkert, Michael C.J. Putnam, *Arktouros*, Hellenic Studies Presented to Bernard M.W. Knox (Berlin and

agreed that his commentaries show far less bias than the full-blown Neoplatonist ones. They are also far more informative than the designation 'paraphrase' might suggest, and it has been estimated that Philoponus' *Physics* commentary draws silently on Themistius six hundred times.[7] The pseudo-Alexandrian commentary on *Metaphysics* 6–14, of unknown authorship, has been placed by some in the same group of commentaries as being earlier than the fifth century.[8]

By far the largest group of extant commentaries is that of the Neoplatonists up to the sixth century A.D. Nearly all the major Neoplatonists, apart from Plotinus (the founder of Neoplatonism), wrote commentaries on Aristotle, although those of Iamblichus (*c.* 250 – *c.* 325) survive only in fragments, and those of three Athenians, Plutarchus (died 432), his pupil Proclus (410-485) and the Athenian Damascius (*c.* 462 – after 538), are lost.[9] As a result of these losses, most of the extant Neoplatonist commentaries come from the late fifth and the sixth centuries and a good proportion from Alexandria. There are commentaries by Plotinus' disciple and editor Porphyry (232 – 309), by Iamblichus' pupil Dexippus (*c.* 330), by Proclus' teacher Syrianus (died *c.* 437), by Proclus' pupil Ammonius (435/445 – 517/526), by Ammonius' three pupils Philoponus (*c.* 490 to 570s), Simplicius (wrote after 532, probably after 538) and Asclepius (sixth century), by Ammonius' next but one successor Olympiodorus (495/505 – after 565), by Elias (*fl.* 541?), by David (second half of the sixth century, or beginning of the seventh) and by Stephanus (took the chair in Constantinople *c.* 610). Further,

N.Y., 1979), 391-400; E.P. Mahoney, 'Themistius and the agent intellect in James of Viterbo and other thirteenth-century philosophers: (Saint Thomas Aquinas, Siger of Brabant and Henry Bate)', *Augustiniana* 23 (1973), 422-67, at 428-31; id., 'Neoplatonism, the Greek commentators and Renaissance Aristotelianism', in D.J. O'Meara (ed.), *Neoplatonism and Christian Thought* (Albany N.Y. 1982), 169-77 and 264-82, esp. n. 1, 264-6; Robert Todd, introduction to translation of Themistius *in DA 3,4-8,* forthcoming in a collection of translations by Frederick Schroeder and Robert Todd of material in the commentators relating to the intellect.

[7] H. Vitelli, *CAG* 17, p. 992, s.v. Themistius.

[8] The similarities to Syrianus (died *c.*437) have suggested to some that it predates Syrianus (most recently Leonardo Tarán, review of Paul Moraux, *Der Aristotelismus,* vol. 1, in *Gnomon* 46 (1981), 721-50 at 750), to others that it draws on him (most recently P. Thillet, in the Budé edition of Alexander *de Fato*, p. lvii). Praechter ascribed it to Michael of Ephesus (eleventh or twelfth century), in his review of *CAG* 22.2, in *Göttingische Gelehrte Anzeiger* 168 (1906), 861-907.

[9] The Iamblichus fragments are collected in Greek by Bent Dalsgaard Larsen, *Jamblique de Chalcis, Exégète et Philosophe* (Aarhus 1972), vol.2. Most are taken from Simplicius, and will accordingly be translated in due course. The evidence on Damascius' commentaries is given in L.G. Westerink, *The Greek Commentaries on Plato's Phaedo*, vol.2., Damascius (Amsterdam 1977), 11-12; on Proclus' in L.G. Westerink, *Anonymous Prolegomena to Platonic Philosophy* (Amsterdam 1962), xii, n.22; on Plutarchus' in H.M. Blumenthal, 'Neoplatonic elements in the de Anima commentaries', *Phronesis* 21 (1976), 75.

a commentary on the *Nicomachean Ethics* has been ascribed to Heliodorus of Prusa, an unknown pre-fourteenth-century figure, and there is a commentary by Simplicius' colleague Priscian of Lydia on Aristotle's successor Theophrastus. Of these commentators some of the last were Christians (Philoponus, Elias, David and Stephanus), but they were Christians writing in the Neoplatonist tradition, as was also Boethius who produced a number of commentaries in Latin before his death in 525 or 526.

The third group comes from a much later period in Byzantium. The Berlin edition includes only three out of more than a dozen commentators described in Hunger's *Byzantinisches Handbuch*.[10] The two most important are Eustratius (1050/1060 – c. 1120), and Michael of Ephesus. It has been suggested that these two belong to a circle organised by the princess Anna Comnena in the twelfth century, and accordingly the completion of Michael's commentaries has been redated from 1040 to 1138.[11] His commentaries include areas where gaps had been left. Not all of these gap-fillers are extant, but we have commentaries on the neglected biological works, on the *Sophistici Elenchi*, and a small fragment of one on the *Politics*. The lost *Rhetoric* commentary had a few antecedents, but the *Rhetoric* too had been comparatively neglected. Another product of this period may have been the composite commentary on the *Nicomachean Ethics* (*CAG* 20) by various hands, including Eustratius and Michael, along with some earlier commentators, and an improvisation for Book 7. Whereas Michael follows Alexander and the conventional Aristotelian tradition, Eustratius' commentary introduces Platonist, Christian and anti-Islamic elements.[12]

The composite commentary was to be translated into Latin in the next century by Robert Grosseteste in England. But Latin translations of various logical commentaries were made from the Greek still earlier by James of Venice (*fl. c.* 1130), a contemporary of Michael of Ephesus, who may have known him in Constantinople.

---

[10] Herbert Hunger, *Die hochsprachliche profane Literatur der Byzantiner*, vol.1 (= *Byzantinisches Handbuch*, part 5, vol.1) (Munich 1978), 25-41. See also B.N. Tatakis, *La Philosophie Byzantine* (Paris 1949).

[11] R. Browning, 'An unpublished funeral oration on Anna Comnena', *Proceedings of the Cambridge Philological Society* n.s. 8 (1962), 1-12, esp. 6-7.

[12] R. Browning, op. cit. H.D.P. Mercken, *The Greek Commentaries of the Nicomachean Ethics of Aristotle in the Latin Translation of Grosseteste, Corpus Latinum Commentariorum in Aristotelem Graecorum* VI 1 (Leiden 1973), ch.1, 'The compilation of Greek commentaries on Aristotle's Nicomachean Ethics'. Sten Ebbesen, 'Anonymi Aurelianensis I Commentarium in *Sophisticos Elenchos*', *Cahiers de l'Institut Moyen Age Grecque et Latin* 34 (1979), 'Boethius, Jacobus Veneticus, Michael Ephesius and "Alexander"', pp. v-xiii; id., *Commentators and Commentaries on Aristotle's Sophistici Elenchi*, 3 parts, *Corpus Latinum Commentariorum in Aristotelem Graecorum*, vol. 7 (Leiden 1981); A. Preus, *Aristotle and Michael of Ephesus on the Movement and Progression of Animals* (Hildesheim 1981), introduction.

And later in that century other commentaries and works by commentators were being translated from Arabic versions by Gerard of Cremona (died 1187).[13] So the twelfth century resumed the transmission which had been interrupted at Boethius' death in the sixth century.

The Neoplatonist commentaries of the main group were initiated by Porphyry. His master Plotinus had discussed Aristotle, but in a very independent way, devoting three whole treatises (*Enneads* 6.1–3) to attacking Aristotle's classification of the things in the universe into categories. These categories took no account of Plato's world of Ideas, were inferior to Plato's classifications in the *Sophist* and could anyhow be collapsed, some of them into others. Porphyry replied that Aristotle's categories could apply perfectly well to the world of intelligibles and he took them as in general defensible.[14] He wrote two commentaries on the *Categories*, one lost, and an introduction to it, the *Isagôgê*, as well as commentaries, now lost, on a number of other Aristotelian works. This proved decisive in making Aristotle a necessary subject for Neoplatonist lectures and commentary. Proclus, who was an exceptionally quick student, is said to have taken two years over his Aristotle studies, which were called the Lesser Mysteries, and which preceded the Greater Mysteries of Plato.[15] By the time of Ammonius, the commentaries reflect a teaching curriculum which begins with Porphyry's *Isagôgê* and Aristotle's *Categories*, and is explicitly said to have as its final goal a (mystical) ascent to the supreme Neoplatonist deity, the One.[16] The curriculum would have progressed from Aristotle to Plato, and would have culminated in Plato's *Timaeus* and *Parmenides*. The latter was read as being about the One, and both works were established in this place in the curriculum at least by

[13] For Grosseteste, see Mercken as in n. 12. For James of Venice, see Ebbesen as in n. 12, and L. Minio-Paluello, 'Jacobus Veneticus Grecus', *Traditio* 8 (1952), 265-304; id., 'Giacomo Veneto e l'Aristotelismo Latino', in Pertusi (ed.), *Venezia e l'Oriente fra tardo Medioevo e Rinascimento* (Florence 1966), 53-74, both reprinted in his *Opuscula* (1972). For Gerard of Cremona, see M. Steinschneider, *Die europäischen Übersetzungen aus dem arabischen bis Mitte des 17. Jahrhunderts* (repr. Graz 1956); E. Gilson, *History of Christian Philosophy in the Middle Ages* (London 1955), 235-6 and more generally 181-246. For the translators in general, see Bernard G. Dod, 'Aristoteles Latinus', in N. Kretzmann, A. Kenny, J. Pinborg (eds). *The Cambridge History of Latin Medieval Philosophy* (Cambridge 1982).

[14] See P. Hadot, 'L'harmonie des philosophies de Plotin et d'Aristote selon Porphyre dans le commentaire de Dexippe sur les Catégories', in *Plotino e il neoplatonismo in Oriente e in Occidente* (Rome 1974), 31-47; A.C. Lloyd, 'Neoplatonic logic and Aristotelian logic', *Phronesis* 1 (1955-6), 58-79 and 146-60.

[15] Marinus, *Life of Proclus* ch.13, 157,41 (Boissonade).

[16] The introductions to the *Isagôgê* by Ammonius, Elias and David, and to the *Categories* by Ammonius, Simplicius, Philoponus, Olympiodorus and Elias are discussed by L.G. Westerink, *Anonymous Prolegomena* and I. Hadot, 'Les Introductions', see n. 2. above.

the time of Iamblichus, if not earlier.[17]

Before Porphyry, it had been undecided how far a Platonist should accept Aristotle's scheme of categories. But now the proposition began to gain force that there was a harmony between Plato and Aristotle on most things.[18] Not for the only time in the history of philosophy, a perfectly crazy proposition proved philosophically fruitful. The views of Plato and of Aristotle had both to be transmuted into a new Neoplatonist philosophy in order to exhibit the supposed harmony. Iamblichus denied that Aristotle contradicted Plato on the theory of Ideas.[19] This was too much for Syrianus and his pupil Proclus. While accepting harmony in many areas,[20] they could see that there was disagreement on this issue and also on the issue of whether God was causally responsible for the existence of the ordered physical cosmos, which Aristotle denied. But even on these issues, Proclus' pupil Ammonius was to claim harmony, and, though the debate was not clear cut,[21] his claim was on the whole to prevail. Aristotle, he maintained, accepted Plato's Ideas,[22] at least in the form of principles (*logoi*) in the divine intellect, and these principles were in turn causally responsible for the beginningless existence of the physical universe. Ammonius wrote a whole book to show that Aristotle's God was thus an efficient cause, and though the book is lost, some of its principal arguments are preserved by Simplicius.[23] This tradition helped to make it possible for Aquinas to claim Aristotle's God as a Creator, albeit not in the sense of giving

---

[17] Proclus *in Alcibiadem 1* p.11 (Creuzer); Westerink, *Anonymous Prolegomena*, ch. 26, 12f. For the Neoplatonist curriculum see Westerink, Festugière, P. Hadot and I. Hadot in n. 2.

[18] See e.g. P. Hadot (1974), as in n. 14 above; H.J. Blumenthal, 'Neoplatonic elements in the de Anima commentaries', *Phronesis* 21 (1976), 64-87; H.A. Davidson, 'The principle that a finite body can contain only finite power', in S. Stein and R. Loewe (eds), *Studies in Jewish Religious and Intellectual History presented to A. Altmann* (Alabama 1979), 75-92; Carlos Steel, 'Proclus et Aristote', Proceedings of the Congrès Proclus held in Paris 1985, J. Pépin and H.D. Saffrey (eds), *Proclus, lecteur et interprète des anciens* (Paris 1987), 213-25; Koenraad Verrycken, *God en Wereld in de Wijsbegeerte van Ioannes Philoponus*, Ph.D. Diss. (Louvain 1985).

[19] Iamblichus ap. Elian *in Cat.* 123,1-3.

[20] Syrianus *in Metaph.* 80,4-7; Proclus *in Tim.* 1.6,21-7,16.

[21] Asclepius sometimes accepts Syranius' interpretation (*in Metaph*, 433,9-436,6); which is, however, qualified, since Syrianus thinks Aristotle is really committed willy-nilly to much of Plato's view (*in Metaph*, 117,25-118,11; ap. Asclepium *in Metaph.* 433,16; 450,22); Philoponus repents of his early claim that Plato is not the target of Aristotle's attack, and accepts that Plato is rightly attacked for treating ideas as independent entities outside the divine Intellect (*in DA* 37,18-31; *in Phys.* 225,4-226,11; *contra Procl.* 26,24-32,13; *in An. Post.* 242,14–243,25).

[22] Asclepius *in Metaph* from the voice of (i.e. from the lectures of) Ammonius 69,17-21; 71,28; cf. Zacharias *Ammonius*, *Patrologia Graeca* vol. 85, col. 952 (Colonna).

[23] Simplicius *in Phys.* 1361,11-1363,12. See H.A. Davidson; Carlos Steel; Koenraad Verrycken in n.18 above.

the universe a beginning, but in the sense of being causally responsible for its beginningless existence.[24] Thus what started as a desire to harmonise Aristotle with Plato finished by making Aristotle safe for Christianity. In Simplicius, who goes further than anyone,[25] it is a formally stated duty of the commentator to display the harmony of Plato and Aristotle in most things.[26] Philoponus, who with his independent mind had thought better of his earlier belief in harmony, is castigated by Simplicius for neglecting this duty.[27]

The idea of harmony was extended beyond Plato and Aristotle to Plato and the Presocratics. Plato's pupils Speusippus and Xenocrates saw Plato as being in the Pythagorean tradition.[28] From the third to first centuries B.C., pseudo-Pythagorean writings present Platonic and Aristotelian doctrines as if they were the ideas of Pythagoras and his pupils,[29] and these forgeries were later taken by the Neoplatonists as genuine. Plotinus saw the Presocratics as precursors of his own views,[30] but Iamblichus went far beyond him by writing ten volumes on Pythagorean philosophy.[31] Thereafter Proclus sought to unify the whole of Greek philosophy by presenting it as a continuous clarification of divine revelation,[32] and Simplicius argued for the same general unity in order to rebut Christian charges of contradictions in pagan philosophy.[33]

Later Neoplatonist commentaries tend to reflect their origin in a teaching curriculum:[34] from the time of Philoponus, the discussion is often divided up into lectures, which are subdivided into studies of doctrine and of text. A general account of Aristotle's philosophy is prefixed to the *Categories* commentaries and divided, according to a formula of Proclus,[35] into ten questions. It is here that commentators explain the eventual purpose of studying Aristotle (ascent to the One) and state (if they do) the requirement of

[24] See Richard Sorabji, *Matter, Space and Motion* (London and Ithaca N.Y. 1988), ch. 15.

[25] See e.g. H.J. Blumenthal in n. 18 above.

[26] Simplicius *in Cat.* 7,23-32.

[27] Simplicius *in Cael.* 84,11-14; 159,2-9. On Philoponus' *volte face* see n. 21 above.

[28] See e.g. Walter Burkert, *Weisheit und Wissenschaft* (Nürnberg 1962), translated as *Lore and Science in Ancient Pythagoreanism* (Cambridge Mass. 1972), 83-96.

[29] See Holger Thesleff, *An Introduction to the Pythagorean writings of the Hellenistic Period* (Åbo 1961); Thomas Alexander Szlezák, *Pseudo-Archytas über die Kategorien*, Peripatoi vol. 4 (Berlin and New York 1972).

[30] Plotinus e.g. 4.8.1; 5.1.8 (10-27); 5.1.9.

[31] See Dominic O'Meara, *Pythagoras Revived: Mathematics and Philosophy in late Antiquity*, forthcoming.

[32] See Christian Guérard, 'Parménide d'Elée selon les Néoplatoniciens', forthcoming.

[33] Simplicius *in Phys.* 28,32-29,5; 640,12-18. Such thinkers as Epicurus and the Sceptics, however, were not subject to harmonisation.

[34] See the literature in n. 2 above.   [35] ap. Elian *in Cat.* 107,24-6.

displaying the harmony of Plato and Aristotle. After the ten-point introduction to Aristotle, the *Categories* is given a six-point introduction, whose antecedents go back earlier than Neoplatonism, and which requires the commentator to find a unitary theme or scope (*skopos*) for the treatise. The arrangements for late commentaries on Plato are similar. Since the Plato commentaries form part of a single curriculum they should be studied alongside those on Aristotle. Here the situation is easier, not only because the extant corpus is very much smaller, but also because it has been comparatively well served by French and English translators.[36]

Given the theological motive of the curriculum and the pressure to harmonise Plato with Aristotle, it can be seen how these commentaries are a major source for Neoplatonist ideas. This in turn means that it is not safe to extract from them the fragments of the Presocratics, or of other authors, without making allowance for the Neoplatonist background against which the fragments were originally selected for discussion. For different reasons, analogous warnings apply to fragments preserved by the pre-Neoplatonist commentator Alexander.[37] It will be another advantage of the present translations that they will make it easier to check the distorting effect of a commentator's background.

Although the Neoplatonist commentators conflate the views of Aristotle with those of Neoplatonism, Philoponus alludes to a certain convention when he quotes Plutarchus expressing disapproval of Alexander for expounding his own philosophical doctrines in a commentary on Aristotle.[38] But this does not stop Philoponus from later inserting into his own commentaries on the *Physics* and *Meteorology* his arguments in favour of the Christian view of Creation. Of course, the commentators also wrote independent works of their own, in which their views are expressed independently of the exegesis of Aristotle. Some of these independent works will be included in the present series of translations.

The distorting Neoplatonist context does not prevent the commentaries from being incomparable guides to Aristotle. The

---

[36] English: Calcidius *in Tim.* (parts by van Winden; den Boeft); Iamblichus fragments (Dillon); Proclus *in Tim.* (Thomas Taylor); Proclus *in Parm.* (Dillon); Proclus *in Parm.*, end of 7th book, from the Latin (Klibansky, Labowsky, Anscombe); Proclus *in Alcib. 1* (O'Neill); Olympiodorus and Damascius *in Phaedonem* (Westerink); Damascius *in Philebum* (Westerink); *Anonymous Prolegomena to Platonic Philosophy* (Westerink). See also extracts in Thomas Taylor, *The Works of Plato*, 5 vols. (1804). French: Proclus *in Tim.* and *in Rempublicam* (Festugière); *in Parm.* (Chaignet); Anon. *in Parm.* (P. Hadot); Damascius *in Parm.* (Chaignet).

[37] For Alexander's treatment of the Stoics, see Robert B. Todd, *Alexander of Aphrodisias on Stoic Physics* (Leiden 1976), 24-9.

[38] Philoponus *in DA* 21,20-3.

introductions to Aristotle's philosophy insist that commentators must have a minutely detailed knowledge of the entire Aristotelian corpus, and this they certainly have. Commentators are also enjoined neither to accept nor reject what Aristotle says too readily, but to consider it in depth and without partiality. The commentaries draw one's attention to hundreds of phrases, sentences and ideas in Aristotle, which one could easily have passed over, however often one read him. The scholar who makes the right allowance for the distorting context will learn far more about Aristotle than he would be likely to on his own.

The relations of Neoplatonist commentators to the Christians were subtle. Porphyry wrote a treatise explicitly against the Christians in 15 books, but an order to burn it was issued in 448, and later Neoplatonists were more circumspect. Among the last commentators in the main group, we have noted several Christians. Of these the most important were Boethius and Philoponus. It was Boethius' programme to transmit Greek learning to Latin-speakers. By the time of his premature death by execution, he had provided Latin translations of Aristotle's logical works, together with commentaries in Latin but in the Neoplatonist style on Porphyry's *Isagôgê* and on Aristotle's *Categories* and *de Interpretatione*, and interpretations of the *Prior* and *Posterior Analytics, Topics* and *Sophistici Elenchi*. The interruption of his work meant that knowledge of Aristotle among Latin-speakers was confined for many centuries to the logical works. Philoponus is important both for his proofs of the Creation and for his progressive replacement of Aristotelian science with rival theories, which were taken up at first by the Arabs and came fully into their own in the West only in the sixteenth century.

Recent work has rejected the idea that in Alexandria the Neoplatonists compromised with Christian monotheism by collapsing the distinction between their two highest deities, the One and the Intellect. Simplicius (who left Alexandria for Athens) and the Alexandrians Ammonius and Asclepius appear to have acknowledged their beliefs quite openly, as later did the Alexandrian Olympiodorus, despite the presence of Christian students in their classes.[39]

The teaching of Simplicius in Athens and that of the whole pagan Neoplatonist school there was stopped by the Christian Emperor Justinian in 529. This was the very year in which the Christian

---

[39] For Simplicius, see I. Hadot, *Le Problème du Néoplatonisme Alexandrin: Hiéroclès et Simplicius* (Paris 1978); for Ammonius and Asclepius, Koenraad Verrycken, *God en Wereld in de Wijsbegeerte van Ioannes Philoponus*, Ph.D. Diss. (Louvain 1985); for Olympiodorus, L.G. Westerink, *Anonymous Prolegomena to Platonic Philosophy* (Amsterdam 1962).

Philoponus in Alexandria issued his proofs of Creation against the earlier Athenian Neoplatonist Proclus. Archaeological evidence has been offered that, after their temporary stay in Ctesiphon (in present-day Iraq), the Athenian Neoplatonists did not return to their house in Athens, and further evidence has been offered that Simplicius went to Ḥarrān (Carrhae), in present-day Turkey near the Iraq border.[40] Wherever he went, his commentaries are a treasure house of information about the preceding thousand years of Greek philosophy, information which he painstakingly recorded after the closure in Athens, and which would otherwise have been lost. He had every reason to feel bitter about Christianity, and in fact he sees it and Philoponus, its representative, as irreverent. They deny the divinity of the heavens and prefer the physical relics of dead martyrs.[41] His own commentaries by contrast culminate in devout prayers.

Two collections of articles by various hands are planned, to make the work of the commentators better known. The first is devoted to Philoponus;[42] the second will be about the commentators in general, and will go into greater detail on some of the issues briefly mentioned here.[43]

---

[40] Alison Frantz, 'Pagan philosophers in Christian Athens', *Proceedings of the American Philosophical Society* 119 (1975), 29-38; M. Tardieu, 'Témoins orientaux du *Premier Alcibiade* à Ḥarrān et à Nag 'Hammādi', *Journal Asiatique* 274 (1986); id., 'Les calendriers en usage à Ḥarrān d'après les sources arabes et le commentaire de Simplicius à la *Physique* d'Aristote', in I. Hadot (ed.), *Simplicius, sa vie, son oeuvre, sa survie* (Berlin 1987), 40-57; *Coutumes nautiques mésopotamiennes chez Simplicius*, in preparation. The opposing view that Simplicius returned to Athens is most fully argued by Alan Cameron, 'The last days of the Academy at Athens', *Proceedings of the Cambridge Philological Society* 195, n.s. 15 (1969), 7-29.

[41] Simplicius *in Cael.* 26,4-7; 70,16-18; 90,1-18; 370,29-371,4. See on his whole attitude Philippe Hoffmann, 'Simplicius' polemics', in Richard Sorabji (ed.), *Philoponus and the Rejection of Aristotelian Science* (London and Ithaca, N.Y. 1987).

[42] Richard Sorabji (ed.), *Philoponus and the Rejection of Aristotelian Science* (London and Ithaca, N.Y. 1987).

[43] The lists of texts and previous translations of the commentaries included in Wildberg, *Philoponus Against Aristotle on the Eternity of the World* (pp.12ff.) are not included here. The list of translations should be augmented by: F.L.S. Bridgman, Heliodorus (?) in *Ethica Nicomachea*, London 1807.

I am grateful for comments to Henry Blumenthal, Victor Caston, I. Hadot, Paul Mercken, Alain Segonds, Robert Sharples, Robert Todd, L.G. Westerink and Christian Wildberg.

English-Greek Glossary

This glossary gives the more important of the Greek words on which the translations are based, and will serve as a key from the English translation to the full Greek-English index. As explained in the Introduction, the same Greek word has not always been translated by the same English one; nor is the idiomatic English term always the syntactical equivalent of the Greek one, notably in cases where the Greek uses the neuter form of an adjective, or the infinitive of a verb, where we would rather use an abstract noun. In cases such as these, if more than one Greek word has been translated by the same English one, or vice versa, the syntactically similar forms have generally been given first. 'To' has only been prefixed to the infinitives of English verbs where there is a noun of similar form which might lead to ambiguity.

able, be able: *dunasthai, hoios te (einai)*
above: *anô*
absence: *apousia, sterêsis*
absurd: *atopos*
accept: *sunkhôrein*
be accepted: *keisthai*
accident, accidental: *sumbebêkos*; be accident of: *sumbainein*
accompany: *hepesthai, parakolouthein, suneinai, epi ... ginesthai*; accompany reciprocally: *antakolouthein*
account: *logos*; summary account: *epidromê*
take into account: *lambanein*
on its/their own account: *di' hauto, di' hautên*, etc.
accustom: *ethizein*
acquire: *dekhesthai, ktasthai*; able to acquire: *dektikos*
acquisition: *ktêsis*
acquit: *aphienai*
act: *energein, poiein, prattein*
act wrongly: *hamartanein*
be acted on: *paskhein*
action: *praxis*
perform action: *prattein*; performing actions: *praktikos*
do wrong action: *hamartanein*
be active, have or perform activity; *energein*
activity, actuality: *energeia, energein*
absence of activity: *anenergein*
be added: *proskeisthai*

addition, being added: *prosthêkê, prosthesis*
adequate, adequately: *hikanos, –ôs*
admit: *homologein*; admit of: *dekhesthai, endekhesthai, epidekhesthai, ekhein*
adultery: *moikheia*; commit adultery: *moikheuein*
advance: *probainein*
be advantageous: *sumpherein*
advise; *parainein*
adze: *skeparnon*
affect: *haptesthai*; be affected *paskhein*
affection, being affected: *pathos*
affinity: *oikeiotês*; having an affinity: *oikeios*
affliction: *thlipsis*
affluence: *periousia*
be afraid: *phobeisthai*
age, time of life: *hêlikia*
be agent: *prattein*
agree: *homologein*; be agreed: *homologeisthai*; agree to: *sunkhôrein*
aiming at: *stokhastikos*
alien, alienated, (sign of) alienation: *allotrios*
alienation: *allotriotês*
by this alone, already: *êdê*
alter: *ameibein, kinein*; alteration: *alloiôsis*
always: *aei*
amass: *athroizein*
ambiguous, ambiguity: *homônumos*
ambition, ambitious: *philotimia*

amusement: *paidia*
anger: *orgê, thumos*
be angry: *orgizesthai*
be annoyed: *akhthesthai*
antithesis: *antithesis*
apart from: *khôris*
be apart: *diistasthai*
be apparent: *phainesthai*
appear: *dokein, phainesthai*
appearance, how things appear:
　phantasia
appetite, appetition: *orexis*; have appe-
　tite: *oregesthai*; object of appetite:
　orektos; appetitive: *orektikos*
apply (a term): *legein*; apply to:
　sumbainein
be apprehensive: *hupopteuesthai*
approach: *prosodos*
appropriate: *oikeios*
argue syllogistically: *sullogizesthai*
argument: *logos*
Aristotle: *Aristotelês*; see also *autos*
arm: *kheir*
arrive at: *tunkhanein*
art: *tekhnê*; see also names of individual
　arts and crafts
ascertain: *heuriskein*
be ashamed: *aideisthai*
ask questions: *zêtein*
assert: *axioun*
assessment, assess: *metron*
give assistance: *sunairesthai*
associate, be associated: *suneinai*
at Athens: *Athênêsin*
attain: *tunkhanein*
attend on: *parakolouthein*
attend to: *prosekhein*
attract: *parakalein*
avoid: *pheugein, phulassesthai*; to be
　avoided: *pheukteos, pheuktos*
avoidance: *phugê*; matter of avoidance:
　pheuktos

bad: *kakos, mokhthêros*
badly: *kakôs*
base: *phaulos*; baseness: *phaulotês*
be, exist: *einai* (not generally indexed),
　phuein
bear: *pherein*
beauty: *kallos*
become *as opposed to* be: *ginesthai* (not
　generally indexed) opposed to *einai*
begin, be at the beginning: *arkhesthai*
beginning: *arkhê*; in the beginning: *tên
　arkhên*
being, the being of a thing: *einai*. See
　also essence

beings: *onta*
belong to: *huparkhein*
below: *katô*
beneficial: *ôphelimos*
best: *aristos, beltistos, kratistos*
bestial: *thêriôdês*
better: *ameinôn, beltiôn, kalos, agathos*
beyond: *exô*
black: *melas*
blame: *psogos*
blunt, bluntness: *amblus*
blush: *eruthainesthai, eruthrian*
bodily, of the body: *organikos, sômatikos,
　sôma*
body: *sôma*
boldness: *tharros, tharrein, thrasutês*
be born: *gennasthai, ginesthai* (not gen-
　erally indexed), *phuesthai*
build: *oikodomein*
builder: *oikodomos*
building (art of): *oikodomikê*

calculating: *logistikos*
call (apply a term); *legein, phanai*;
　should be called: *rhêteon*
can, cannot: *dunasthai, einai, hoios te
　(einai)*
capable of being: *dektikos, epidekhesthai,
　epidektikos*; be capable: *dunasthai*;
　not capable of: *adunatos*
capacity: *dunamis*; having capacity for:
　dektikos
cargo: *phortion*
carpenter: *tektôn*; of a carpenter:
　tektonikos
carpentry (art of): *tektonikê*
carry: *pherein*
cattle: *boskêmata*
cause: *aitia, aitios, aition*; contributory
　cause: *sunaitios*; to cause: *apo-
　didonai*; causing: *aitios*
cease: *pauesthai*
centre: *kentron*
chance: *tukhê*; chance to be, happen to
　be: *tunkhanein*
change: *metabolê*; to change: *metaball-
　ein*; easy to change, easily changed:
　eukinêtos, eumetabolos; hard to
　change: *duskinêtos*
child, children: *pais, paidion*
choice, being chosen: *hairesis, proairesis*;
　matter or object of choice: *hairetos,
　proairetos*
choose, choosing: *haireisthai, pro-
　aireisthai, proairetikos*
chosen by self, that we choose ourselves:
　authairetos

to be chosen, deserving, worthy, worthiness to be chosen: *hairetos*
circle: *kuklos*
circumstance: *peristasis*
city-state, inclined to live in: *politikos*
claim: *axioun*
clear: *dêlos, enargês, phaneros*: it is clear that: *dêlonoti*; quite clear: *prodêlos*
clearly: *dêlôs, dêlonoti, enargôs, phanerôs, saphôs*
cleverness: *deinotês*
colour: *khrôma*
combination: *sunthesis, sunkeisthai*
combine: *sullambanein, suntithenai*; be combined: *sunkeisthai*
come, come about: *ginesthai* (not indexed), *periginesthai, sumbainein*; come about in: *engignesthai*
having come to be, that has come to be: *genêtos*
not having come to be: *agenêtos*
perform comedy: *kômôidein*
coming-to-be: *genesis*
commit: *poiein*
common: *koinos*
commonplace: *topos*
community: *koinônia*
community, inclined to live in: *koinônikos*
compel: *biazein*; being compelled: *bia*
complete: *teleios*; completely: *holoklêrôs, pantapasin*
completion: *teleiôsis*
be composed: *sunkeisthai*
compulsion: *bia, biaios*; put or be under compulsion: *biazein, biazesthai*
compulsory: *biaios*
concede: *sunkhôrein*
conception: *prolêpsis*
concern, being concerned: *spoudê*
concern, lack of: *ameleia, amelein*; to lack concern: *amelein*
be concomitant: *hepesthai*
concrete: *sunamphoteros*
condition: *katastasis; ekhein* (with adverb, not generally indexed); good condition, sound physical condition: *euexia*; be in good condition: *eu ekhein*
conditional (proposition): *sunêmmenon*
be conquered: *hêttasthai*
be conscious: *suneidenai*
be consequence: *hepesthai*
consider: *theôrein*
be constituted: *sunistasthai*; constitution, constituted: *sustasis*
construct: *sunistanai*
contemplation: *theôria*

continuously, continuous: *sunekhôs*
contract (agreement): *sunallagma*
contraction: *sustolê*
contradiction, contradictory: *antiphasis*
on the contrary: *enantios*
contrast, what is contrasted: *antithesis*
contribute: *sumballein, suntelein, sunteleia*; contribution: *sunteleia*
adopt a contrivance: *paraskeuazesthai*; contrive: *heuriskein*
in one's control: *epi* plus dative
conversely: *empalin*
be convertible: *antistrephein*
conviction: *pistis*; convince: *peithein*
co-operate: *sumprattein*
corrupt: *diastrephein, pêroun*
courage, courageous: *andreia, andria*
covering: *epi*
cowardice: *deilia, deilian*
craftsman: *tekhnitês*
create: *poiein, poiêtikos*
living creature: *zôion*

damaging, damage: *phthartikos*
death: *thanatos*
deceit, being deceived: *apatê*; deceive: *apatan*
decide: *diakrinein, dialambanein, dokein*
deed: *praxis, prattein*
defect: *kakia*
defend: *proistasthai*
deficiency, deficient, be deficient: *elleipsis, elleipein, endeia, endein*
to define: *diorizein, horizein, horos*; definite, definitely fixed: *horizein, hôrismenos*
definition: *horos, horismos, logos*
to deliberate: *bouleuesthai*; to deliberate beforehand: *probouleuesthai*; deliberation: *boulê, bouleuesthai*; object of deliberation: *bouleutos*; deliberative: *bouleutikos*
deny: *arneisthai*
be deprived of: *apostereisthai*
derive: *lambanein*
deserving: *axios*; deserving to be chosen: *hairetos*
desirable: *hairetos*
desire (noun): *ephesis, epithumia*; to desire: *ephiesthai, epithumein*
destroy: *diaphtheirein, phtheirein, phthartikos*; destroying, able to destroy, destructive: *phthartikos*
deviation: *ekbasis, ektropê, parabasis*
differ, make a difference: *diapherein*; difference: *diaphora, diapherein*

different: *allos, diaphoros, heteros*; be
different: *diapherein, diaphoros*; at
different times: *allote*; in different
ways: *allôs, diaphorôs*
differentiate: *diairein*; differentiate in a
corresponding way: *sundiairein*; be
differentiated correspondingly: *sun-
diaireisthai*
differentiation: *diairesis*
difficulty: *aporia*; raise difficulty:
aporein
diminution: *meiôsis*
directed towards: *kharin*
disable, be disabled: *pêroun, pêrousthai*
disagreeable: *duskherês*
lack of discipline: *anaskêsia*
discovery, discover: *heuresis*; able to,
such as to discover: heuretikos
discussion: *logos*
disease: *nosos*; diseased: *nosêmatôdês*;
be diseased: *nosein*
dislike: *akhthesthai*
be disposed: *diakeisthai*
disposition: *diathesis, hexis*
dissolute, in a dissolute manner:
aneimenôs
distance: *apostasis*
distraction: *askholia*
distress: *lupê*; cause or give or produce
distress: *lupein*; be distressed:
lupeisthai: distressing, causing distress: *epilupos, lupêros*; absence of
distress: *alupia, alupos*
distribution: *nomê*
divide: *diairein*
do, doing: *poiein, prattein, praxis*; doing,
capable of doing: *praktikos*; able to be
done, can be done: *praktos*; to be
done, what ought to be done: *poiêteos*;
do away with: *anairein*; do wrong, do
wrongly, do wrong action: *hamartanein*
dog: *kuôn*
double: *diplous, dittos*
drive off course: *exôthein*
drought: *aukhmos*
be drunk: *methuein*; drunkenness: *methê*
dryness: *xêrotês*
due measure, proportion: see measure,
proportion

be eager: *speudein, spoudazein*; eagerly:
diatetamenôs
easy, easily: *euemptôtôs, prokheiros,
rhâidios*
eat sweetmeats: *tragêmatizein*
economic: *oikonomikos*

educate: *paidagôgein*
have effect: *poiein*
efficient (cause): *poiêtikos; poiein*
make effort: *ponein*
enact: *prattein*
encourage: *sunauxein*
end: *telos*
endear: *oikeioun*
endure: *pherein*
enemy: *polemioi*
engage in (activity): *energein*
enjoy: *hêdesthai, khairein*
enjoyment: *apolausis*; of enjoyment: *apolaustikos*
give enjoyment: *terpein*
enquire, hold enquiry: *epizêtein, zêtein*;
such as to enquire: *zêtêtikos*
envy: *phthonos*
equal: *isos*; equality: *isotês, isos*
equivalent: *isos*
be in error: *pseudesthai, diapseudesthai*
essence: *einai, ousia*
be established: *keisthai, sunistasthai*;
establishment: *sustasis*
esteem: *krinein*
eternal: *aidios*; eternity: *aidiotês*
ethics: *êthika*
even: *artios*
evidence: *pistis*
evil, an evil: *kakos*
examine: *exetazein, prokheirizesthai*
exceed: *huperballein*
excellence, excellently: *aretê*
excess: *huperbolê, huperballein*; be
excessive: *huperballein*
exclude: *anairein, apokleiein*
excuse: *paramutheisthai*
exercise: *gumnasia*
exist: *einai* (not generally indexed),
huphistasthai; exist together: *sunuparkhein*; existence: *hupostasis*
experience (a feeling): *paskhein*
explanation: *exêgêsis, logos*
extend: *proienai*
external: *ektos, exôthen*
extreme, extremely: *akros, –ôs*; an
extreme: *akrotês*
eye: *omma, ophthalmos*

faculty: *dunamis*
fail: *apoleipesthai*
fall on: *empiptein*
fall short of: *deisthai*
false, falsehood: *pseudos*
familiarity: *sunêtheia*
find fault: *aitiasthai*; without fault:
anaitios

fear: *phobos*; to fear: *phobeisthai*
feeling: *pathos*
final (cause): *telos, telikos*
find: *heuriskein, heuretikos*
finely: *kalôs*
fire: *pur*
first: *prôtos*; in the first place: *arkhê, tên arkhên*
to fit: *epharmozein*; be fitting: *prosêkein, sumpherein*
flavour: *khumos*
follow, follow on: *akolouthein, epakolouthein, hepesthai*
folly: *aphrosunê*
food: *sitia*
foolish: *aphrôn*
for the sake of: *heneka, kharin*; for the sake of which: *hou heneka*; for the sake of something: *heneka tou*
form: *eidos*
free: *eleutheros*; free from: *exô*

gaze intently: *emblepein*
general, in general, generally, in the general sense: *koinos, katholou, holôs*
genus: *genos*
geometry: *geômetria*; do geometry: *geômetrein*
get: *lambanein*
give: *didonai*; giving: *dosis*
gloating: *epikhairekakia*
go on: *proienai*; be going to: *mellein*
goal: *skopos*; be a goal: *prokeisthai*
god: *theos*
good, a good: *agathos, spoudaios, eu*; goodness: *to eu*; good condition: *euexia*; be in good condition: *eu ekhein*; good man: *spoudaios*
govern selves: *politeuesthai*
greatness of spirit: *megalopsukhia*
growth: *auxêsis*
guard: *phulattein*; guard against: *phulattesthai*; guarding against: *phulakê*
gymnastic art: *gumnastikê*

habit: *ethos, hexis*; develop habit: *ethizein*
in hand, immediate: *en posin*; in their hands: *par' autois*
happen, happen to be: *sumbainein, tunkhanein*
happiness: *eudaimonia, eudaimonein*; be happy: *eudaimonein*
hard to change: *duskinêtos*
harm: *blaptein*; harmful: *blaberos*
hate: *misein*; hateful: *misêtos*
head: *kephalê*

health: *hugeia*; healthy: *hugieinos*; be healthy: *hugiainein*
hear: *akouein*; hearing, act of hearing: *akoê*
heavy, heaviness: *barus*
hinder: *empodizein*; hindering: *empodôn*
hold out: *antekhein*
honour: *timê*; honourable: *timios*
horse: *hippos*
hot: *thermos*; hotness: *thermotês*
house: *oikia*
(house-)building, art of: *oikodomikê*
human, human being: *anthrôpos*; human: *anthrôpeios*
to hunt: *thêran*

ignorance: *agnoia*; be ignorant, be in ignorance: *agnoein*
ill repute: *adoxia*
imitate: *mimeisthai*
immediate, in hand: *en posin*; immediately: *euthus*
immoderate: *ametros*
immoral earnings, living off: *pornoboskia*
impede: *empodizein*; without impediment, absence of impediment: *anempodistos,-ôs*
imply: *emphainein*; imply one another: *antakolouthein*
important: *kurios*
impossible: *adunatos*
impression: *phantasia*
impugn: *diaballein*
impulse: *hormê*
be inactive: *anenergein*
inappropriateness, inappropriate: *atopia*
be incapable: *adunatein*
to incline: *neuein*
incomplete: *atelês*
inconsistent: *apemphainôn*
indefinitely, indefinite: *adioristôs*
indicate: *deiknunai, dêloun, emphainein, sêmainein*; indication: *mênusis*
indifferent: *adiaphoros*
individual: *kathekastos*
infinite, infinity: *apeiros*
have influence: *iskhuein*
injustice, being unjust: *adikia, adikos*; do, commit injustice: *adikein*
insensitivity: *anaisthêsia*
instrument: *organon*
intellect: *nous*; intellectual: *noêtikos*
be intensified: *epi pleon ginesthai*
intermediate: *mesos, metaxu*
interpret as: *lambanein*; interpretation:

exêgêsis
introduce: *paraspeirein*
involuntary, involuntarily: *akousios,*
   akousiôs
irrational, irrational creature: *alogos*
isolated: *monos*
in itself: *kath' hautên*

to judge: *krinein, krisis*; judgement:
   krisis
just: *dikaios*; justice, being just: *dikaio-*
   sunê, dikaios
be just any: *tunkhanein*
just because, just for this reason: *êdê*

keep: *phulassein*
kind: *eidos*; make of a particular kind:
   eidopoiein; the same in kind:
   homoeidês
kiss: *kataphilein*
knock down: *kataballein*
know: *gignôskein, eidenai*; not to know,
   without knowing: *agnoein*
knowledge, coming to know, come to
   know: *gnôsis*
known, well known: *gnôrimos, gnôrizein*

lack, be lacking, a lack: *elleipein, endein,*
   endeia; see concern, lack of
be laid down: *keisthai*
land, piece of: *khôrion*
last: *teleutaios*
law: *nomos*; lawgiver: *nomothetês*
lay down: *horizein*
lead: *agein, pherein*; lead away: *apagein*;
   lead on: *parapempein*
learn: *manthanein*; learning: *mathêma,*
   mathêsis
leave behind: *kataleipein*
leg: *skelos*
liberality: *eleutheriotês*
life: *bios, zên*; have good life: *eu zên*
light, lightness: *kouphos*
limit: *peras*; to limit, be limited: *per-*
   ainein; limited: *peperasmenos*
listen: *akouein*
to live, living: *bioun, zên*; to live well: *eu*
   zên
living creature: *zôion*
locate: *heuriskein, tithenai, tithesthai*; be
   located: *keisthai*
lose, easy to: *euapoblêtos*
lost, unable to be: *anapoblêtos*
love: *erôs*; to love: *philein*; fall or be in
   love: *eran*
lyre: *kithara*; play the lyre: *kitharizein*;
   lyre-playing: *kitharizein, kitharistikê*

magnificence: *megaloprepeia*
maintain: *sôizein*
make: *poiein*
man: *anêr*; man (human being), mankind: *anthrôpos*
mating: *sunduasmos*
matter: *hulê*
mean (a): *mesotês, meson*; mean (adjective): *mesos*
mean (to): *sêmainein*
measure: *metron*; due measure: *summe-*
   tria; in due measure: *summetros, –ôs*;
   lack of due measure: *ametria,*
   asummetria; lacking in due measure:
   ametros
medicine: *iatrikê*
mention: *mimnêskein*
middle: *mesos*
mildness: *praotês*
mind, be in a state of: *phronein*
mischance: *apotuchia*
misrepresentation: *diabolê*; misrepresent: *diaballein*
mix, mixture: *meignunai*; mixed: *miktos*;
   mixture: *mixis*; free from mixture,
   unmixed: *amiktos*
to moderate: *metrein*; moderate,
   moderately: *mesos,-ôs*; moderation:
   metron
money: *khrêmata*
moral: *êthikos*
move: *kinein*; movement: *kinêsis, kinein*;
   movement, way of moving:
   metaphora
murder: *androphonia*
must: *dein, khrênai*
of Mytilene (on the spelling cf. *Oxford*
   Classical Dictionary): *Mitulênaios*

to name: *onomazein*
nature: *phusis*; natural: *phusikos, kata*
   phusin; nature, from the point of view
   of: *phusikôs*; naturally be, naturally
   do: *phuein*; be formed or endowed by
   nature: *phuesthai*; well endowed by
   nature: *euphuês*; good natural endowment: *euphuia*; in accordance with
   nature: *kata phusin*; contrary to
   nature: *para phusin*
navigation, art of: *kubernetikê*
necessary, necessarily: *anankê,*
   anankaios, –on, –ôs, ex anankês;
   necessity: *anankê, endeia*; be necessary: *dein, khrênai*
need: *endeia*; to need: *dein, deisthai*
to neglect, be negligent: *amelein,*
   paramelein

neighbours: *plêsion, hoi*
Nicomachean (Ethics): *Nikomakheios*
noble, nobility: *kalos*; nobly: *kalôs*
normal: *sunêthês*
to note, notice: *katanoein*
notion: *ennoia*
nourish, take nourishment: *trephein, trephesthai*; nourishment: *trophê*
novel: *kainos*
number, numerically: *arithmos, kat' arithmon*

obey: *peithesthai*
object of sensation, object of sense: *aisthêton*
object of: *hupo*
observe: *lambanein, noein*; not be observed: *lanthanein*
obtaining: *analêpsis*
odd: *atopos, perittos*
odour: *osmê*
offspring, production of: *teknopoiia*
on its own account: *di' hauto*
opinion: *doxa*; hold opinions: *doxazein*
opposite, opposed: *antikeimenos, enantios, enantiotês*; be opposed: *antikeisthai*; in the opposite way to: *empalin*; opposition, being opposed: *enantiôsis, enantiotês*
be ordered: *rhuthmizesthai*
ordering: *taxis*
origin: *arkhê*
be otherwise: *allôs ekhein*
ought: *dein, khrênai*
outside, from outside: *ektos, exô, exôthen*
own account, on its/their: *di' hauto, di' hautên*, etc.
own efforts, by our: *par' hautôn*
own right, in its: *autê kath' hautên, kath' hautên, kath' hauto*

pain: *odunê, ponos*; painstaking: *philoponos*
pardon: *sungnômê*; to pardon: *sungignôskein*
part: *meros, morion*; not having parts similar to one another: *anomoiomerês*
particular: *hode, idios, kath' hekasta, en merei*; particularly: *idiôs*
pass over: *paroran*
passage: *lexis*
passion: *thumos*
peculiar: *idios*
penalty: *epitimion, zêmia*; suffer penalties: *zêmiousthai*
perceive: *aisthanesthai*; perception: *aisthêsis*

perfect: *teleios, teleos*; perfection: *teleiotês*; bring to perfection: *apotelein*; perfectly: *teleiôs*
perform (action, activities): *apodidonai, energein, poiein, prattein*; perform comedy: *kômôidein*
persevere in: *proelthein*
persist: *menein*
personal: *idios*
persuade: *peithein*; persuasion: *pistis*
philosophy: *philosophia*
physical condition, sound: *euexia*
piece of land: *khôrion*
pipe: *aulos*; to pipe, play the pipe: *aulein*
Pittacus: *Pittakos*
place: *topos*; to place: *tithenai*; be placed, be set: *keisthai*
pleasure: *hêdonê*; pleasant, causing pleasure: *hêdus*; be pleased, experience pleasure, take pleasure in: *hêdesthai*; give pleasure: *hêdein*; with pleasure: *hêdeôs*; without pleasure: *aêdês*
political: *politikos*
poorly: *phaulôs*
(fact of) possession, possessing: *hexis*; possessions: *ktêmata*
possible: *hoios te*; be possible: *dunasthai, einai, eneinai*
potentiality, potentially: *dunamis*; have or be potentiality, have potential: *dunasthai*
poverty: *penia*
power: *exousia*; in one's power: *epi* plus dative; powerful, having power: *kurios*
practical: *praktikos*
practice: *askêsis*
to praise: *epainein*; praiseworthy: *epainetos*
precautions, take: *phulassesthai*
preconception: *prolêpsis*
to predicate: *katêgorein*
prefer: *prokrinein*; preferable: *hairetôteros*
premiss: *protasis*
presence: *parousia*
be present: *pareinai*
preservation: *sôtêria*; to preserve: *phulassein, sôzein*; preserving, that preserves: *sôstikos, têrêtikos*
prevent: *kôluein*; preventing, that prevents: *empodôn*
prime, primary: *proêgoumenos, prôtos*; primarily: *proêgoumenôs*
principle: *arkhê*; (one's) principles: *haireseis*

privation: *sterêsis*
proceed: *proienai*
proclaim: *kêruttein*
produce, be productive of: *poiein*; producing, productive of, produce: *poiêtikos, peripoiêtikos*
profligacy: *asôtia, akolastainein*; profligate: *akolastos*; be profligate: *akolastainein*
progress: *epidosis*
proof: *apodeixis*; capable of giving proofs: *apodeiktikos*
proper, proper to: *oikeios*; proper, in the proper sense: *kurios, kuriôs*
be property of: *huparkhein*
proportionate, due proportion: *summetros*
be proposed: *prokeisthai*
prosperity: *euporia*
prove, such as to: *apodeiktikos*
provide: *paraskeuazein*
prudent: *phronimos*
punish: *kolazein, zêmioun*; punishment: *kolasis*
pure: *eilikrinês, katharos*; keep pure: *kathareuein*
purpose: *prothesis*
pursue: *diôkein, metienai*; pursue eagerly: *spoudazein*
push: *apôthein*

qualification, without: *haplôs*
quality: *poiotês*
quantity, quantitative aspect: *posos, posotês*
be in question: *prokeisthai*

rainstorm: *ombros*
rational: *logikos*; rationally: *kata logon*; being rational: *logos*
reach (a goal): *tunkhanein*
real existence: *hupostasis*
really: *alêthôs, ontôs*
reason (argument, account; reasoning, being rational): *logos*; reason, cause: *aitia*; of reasoning, reason: *dianoêtikos, logikos*; in accordance with reason: *kata logon*; right reasoning: *orthos logos*
reasonable, reasonably: *eikotôs, eulogos, eulogôs*
receive: *tunkhanein*; (a) receiving: *lêpsis*
reckon: *katalegein*
recognise: *gignôskein, gnôrizein*
recommend: *proxenoun*
reference, being referred: *anaphora*
refrain: *apekhesthai*

regard: *lambanein*
region: *khôra*
regret: *metaginôskein, metameleia, metanoia*
reject: *apostrephesthai*
relaxation: *anapausis, diakhusis*
remain: *menein, hupomenein*
removal: *aposkeuê*; remove: *anairein, aphairein, apoballein*; remove along with: *sunanairein*; be removed, distant: *apekhein, aphistasthai*
render: *apodidonai*
to reproach: *epikalein*
reputation: *doxa*; be reputed: *dokein*
require: *apaitein*
resist: *enistasthai; menein*
resolve: *luein*
respectable: *epieikês*
respected: *semnos*
responsibility, one's: *epi* plus dative; responsible: *aitios*
to result: *periginesthai*
retain: *sôzein*
the reverse: *enantios*
get rid of: *apoballein*; easy to get rid of: *euapoblêtos*
rider: *epibatês*
right: *orthos*; right reasoning: *orthos logos*; be right: *katorthoun*; rightly: *kalôs*; rightness: *orthotês*
rising: *anatolê*
rule out: *anairein*
run: *trekhein, dramein*

say, one should: *rhêteon*; be said in many ways: *pollakhôs legesthai*; be said in relation to one thing: *pros hen legesthai*
for the sake of: *kharin*
same in kind: *homoeidês*
Sardanapulus: *Sardanapalos*
saw: *priôn*; to saw: *priein*
science, (scientific) understanding: *epistêmê*; scientific: *epistêmonikos*
sculpture (art of): *plastikê*
Scythians: *Skuthai*
sea: *thalassa*
second: *deuteros*
see: *horan, idein*; (act of) seeing: *opsis*
seek: *zêtein*
seem: *dokein, eoikenai, phainesthai*; seem right: *dokein*
self: in itself, in its own right: *autê kath' hautên, kath' hautên, kath' hauto*; him(self) = Aristotle: *autos*
sense, sensation: *aisthêsis*; in the general sense: *katholou*; in a single

sense: *sunônumôs*; in the strict sense: *kurios, kuriôs*; have several senses *pollakhôs (legesthai)*

sense-perception, a matter of: *aisthêtikos*

separable: *khôristos*; to separate: *khôrizein*; separately: *khôris*

serious: *spoudaios*; seriousness: *spoudê, spoudazein*; take seriously: *spoudazein*

be set: *keisthai*; be set before: *prokeisthai*

settle: *diakrinein*

setting (of heavenly body): *dusis*

sex, sexual intercourse: *aphrodisia*

shame: *aidôs*; shameful, shamefulness: *aiskhros*; shamelessness: *anaiskhuntia*

shape: *skhêma*

share in: *metekhein*

sharp, sharpness: *oxus*

shelter: *skepê*

ship: *naus*

short time, for a: *ep' oligon*

should: *dein, khrênai*

show: *deiknunai, endeiknusthai*; showing: *deixis*

shrink from: *oknein*

sight: *opsis*

sign: *sêmeion*

single kind, of a: *monoeidês*

skill: *tekhnê*

slacken: *aniênai*; slackening: *anesis*

slave: *andrapodon*; characteristic of a slave: *andrapodôdês*

sleep: *hupnos*

smell, act of smelling, sense of smell: *osphrêsis*; to smell, have sense of smell: *osmasthai*; object of smell: *osphrantos, osphrêtos*

softness: *malakia*

solution: *lusis*

soul: *psukhê*; of the soul: *psukhikos*

sound: *hugiês*; sound condition: *eustheneia, euexia*

speak of: *legein*

species: *eidos*

speculative thought: *theôria*

speech: *logos*; capable of speech: *logikos*

spend life: *katazên*

spirit, greatness of: *megalopsukhia*

stable: *monimos*

star: *astron*

start: *arkhê*

state: *hexis*; be in the same state: *homoiôs ekhein*

statue: *andrias*

stop: *pauesthai*

tell stories: *muthologein*

strict, in the strict sense: *kurios, kuriôs*

be subject: *hupokeisthai*

subordinate to: *hupo*

substance: *ousia*

to substitute, make a substitution: *metalambanein*

subtraction: *aphairesis*

suffer: *paskhein*

sufficient, sufficiently: *autarkês, hikanos, hikanôs*

summary account: *epidromê*

summer: *theros*

summon help: *epikaleisthai*

superior: *ameinôn*

supervene: *epiginesthai, epi … (ginesthai)*

support: *pistis*

suppose: *lambanein, hupolambanein, tithenai, hupotithesthai, hupolêpsis*; supposition: *hupolêpsis*

surpass: *huperekhein*

survive, be preserved: *sôzesthai*

suspect, suspicion: *hupopteuein*

sweetmeats, eat: *tragêmatizein*

synonymously: *sunônumôs*

take: *agein, lambanein*

teach: *didaskein*; teacher: *didaskalos*

temperance: *sôphrosunê*; temperate: *sôphrôn, sôphronikos*

theatre: *theatron*

theft: *klopê*

theoretical: *theôrêtikos*

thing: *pragma*

think: *dokein, hêgeisthai, oiesthai, phronein*; think little of: *kataphronein*; think right, think worth: *axioun*

thought: *dianoia, noêma*; be thought: *dokein*

time (of life); *hêlikia*; at different times: *allote*

total, totality: *holos, sunamphoteros*

touch, act of touching: *haphê*

transgression: *parabasis*

be treated (medically): *iatreuesthai, therapeuesthai*

trouble: *enokhlêsis*; be troubled: *enokhleisthai*

true: *alêthês, alêthinos*; truly: *alêthôs, kat' alêtheian*; truth: *alêtheia, alêthês*

try: *peirasthai*

turn: *trepein*; turn away from: *apostrephesthai*; turn out: *sumbainein*; in turn: *para meros*; turning: *tropê*

tutor: *paidagôgos*

ugliness: *aiskhos*
ultimate: *eskhatos*
unconvincingly: *apithanôs*
under, falling under: *hupo*
underlie: *hupokeisthai*
understand: *lambanein*; understanding:
    epistêmê, ennoia, sophia; lacking
    understanding: *anennoêtos*
uniform: *homoiomerês*
unimpeded: *anempodistos*
unjust: *adikos*
unlimited: *apeiros*
unmixed: *amiktos*
unnatural, contrary to nature: *para
    phusin*
be unobserved: *lanthanein*
unpleasant: *aêdês*
unqualified, without qualification, in an
    unqualified sense: *haplôs*
use: *khreia*; to use, make use of:
    khrasthai; useful, usefulness:
    khrêsimos
utterance: *phêmê*

valuable, value, to be valued: *hairetos*
be at variance with: *diaballein*
varied: *allos*
vice: *kakia*
vice versa: *empalin*
with a view to: *kharin*
virtue, virtuous, being virtuous: *aretê,
    kat' aretên*; virtuous man: *spoudaios*;
    be on the way to virtue: *prokoptein*
voice: *phônê*
voluntary, voluntarily: *hekôn, hekousios,
    –ôs*
voyage, be voyager, make a voyage:
    plein; voyaging well: *euploia*

vulgar: *phortikos*

walk: *peripatein*; of walking: *peri-
    patêtikos*
want: *ephiesthai*; wanting: *ephesis*
be on the way to virtue: *prokoptein*
weaken: *amauroun*; weakening:
    amaurôsis
wealth: *ploutos*
be wearied: *kamnein*
well: *aristos, eu, kalôs*
white: *leukos*
whole: *holos, pas*
wicked: *kakos, mokhthêros*; wickedness,
    being wicked: *kakia, okhthêria*
wider (in application): *koinoteros*
wind: *pneuma*
winter: *kheimôn*
wisdom: *phronêsis*
wish: *boulesthai*; wished for: *boulêtos*
without: *khôris*; without qualifica-
    tion: *haplôs*
withstand: *menein*
bear witness: *marturein*
work: *ergon*
world: *kosmos*
worse: *kheirôn*
worth: *axia, axios*; worth while, worthy:
    axios; worthy to be chosen, worthi-
    ness to be chosen: *hairetos*
wrestle: *palaiein*; art of wrestling:
    palaistikê
be wrong, do or act wrongly: *hamar-
    tanein*; wrong action, wrongdoing,
    going wrong: *hamartêma*

yield: *eikein*
young: *neos*

Greek-English Index

This index contains all occurrences of the more important words in the Greek text, and the translations used. There are errors in the printed line numbers of Bruns' text at 148,10 and 163,10; in both places the printed rather than the actual line numbers have been followed. References are to the page and line numbers of the Greek text. Bold type is used for the problem numbers.

adiaphoros, indifferent, 117,11; **1** 118,26; **5** 124,2.5.6.9.10.11.17.21.25. 26;125,4-5.7.9.31.32

adikein, do or commit injustice, **27** 156,34

adikia, injustice, being unjust, 117,6; 118,20; **3** 121,12.14.15.23.25.32; 122.5; **30** 161,31.33; 162,10

adikos, unjust, injustice, **3** 121,16.17. 18.20.22.31.33; **30** 162,11

adioristôs, indefinitely, **4** 123,2

adoxia, ill repute, **21** 141,21.25.27.29. 30.32; 142,3.4.[5-6].8.10.12.14.18.21

adunatein, be incapable, **14** 135,29

adunatos, impossible, **1** 119,9; **23** 144,21; **25** 148,8; **30** 162,16.23; not capable of, **3** 122,23

aêdês, without pleasure, unpleasant, **2** 120,28; **18** 139,1

aei, always, **9** 130,24; **23** 144,31

agathos, good, a good, better, goodness, 117,4.10.14; 118,1,2; **1** 118,22.23.24.25.26; 119.25.26; **4** 123,29; **5** 124,2.3.4.6.8.10.11.17.20. 24.25.26.31.32.33.34.35; 125,2.3.4.5. 8.22.24.30. 31; 126,1.4; **6** 126,21. 27.31; **7** 127,2.5.7.19.22.35; 128,2; **9** 130,22.24.25.26; **16** 136,29.31; 137,1. 2.3.4.5.7.8.9. 11.12.13.14.15.16.18; **17** 21.22.24.25; 138,1.4.5; **18** 138,12.28. 30; **20** 140,1.3.4.5.6.7.8.9.10.13.19. 24; **21** 141,30; **23** 143,17; **25** 148,7.13. 16.17.19.20.24.29; 150,12.13.14; 151,4; **27** 153,3; 156,8; **29** 158,6.14. 19; 161,6.9.12.18

agein, lead (to a thing), lead, take, **9** 129,14; **12** 133,4; **29** 160,18.21

agenêtos, not having come to be, **15** 136,22

agnoein, be ignorant, be in ignorance, not know, without knowing, **9** 128,28.29; 129,3; 130,8.

22; **11** 132,5; **15** 136,17; **21** 142,2; **25** 148,9a; **29** 158,25.28; 159,3.4.6.11; 161,10.12

agnoia, ignorance, 117,16.19.24; **9** 128,23.<25>; 129,19; 130,9.13. <14>.19.21.27.29.30.33; **11** 131,18. 22; 132,2.6; **15** 136,14.17; **27** 154,15; **29** 158,11.24.25.26.29; 159,4.7.8.10. 23.24.26; 161,10.11

aideisthai, be ashamed, **9** 129,5.25; **21** 141,16.26.32; 142,11.17.19

aidios, eternal, **25** 149,14; 150,25.37; 151,3; **29** 160,6

aidiotês, eternity, **23** 144,30

aidôs, shame, 118,9; **21** 141,13.16.19. 21; 142,[6].8.12.14

aiskhos, ugliness, **27** 156,17

aiskhros, shameful, shamefulness, **7** 127,16-17; **13** 134,20.22.26; **18** 138,11.15.17.18.20.21.23.25; 139,3.4. 6.10.11.12.14; **21** 141,21-2.24.31; 142,3-4.9.11.13.17.20.21; **23** 144,12; 145,3.5.7.9.19.24.31; 146,1.2.5.7.11- 12; **26** 151,22.25.26.28; 152,6.11.17. 21.26.28.33; **29** 159,4

aisthanesthai, perceive, **14** 136,4- 5.7.9.10.12

aisthêsis, sense, sensation, **14** 135,3.5. 9.15.17; 136,9.11.12; **29** 161,19.22; in Aristotelian book title, **27** 155,32; perception, **20** 141,7

aisthêtikos, matter of sense- perception, **29** 161,24

aisthêton, object of sensation, object of sense, **14** 135,3; 136,11

aitia, cause, reason, **1** 119,29; **9** 129,9; **12** 132,27.30; **23** 143,16.18.20.23.24; 144,11; 145,8; 146,6; **26** 151,27; 152,27; **29** 158,27; 159,1.9.14.16.19.22

aitiasthai, find fault, **27** 155,28

aitios, aition, cause, causing, respon- sible, **9** 129,27; 130,1.4.8.20.29;

12 133,18; **13** 134,27; **21** 141,25;
23 143,14. <18>; 144,29; 146,2;
26 152,27; **28** 158,9.10.26.28; 159,3.
4.7; **161**,4.5.7.8.12
akhthesthai, be annoyed, dislike, **13**
134,7; **25** 150,19
akoê, hearing, act of hearing, **14** 135,25
akolasia, profligacy, **25** 150,1
akolastainein, be profligate, profligacy,
27 156,35
akolastos, profligate, **2** 120,27-8;
121,11; **6** 126,25; **7** 128,2; **13** 134,21;
19 139,26.27
akolouthein, follow, **7** 127,21
akouein, hear, listen, **2** 121,2; **17**
137,31; **19** 139,20
akousios, –ôs, involuntary, involuntarily, 117,19; **9** 129,26; 130,4.5.11.12.
13.32; **11** 131,18.21.22.23.25.33;
132,3.5; **29** 158,23.26.27.29; 159,9.
11.20.24.26.29.31.33; 161,11
akros, –ôs, extreme, extremely, **3**
122,26; **27** 153,32; 154,1.18.24.25.26;
155,8.20.23.24.26; 156,1; 157,4; **30**
162,3.4
akrotês, an extreme, **27** 155,22.25
alêtheia, truth, **20** 141,8.11; **25** 149,13;
150,29.30
kat' alêtheian, truly, **29** 158,13-14;
161,18
alêthês, –ôs, true, truth, truly, **1**
118,25; **18** 138,28.30; **23** 145,6; **25**
149,14; 150,37-151,1; 151,2.3.4.6;
26 151,26; **27** 153,11; **29** 158,19.20;
161,3.5; *alêthôs*, really, **5** 125,21-2
alêthinos, true, **29** 158,17
alloiôsis, alteration, **34** 163,7
allos, different, varied, **3** 122,23; **13**
134,6; **17** 137,33.34
allôs, in different ways, in a different
way, **2** 121,7; **3** 122,23; **29** 160,8.15;
allôs ekhein, be otherwise, **25** 149,12;
150,26.31
allote, at different times, **2** 121,7; **29**
160,8.14
allotrios, alien, alienated, (sign of)
alienation, **5** 124,32.33; **21** 141,20;
142,6
allotriotês, alienation, **5** 124,30.35;
21 142,13
alogos, irrational, **3** 122,1.3.19.20.22.
23.24.25.29; **5** 124,14; **11** 131,20;
25 149,4; **29** 159,29; irrational
creature, **18** 138,19
alupia, alupos, absence of
distress, **14** 134,31; 136,4
amaurôsis, weakening, **14** 136,3-4

amauroun, weaken, **14** 136,2
amblus, blunt, bluntness, **4** 123,25
ameibein, alter, **30** 162,24
ameinôn, better, superior, **1** 119,32.33.
34; **10** 131,2-3.4.10.15; **29** 160,33
ameleia, neglect, lack of concern, **9**
129,30; **29** 159,5-6
amelein, neglect, lack of concern, **9**
130,7.22; **29** 159,7
ametria, lack of due measure, **25**
149,20; **27** 154,20
ametros, immoderate, lacking in due
measure, **24** 146,15; **25** 150,15
amiktos, free from mixture, unmixed,
23 145,29; 146,6; **26** 152,16.27
anairein, remove, rule out, exclude, do
away with, **8** 128,4-5.6.8.13.16; **11**
132,2.7.10; **20** 139,31; 140,7.8.11.23.
24.26; **24** 146,30; **28** 157,12.13.14
anaiskhuntia, shamelessness, **27**
156,28
anaisthêsia, insensitivity, **25** 150,1;
27 154,12
anaitios, without fault, **27** 155,28
analêpsis, obtaining, **29** 160,35
anankaios, –on, –ôs, necessary, necessarily, **4** 123,3; **5** 124,11; **6** 126,24.25
anankê, ex anankês, necessity, necessary, necessarily, **1** 119,12; **7** 127,21;
16 136,31; **22** 142,31; 143,2; **23**
145,16; **26** 152,3
anapausis, relaxation, **14** 135,18
anaphora, reference, being referred, **20** 140,15; **24** 147,5; **25** 151,2
anapoblêtos, unable to be lost, **3**
121,16.24
anaskêsia, lack of discipline, **9** 128,27
anatolê, rising (of heavenly body), **29**
160,8
andrapodôdês, characteristic of a
slave, **23** 144,4
andrapodon, slave, **10** 131,12; **18**
138,9; **20** 140,31; **23** 144,6
andreia, courage, courageous, **18**
157,23.32; **23** 144,12; **27** 154,3;
156,21.22;157,3
andria, courage, courageous, **18**
138,14; **24** 146,16; 147,9; **25** 150,2
andrias, statue, **28** 157,17
androphonia, murder, **27** 156,29
aneimenôs, in a dissolute manner, **29**
159,15
anempodistos, –ôs, unimpeded, without impediment, absence of impediment, 118,12;'**14** 134,29; 135,1; **23**
143,10.13.15.16.19.22.24-5.31.32-3;
144,2

anenergein, be inactive, absence of
    activity, **14** 135,16
anennoêtos, lacking understand-
    ing, **9** 129,10.18
anêr, man, **29** 159,7
anesis, slackening, **14** 135,22; 136,3
anienai, slacken, **14** 135,24
anô, above, **15** 136,24
anomoiomerês, not having parts
    similar to one another, **8** 128,11
antakolouthein, imply one another;
    accompany reciprocally, 118,10; **8**
    128,5.8; **22** 142,22.23
antekhein, hold out, **9** 128,27; 129,8
anthrôpeios, human, **14** 135,29
anthrôpos, man, mankind, human,
    117,18; **1** 119,31.34.35; **3** 121,27.28.
    29-30; **4** 123,30; **5** 125,14.24.25; **7**
    127,30; **9** 129,15; **10** 130,34; 131,4.5.
    6.7.8.9.10.11; **14** 136,7; **18** 138,16.26;
    20 140,30; 141,5.9; **23** 143,18.20.21.
    22.24; **24** 147,17.21.24-5.27.30.31;
    148,2; **25** 148,6.24.25.26.28.29;
    150,12.13.14; **27** 153,6.12.13; **29**
    160,5.10.36; 161,16
antikeimenos, antikeisthai,
    opposite, be opposed, **1** 118,25; 119.
    10,12; **7** 127,5; **11** 131,30; 132,3; **29**
    161,1.2.3
antiphasis, contradiction, contra-
    dictory, **34** 163,11
antistrephein, be convertible, **23**
    145,16; **26** 152,2-3
antithesis, antithesis, what is contras-
    ted, **11** 131,34; **30** 163,11
apagein, lead away, **13** 134,7-8
apaitein, require, 118,7-8; **18** 139,6.7;
    20 139,30; 140,7
apatan, deceive, **15** 136,19
apatê, deceit, being deceived, **15**
    136,19.21.26
apeiros, infinite, infinity,
    unlimited, **15** 136,22; **20** 140,15; **25**
    151,7
apekhein, be removed, **27** 154,25
apekhesthai, refrain, **9** 130,7; **18** 138,18
apemphainôn, inconsistent, **1** 119,23
aphairein, remove, **27** 156,21.22
aphairesis, subtraction, **27** 153,16.27
aphienai, acquit, **29** 159,10
aphistasthai, be removed, **2** 120,17.19;
    27 154,18; 155,8; 156,7
aphrodisia, sex, sexual inter-
    course, **17** 138,4; **23** 144,27
aphrôn, foolish, **15** 136,17.19
aphrosunê, folly, 117,24; **15** 136,14.
    17.27

apithanôs, unconvincingly, **23** 145,26;
    26 152,12
apoballein, remove, get rid of, **3**
    122,11-12
apodeiktikos, such as to prove, capable
    of giving proofs, **25** 151,5.16
apodeixis, proof, **25** 151,5
apodidonai, cause, render,
    perform an activity, **27** 152,36;
    153,7.12.14
apokleiein, exclude, **21** 142,3
apolausis, enjoyment, **18** 138,8
apolaustikos, of enjoyment, **23** 144,5
apoleipesthai, fail, **23** 144,3
aporein, raise difficulty, **27** 157,9
aporia, difficulty, 117,4.8.10; **1** 118,22;
    4 122,30; **5** 124,1; **8** 128,22; **14**
    135,2.13; **27** 157,8
aposkeuê, removal, **24** 146,16
apostasis, distance, **27** 154,26; 156,1
apostereisthai, be deprived of, **18**
    138,27
apostrephesthai, reject, turn away
    from, **18** 139,3; **25** 149,19
apotelein, bring to perfection, **27**
    152,35; 153,12
apôthein, push, **12** 133,7
apotukhia, mischance, **1** 118,28; 119,3
apousia, absence, **4** 123,29
aretê, virtue, virtuous, excellence,
    excellently, 117,15.18; 118,6.10.13.
    14.16.17.18; **1** 119,32; **3** 121,12.14.
    23.26.30; 122,2.7.8.10.11.13.15.17.18.
    21.28; **4** 123,30; **6** 126,30; **7** 127,8; **8**
    128,3.5.6.9.10.12.15.17.18.20.21; **10**
    130,34; 131,7.8.9.10.11.13.15.16; **11**
    131,30.31.32; **15** 136,26; **17** 138,3; **21**
    141,15.23; **22** 142,22.23.24.26.28.29.30;
    143,1.2.3.5; **23** 143,16.19.23; 144,2.
    3.9.11.13.15.16; **24** 146,13.14.18.28.
    30.31; 146,30-147,1; 147,2.7; **25**
    148,5.22.23.24.28.30; 149,2.3-4.8.10.
    12.14.15.24.31.32.34; 150,7.11.12.14.
    16.21.23.28.29.30.33.35; 151,4-5.10-
    11.<14>; **27** 152,34.35.36; 153,1.3.6.
    8.13.15.18.19.24-5.26.28.32; 154,3.
    13.15.17; 155,6.10.11.12.19.20.25.29;
    156,9.10.11.12.13.19.20.24.25; **28**
    157,10.11.13.18.20.22.27.29; 158,1.2;
    29 158,5; 160,30.36.37; 161,1.15.18.
    19.20.21.24.25.28; **30** 161,32
aristos, best, as well as possible, **1**
    119,21.22; **8** 128,19; **14** 135,7.20; **24**
    147,32; 148,1; **29** 158,12; 160,11
Aristotelês, Aristotle, 117,20-21;
    118,5.11.19; **8** 128,20; **12** 133,11; **13**
    133,23-4; **22** 142,29-30; **23** 143,9.29;

dektikos, capable of being, having capacity for, able to acquire, 1 119,32.33.37; 3 122,21; 20 141,7; 29 161,16.22

dêlonoti, clearly, it is clear that, 30 162,22

dêlos, clear, clearly, 13 134,19; 14 135,16.21.24.26; 136,9.12; 17 137,35; 138,1; 18 139,11; 20 141,8; 23 144,9. 15.35; 24 147,8; 25 148,33; 149,22; 26 151,20; 27 153,12.27; 154,2; 29 160,37; 30 162,20

dêloun, indicate, 5 125,33

deuteros, second, 8 128,13; 9 129,5

diaballein, misrepresent, impugn, be at variance with, 11 131,23-4; 132,11. 12; 21 142,2.9

diabolê, misrepresentation, 21 142,5

diairein, divide, differentiate, 5 125,1; 25 149,15

diairesis, differentiation, 5 124,23-4; 125,10

diakeisthai, be disposed, 14 135,4.8.20

diakhusis, relaxation, 6 126,8.9.14

diakrinein, decide, settle, 23 144,17

dialambanein, decide, 21 141,25

dianoêtikos, reasoning, reason, 25 149,11; 150,24; 151,10

dianoia, thought, 14 135,10.15.32

diapherein, differ, be different, make a difference, 1 119,10; 2 120,8.25; 5 125,27; 8 128,11; 13 133,21.22.23.27; 14 135,6-7; 17 137,34; 19 139,23.24; 20 141,7.10; 22 143,6; 24 147,27; 28 157,18.25.27

diaphora, difference, 2 120,7.10.16.25-6; 23 146,2a

diaphoros, –ôs, different, in different ways, 2 120,11; 121,6-7; 13 134,1(per emend.).2.6

diaphtheirein, destroy, 27 153,22

diapseudesthai, be in error, 15 136,18

diastrephein, corrupt, 9 129,11

diatetamenôs, eagerly, 14 135,32

diathesis, disposition, 3 121,15.16.24; 122,17; 5 125,34.35; 11 132,11; 21 142,15

didaskalos, teacher, 9 129,17

didaskein, teach, 9 129,16.17

didonai, give, 23 144,21

di' hauto, di' hautên (and plurals), on its own account, 118,13; 18 138,10. 11.22.23; 20 140,1.5.18.23; 23 145,1. 22; 24 146,13.14.25.26-7.28.31; 147,1.2.3.12.13.14.15.18.19.21.22.24; 148,3; 26 151,21; 152.8

diistasthai, be apart, 27 155,9

dikaios, just, justice, 3 121,17.20.22. 31.34; 30 161,33; 162,11

dikaiosunê, justice, being just, 117,6; 118,20; 3 121,12.14.15.23.25.30; 24 146,23; 147,18.20.21-2; 148,4; 30 161,31; 162,1.9

diôkein, pursue, 25 149,19

diorizein, define, 27 154,23

diplous, double, 11 131,30; 29 158,30

dittos, double, 25 149,4

dokein, seem, seem right, appear, be reputed, think, decide, 5 124,29; 125,1.9; 8 128,8.17.20; 12 133,5; 14 135,5.13; 18 157,31; 21 141,22.24; 23 143,19; 27 154,16; 29 160,3

dosis, giving, 24 146,20; 147,10

doxa, opinion, 20 140,27; 23 145,28; 26 152,14; 27 157,8; reputation, 21 141,29

doxazein, hold opinions, 29 160,16

dunamis, potentiality, potentially, faculty, capacity, 1 118,25.26.28; 119,9.10.11.14.18.30; 3 122,26; 17 137,22; 138,4; 22 143,5; 25 149,4.8. 17.18; 150,29; 151,13.15; 29 161,20

dunasthai, be able, can, have potentiality, be capable, be possible, 1 118,27.29; 119,6.10.14.15.16.17. 21-2; 2 120,26; 121,2; 3 122,22; 5 124,12; 11 132,4; 13 133,30; 14 134,30-31; 21 142,2.4; 23 143,31; 24 146,16.20; 147,30; 25 149,5; 27 154,17; 155,25-6; 157,9; 29 160,19; 161,26.29; 30 162,25.29

dusis, setting, 29 160,8

duskherês, disagreeable, 5 125,26

duskinêtos, hard to change, 3 122,9.10. 12.14

êdê, just because, just for this reason, by this alone, 3 122,24; 12 133,6.8; 23 143,14; 27 155,33; 156,14

eidenai, know, 9 130,7; 11 132,1; 29 159,21.23

eidopoiein, make of a particular kind, 23 146,6; 26 152,27-8

eidos, species, kind, form; 2 120,24; 8 128,7; 11 131,22.27; 17 138,1; 19 139,24.25; 23 144,30; 28 157,14; 30 162,13.17.18.20.22.25.28.29; 163,2.6

eikein, yield, 9 129,6

eikotôs, reasonably, 18 158,1

eilikrinês, pure, 23 145,29; 26 152,15-16

einai, essence, being of a thing, 2 120,6; 3 122,14; 4 123,24; 8 128,9; 10 131,14; 11 131,33.34; 18 157,32; 23

of (*ep' autois, eph' hêmin* etc.),118,18;
9 129,1.27; 130,6.12.14.17.18.20.25.
28.30.31.32; 29 158,5.23; 159,2.5.7-8;
160,1.26.29; 161,2.9.13
epi, covering, 11 131,27
epibatês, rider, 27 153,4
epidekhesthai, be capable of being,
admit of, 3 122,23; 8 128,11.12; 27
156,26
epidektikos, capable of being, 3 122,23
epidosis, progress, 6 126,29
epidromê, summary account, 118,14; 25
148,5
epieikês, respectable, 21 142,6
epiginesthai, epi ... ginesthai, epi (sc.
ginesthai), supervene on,
accompany, 117,22; 2 120,12.13.(15).
(19).(22).24.25.27.(28).(31); 121,1.3.
(8).9.10.11; 5 124,19.23.24.(25).31.32.
(33).34-5; 125,7.11.17-18.(31).35;
126.2-3; 6 126,(21).(22).29; 7 127,
(12).(13).14.16.19.(27); 13 133,20.25.
28; 134,6-7.10.(11).19; 16 137,3.(4);
17 137,26-7.33-4.35; 19 139,24; 23
144,16.27; 145,5.19.20.21.28-9.(31).
34; 146,(1).(11); 26 151,25; 152,6.7.
15.(17).20.21.22.(33)
epikalein, reproach, 9 128,29
epikaleisthai, summon help, 9 128,30
epikhairekakia, gloating, 27 156,28
epilupos, distressing, causing distress,
9 130,11
epi pleon ginesthai, be intensified, 7
127,26
epistêmê, understanding, scientific
understanding, 117,24.25; 15
136,14-15.16.25; 20 141,7.10-11; 25
151,5; science, 27 153,5
epistêmonikos, scientific, 25 150,26
epithumein, desire, 2 120,17
epithumia, desire, 2 120,4.5.6.9.18.21;
9 130,16.17.18; 16 137,4.5; 29 159,27
epitimion, penalty, 29 158,30
epizêtein, enquire, 5 124,21
ep' oligon, for a short time, 24 147,30
eran, be in love, fall in love, 9 129,1
ergon, work, 25 148,16.18.21.22.23;
149,15.16.17; 27 152,36; 153,1.12.13
erôs, love, 9 129,2
eruthainesthai, blush, 18 139,12
eruthrian, blush, 18 139,14
eskhatos, ultimate, 20 140,18
êthikos, moral, 118,16; 22 142,23.25.28.
29; 143,1.3.4; 25 148,10; 149,10;
150,16.21.23; 27 152,34; 153,26.32;
154,3; *Êthika* as Aristotelian book-
title, 117,20; 118,5.19; 7 127,29-30;

18 138,7; 23 143,26; 29 158,4
ethizein, develop habit, 25 150,18; 29
159,15; 160,31
ethos, habit, 25 149,10; 150,18; 29 161,1
eu, well, good, goodness; 1 118,23.24;
119,18.19.20.22; 14 135,4.11; 25
148,14.17.19.20; 149,8.21.22.26.29.
30; 150,6.11.28.37; 151,4.11.13.16;
27 152,36; 153,1.7.12.32; 154,2.5;
155,20.22; 156,32; 29 158,17
eu ekhein, be in good condition, 27
152,35; 153,7.11.13.(32); 155,23
eu zên, live well, have good life, 1
118,24; 119,18.19.20.22
euapoblêtos, easy to lose, easy to get rid
of, 3 122,8
eudaimonein, being happy, happiness,
23 143,21.28
eudaimonia, happiness, 118,12; 18
138,8; 23 143,10.23.28.32.33;
144,1.4-5; 25 148,6.11.12.29;
149,1.16; 150,10; 151,12.14
euemptôtôs, easily, 21 141,18
euexia, good (bodily) condition, 25
149,24; 27 153,19.20; 156,4
eukinêtos, easy to change, 3 122,8.14.15
eulogos, –ôs, reasonable, reasonably, 5
124,28.31; 6 126,20; 7 127,13; 9
130,18-19.30; 23 144,13.33; 24
146,30.32; 25 149,2; 29 159,32
eumetabolos, easily changed, 30 163,1
euphuês, well endowed by nature, 29
158,14; 161,27-8
euphuia, good natural endowment, 29
158,17
euploia, voyaging well, 1 118,31
euporia, prosperity, 13 134,25
eustheneia, sound condition, 6 126,15
euthus, immediately, 27 156,27
exêgêsis, interpretation, 116,20; 29
158,3
exetazein, examine, 23 144,27
exô, beyond, free from, 20 141,3
exôthein, drive off course, 12 133,3
exôthen, outside, from outside, external,
12 132,19.26.27; 133,1.17; 29
159,14.16
exousia, power, 29 159,19

genesis, coming-to-be, 4 123,32; 30
162,12.27; 163,5.8.10
genêtos, having come to be, 15 136,21-
22; 25 149,11-12
gennasthai, be born, 3 121,27
genos, genus, 117,10.15; 118,17; 5
124,1.3.9.15; 8 128,3.4.21 11 131,27;
27 155,9; 28 157,10.11.14.<19>

geômetrein, do geometry, 13 133,25
geômetria, geometry, 13 133,26
gignôskein, know, recognise, 24 147,25;
25 148,11; 29 161,13
ginesthai = be born, 23 144,19;
ginesthai contrasted with *einai*,
'become' contrasted with 'be', 3 122,4;
not otherwise indexed
gnôrimos, known, well known, 23
144,20; 27 154,27; 155,2
gnôrizein, recognise, 14 135,26; 18
139,10.11; 25 148,8; 29 159,25
gnôsis, knowledge, coming to know, 11
132,6; 15 136,19.21.24; 25 148,10;
149,1.11.12.13.14; 150,25.29.30.32.
36.37; 151,1.3.8; 29 159,5
gumnasia, exercise, 25 149,23, 27
153,20; 156,4
gumnastikê, gymnastic art, 27 153,6

haireisthai, choose, 9 130,25.27; 13
134,7.12; 18 138,21.28.29.30; 139,1.
3.4; 23 144,11.13.16; 24 146,16.18.
23; 25 149,18; 27 154,9; 29 158,14;
161,18
hairesis, choice, being chosen; 9 130,28;
23 145,4-5.8; 24 146,22; 25 150,20;
26 151,24.27; *haireseis*, principles,
23 145,26; 26 152,13
hairetos, to be chosen, deserving or
worthy to be chosen, worthiness to
be chosen, 118,13; 2 120,6.8.15.23; 6
126,23.24.29.31; 7 127,12.13.15.17.
24.27.31; 9 129,30; 13 134,13.16; 16
137,10.16; 17 137,26.36; 18 138,10.
11.12; 23 144,13.15.34; 145,1.2.3.4.6.
9.11.12.13.22.23-4.25.30.32; 146,3.9.
10; 24 146,13.15.25.26.27.28.30.31.
32; 147,1.2.3.4.6.7.12.13.15.18.20.21.
22.25; 148,3; 25 150,33; 26 151,17.
19.20.21.22.23.26.29.30.31-2.33;
152,8.9.10.11.19.24.30.31; 27 153,17;
matter of choice, 1 120,1; desirable,
21 141,18; valuable, value, valued, 5
118,27; 119,1.15.17.21.34; 20 140,1.
3.5.8.9.11.12.19.20.21.22; 141,12;
hairetôteros, preferable, 9 129,7
hamartanein, do wrong, be wrong, do
or act wrongly, do wrong action;
117,16.17; 9 128,23.24.<25>.26.29-
30; 129,3.13.14.24; 130,3.16.17.18.
19.20.27.29.30.31.32; 11 132,5; 27
155,14.16; 156,32.34; 157,5-6; 29
158,25.27.29; 159,1.4.19
hamartêma, wrong action, wrongdoing,
go wrong, 9 129,13.19.29; 130,11.12;
21 141,19

haphê, touch, act of touching, 14
135,26; 24 146,17; 147,10; 27 154,8
haplôs, unqualified, without qualification, in an unqualified sense; 3
122,28; 5 125,20.21.23.27.29.31.34; 6
126,13; 16 137,12.15.16.17.18; 21
142,12.15; 25 150,8; 27 156,33; 30
162,13; 163,10
haptesthai, affect, 27 155,32
hêdesthai, be pleased, experience
pleasure, take pleasure in, enjoy, 2
121,3; 5 125,11.20.22.27; 13 134,18;
14 135,28; 136,5; 19 139,26; 25
150,19; *hêdein*, give pleasure, 23
146,11
hêdeôs, with pleasure, 17 137,30
hêdonê, pleasure, 117,5.10.12.13.22.23;
118,1.2.4.6.11.15; 2 120,3.4.7.9.12.15.
16.19.20.21.22.23.27.29.31;121,2.3.4.
9.11; 5 124,1.3.6.7.16.17.18.22.28;
125,3.9.16.19.20.21.22.23.25.28.30.
31.32.36.37; 126.1.3.4; 6 126,6.8.9.
11.12.13.14.15.17.19.20.21.22.27.28.
31; 7 127,2.3.4.5.6.11.15.18.20.22.23.
24.25.28.30.31.32.33.34; 9 129,7; 12
133,16.17; 13 133,19.20.21.22.24.25.
28; 134,4.5.8.9.11.12.13.14.15.16.19.
20.25.27; 14 134,28.29.31; 135,2.9.
14.15.24.30; 136,2.4.12; 16 136,28.
31; 137,1.6.11.12.15; 17 137,21.23.
24.26.28.29.30.32; 18 138,6.10.11.12.
18.20.29; 19 139,15.18.19.22.23.25.
26.27; 23 143,9.11.13.14.16.17.25.27.
29; 144,5.8.10.12.14.15.19.20.22.23.
26.27.29.31.34.35; 145,2.3.6.7.10.11.
12.13.15.18.19.20.21.22.24.25.29.33.
34; 146,2.3.4.8.9.10; 24 146,18;
147,10; 25 149,18.34; 26 151,17.19.
20.21.23.25.27.30.31.32.33; 152,1.5.6.
7.8.9.11.12.15.20.21.23.24.29.30.31;
27 154,8; 29 159,12.14.16
hêdus, pleasant, causing pleasure, 2
120,5; 5 125,26.27; 12 133,17; 14
135,9.10.19.21.23.27; 136,8.9.10; 18
138,29.31; 139,2.3.5; 23 144,9;
145,17.18; 26 152,4
hêgeisthai, think, 13 133,30
hekôn, voluntary, voluntarily, 9 130,8.
27; 12 133,15
hekousios, –ôs, voluntary, voluntarily, 9
129,2; 130,3.29; 11 131,25.33.34;
132,3; 29 159,1.2.10.20.26.27.29.34;
160,3.25-6.29
hêlikia, age, time of life, 21 141,18.20.
23.26; 142,7.16.20
heneka, for the sake of, 23 144,10;
heneka tou, for the sake of

something, **12** 132,28; see also *hou heneka*

hepesthai, follow, follow on, accompany, be concomitant, be consequence, **1** 119,11; 120,1; **5** 124,20; **7** 127,11; **14** 135,2.30; **17** 137,25; **21** 142,16; **23** 143,25.26; **25** 150,31; **27** 155,7; **28** 157,15; **29** 161,8

heteros, different, **19** 139,25

hêttasthai, be conquered, **12** 133,4; **29** 159,13.15

heuresis, discovery, discover, 118,14; **25** 148,5.9b.33; 150.20.32; 151,1.8.9.10; **27** 154,27

heuretikos, able to or such as to find or discover, **22** 143,7; **25** 150,34; 151,11.16

heuriskein, find, locate, ascertain, contrive, **1** 118,31; **4** 123,24-5; **5** 125,4; **14** 136,4; **23** 144,28; **25** 148,12; 149.4.17; **27** 153,15; 154,26

hexis, state, disposition, habit, 117,6; 118,11; **3** 121,13.15.31; 122,1.16.20. 25.27; **8** 128,19; **9** 129,24.26.31; 130,1.21; **14** 134,29; 135,20; **21** 141,15; 142,15; **23** 143,10; **25** 150,21.33; 151,5; **27** 153,33; 154,6. 11.12; **28** 157,26; **29** 158,8.21.23; 160,26.28.29.30.31.33; 161,3.5.8; **30** 162,1.8.9; 163,1; possession, possessing, **4** 123,31

hikanos, –ôs, sufficient, sufficiently, **9** 129,14.16; 130,9; **23** 144,6; **27** 156,24

hippos, horse, **5** 125,15; **25** 148,16.17; **27** 153,3

hode, tode ti, particular, **16** 137,14; **28** 157,28

hoios te, able, possible, can, **1** 119,2.7. 19.22; **2** 120,10; 121,9.10; **4** 123,31; **5** 124,13; **10** 131,8; **11** 131,29; 132,4; **19** 139,26; **22** 143,4; **23** 145,14; **25** 148,9a; **26** 152,1; **27** 155,26; **28** 157,13; **29** 158,16; 160,12.15; **30** 162,17

holoklêrôs, completely, **30** 162,4

holos, whole, total, a totality, 117,15; 118,17; **4** 123,18; **8** 128,3.10.11.18. 21; **28** 157,10.15.19.21

holôs, generally, in general, 117,6; **3** 121,12.14.25; 122,7; **15** 136,24; **25** 148,8; 149,12; **27** 157,6

homoeidês, same in kind, 117,5; 118,6; **2** 120,3.<4>.10.16; 121,5; **13** 133,21; 134,11-12.16.22; **17** 137,24; **19** 139,15.16.22.27; **23** 145,34a

homoiomerês, uniform, **28** 157,16.19.21. 26.30

homoiôs ekhein, be in same state, **29** 160,6

homologein, agree, admit, **1** 119,31; **3** 122,4; **23** 145,25; **26** 152,12

homônumos, ambiguous, ambiguity, **5** 125,18

horan, idein, see, **18** 139,13; **21** 142,17; **23** 145,19; **25** 149,3; **26** 152,5; **27** 153,2.15.23; **28** 157,29

horismos, definition, **21** 141,16; **27** 154,22

horizein, define, lay down, fix definitely, **7** 127,36; **18** 138,24; **22** 142,27; 143,2.5; **25** 150,9.22; **27** 153,29.30. 31; 154,1.18.20.21.28.31; 155,12; 156,13; **29** 158,30; 159,6; 160,7.15

hormê, impulse, **9** 129,22; **12** 133,9

horos, definition, define, **8** 128,17; **27** 154,24

hou heneka, for the sake of which, **12** 132,27

hugeia, health, **2** 121,6.7; **4** 123,29; **25** 149,27; **27** 153,21; 156,5

hugiainein, be healthy, **27** 153,8

hugieinos, healthy, **5** 125,21; **27** 153,9

hugiês, sound, **8** 128,7; **27** 156,10

hulê, matter, **4** 123,21; **30** 162,12.14.16. 17

huparkhein, belong to, be property of, **4** 123,11.12; **29** 161,23

huper, for the sake of, **23** 144,26

huperballein, exceed, be excessive, excess, **6** 126,25.26; **27** 153,16.19.22; 156,2-3.4.21

huperbolê, excess, **5** 126,2; **6** 126,21.22. 27.28.31; **7** 127,23.25.26.34-5.36; 128,1; **11** 131,20-1.27.28.31; **25** 149,20.21.23.26.29.33; 150,4; **27** 153,24; 154,3.5.9.10.11.14.19; 155,13.18; 156,6.11.17.30.35; 157,1. 2.3.4.6.7

huperekhein, surpass, **27** 156,22

huphistasthai, exist, **30** 162,13

hupnos, sleep, **14** 135,18

hupo, subordinate to, falling under, object of, 118,2; **5** 124,13; **14** 135,5.8. 11.20; **17** 137,21.23.24; 138,1

hupokeisthai, underlie, be subject, **1** 119,3-4; **4** 123,21; **30** 162,14-15

hupolambanein, suppose, **7** 127,14; **9** 129,27; **18** 138,27

hupolêpsis, supposition, suppose, **9** 130,24.26

hupomenein, remain, **30** 162,15.16

hupopteuein, suspect, suspicion, **21** 142,1; *hupopteuesthai*, be apprehensive, **1** 119,29

khrênai, must, should, ought to, be
  necessary, 118,7; **5** 124,21; 125,6.9.
  16; **16** 137,11; **17** 137,23.24; **20**
  139,29; **23** 145,5; **26** 151,24
khrêsimos, useful, usefulness, 118,7; **14**
  135,25; **20** 139,29.30.31; 140,1.2.4.6.
  8.9.11.12.13.14.15.16.17.
  18.20.21.22.25.26.27; 141,2.11-12; **24**
  147,27
khrôma, colour, **11** 132,16; **27** 155,31
khumos, flavour, **27** 155,31
kinein, move, alter, movement, **9**
  129,22; **12** 133,5.8.11.12.14; **27**
  155,10; **29** 159,13
kinêsis, movement, **12** 133,6; **25** 149,10
kithara, lyre, **4** 123,19
kitharistikê, lyre-playing, **13** 133,26-7
kitharizein, play the lyre, lyre-playing,
  13 133,26
klopê, theft, **27** 156,29
koinônia, community, **24** 146,24;
  147,17.20.23.25.26.28.31.32; 148,3
koinônikos, inclined to live in
  community, **24** 146,25
koinos, –ôs, common, general, in
  general, generally, 117,10; **5** 124,1.3.
  4.9.12.15.16; 125,36.37; **8** 128,14.18;
  9 129,11.15.17-18; *koinoteros*, wider,
  7 127,10
kolasis, punishment, **9** 130,17.30; **29**
  159,9-10
kolazein, punish, **9** 130,3.19.31
kôluein, prevent, **1** 119,35; **2** 120,30;
  121,7; **3** 121,25; **4** 123,7; **16** 137,6; **27**
  153,20; 155,3.24
kômôidein, perform comedy, **19** 139,20
kosmos, world, **15** 136,20.24; **23** 144,31
kouphos, light, lightness, **4** 123,26
kratistos, best, **14** 135,8.20.22-3
krinein, judge, esteem, **13** 134,15; **22**
  142,24; **23** 144,7; **29** 158,13; 160,24;
  161,17.18
krisis, judgement, judge, **1** 119,3.12.30.
  35; 120,2; **4** 123,14; **13** 134,15; **24**
  148,1; **29** 160,23
ktasthai, acquire, **10** 131,10.12; **13**
  134,2; **25** 148,7; **29** 160,30.31.33;
  161,25
ktêmata, possessions, **13** 134,3
ktêsis, acquisition, **10** 131,9.13.14.17; **25**
  149,1; **29** 160,35.37
kubernetikê, art of navigation, **1** 118,31
kuklos, circle, **27** 156,7
kuôn, dog, **5** 125,15; **25** 148,18
kurios, kuriôs, properly, in the proper
  or strict sense, **3** 122,24.28; **5** 125,19.
  20.22.29; 126,4; **7** 127,30; **18** 158,2;

20 140,7; **23** 143,17; **25** 151,7; **30**
  162,12.14.27; important, **25** 151,12.
  13; powerful, having power, **12**
  133,4; in control, **29** 158,7.20

lambanein, get, **29** 158,16; 161,27;
  derive, **23** 145,14; **26** 151,33; observe,
  regard, interpret as, take into
  account, understand, suppose,
  117,10; **4** 122,33; 123,2.4.16.28; **5**
  124,1.3; 125,10; **23** 144,18; **25** 150,8;
  151,14; **28** 157,20
lanthanein, not be observed, **9** 129,5
legein, call, speak of, apply (a term); **3**
  121,15; 122.29; **6** 126,16; **7** 127,30; **8**
  128,16; **18** 139,6; (contrasting words
  and deeds) **18** 139,12; not otherwise
  indexed
lêpsis, receiving, **24** 146,21; 147,10
leukos, white, **11** 132,14.15.16; **18**
  139,8; **19** 139,16.17
lexis, passage, 116,20; 118,19; **12**
  132,18; **27** 156,25; **29** 158,3
logikos, rational, of reason, **3** 121,33;
  122,1.3.4.5.6.7.18.19; **5** 124,14; **8**
  128,19; **11** 131,19-20; **18** 138,20.26;
  25 148,26.27.28; 149,1.3.4.5.6-7.17;
  150,24.29; 151,13.15; **27** 155,25;
  capable of speech, **24** 148,2
logistikos, calculating, **25** 150,27
logos, reason, reasoning, being rational,
  3 122,23; **18** 138,27; **25** 149,5.7;
  150,9; **27** 153,29; 154,29; 155,1.14.
  16; **29** 160,2; account, argument,
  discussion, explanation, **7** 127,7; **18**
  139,7.9; **21** 141,28; **23** 143,30; **24**
  147,11; **25** 148,17; **27** 153,2.4.8.9; **30**
  161,32; definition, **4** 123,5; **8** 128,11.
  12.19.20; **27** 153,32; **28** 157,17; **30**
  162,18; speech, **24** 147,28.31.32; *kata
  logon*, rationally, in accordance with
  reason, **16** 137,7; **29** 159,32; see also
  orthos logos
luein, resolve, **27** 156,25; 157,8
lupê, distress, 117,12.13.23; 118,1; **5**
  124,21.30.34.36; 125,1.2.3.5.8.29.33.
  34.37; 126,2.3.4; **6** 126,6.7.11.13.18.
  19.26; **7** 127,1.4.6.8.9.10.14.17.18.20.
  21.22.31.32.33.35; 128,2; **13** 134,20.
  27; **14** 134,28; 135,14.15.24; 136,13;
  16 136,28.30; 137,6.11.16; **19** 139,21;
  23 144,11.14; 145,30.33; 146,6; **25**
  146,18; 147,9; **25** 149,18; **26** 152,16.
  19.27; **27** 154,8
lupein, cause, give or produce distress,
  13 134,7.17; **23** 145,32; 146,11; **26**
  152,17.32; *lupeisthai*, be distressed,

5 124,26; **6** 126,18; **9** 130,10; **14** 136,5; **16** 137,20
lupêros, causing distress, **14** 134,30; 135,26; 136,8.9.10
lusis, solution, 117,8; **4** 122,30

malakia, softness, **9** 128,27
manthanein, learn, **9** 130,6; **20** 139,31; **29** 158,16
marturein, bear witness, **9** 130,2
mathêma, learning, 118,7; **20** 139,30
mathêsis, learning, **3** 122,12
megaloprepeia, magnificence, **4** 123,12; **24** 146,20
megalopsukhia, greatness of spirit, **24** 146,21
meignunai, mix, mixture, **27** 156,8; **28** 157,21.25.26
meiôsis, diminution, **34** 163,8
melas, black, **11** 132,14.16; **19** 139,17
mellein, be going to, **21** 141,22
menein, remain, persist, **7** 127,27; **14** 135,13.23; **20** 140,18; **23** 144,31; **30** 162,23; withstand, resist, **27** 153,4
mênusis, indication, **24** 147,29
meros, part, **7** 127,11; **8** 128,10.19; **9** 129,22; **11** 131,22; 132,3; **12** 133,12; **25** 150,10; **27** 156,17.20.21.22.23.24; **28** 157,15.16.19; *en merei*, particular, **4** 123,2.3; *para meros*, in turn, **30** 162,18.19
mesos, middle, intermediate, **1** 118,26; **3** 121,15.32; 122,1.16.20.25; **14** 135,13. 27; mean, moderate, moderately, **7** 127,8.24; **25** 150,8.20; **27** 153,17.21. 23.28.30; 154,9.18.24.25.27.28.29.30; 155,4.6.7.10.11.20.23.27.29.30.33.34; 156,1.2.12.14.15; 157,4
mesotês, mean, 118,16; **6** 126,27; **7** 127,35-6; **24** 147,8.13.15.18-19.22; **25** 149,25; 150,2.3.6.7.16-17.21-2; **27** 152,34; 153,28.33; 154,13.15.17.22; 155,19.22.24.26; 156,4-5.10.19.26.35; 157,1-2.4.6.7
metaballein, change, **3** 121,25.26; 122,3.6.13; **27** 156,18; **30** 162,1.2.3.5. 6.7.8.9.19.20.21.22.24.29; 163,1.3.4.7
metabolê, change, **3** 121,32; 122,5.8.10. 11.16.25-6.28; **30** 162,23.28-9; 163,2. 6-7.8
metaginôskein, regret, **9** 130,11
metalambanein, substitute, make a substitution, **12** 132,23
metameleia, regret, **9** 130,12; **23** 146,7; **26** 152,29
metanoia, regret, **23** 146,6a

metaphora, movement, way of moving, **12** 133,10-11
metaxu, intermediate, intermediate between, 117,7.23; **1** 119,30.35; **3** 121,13.15.19.21.22; 122,2; **14** 134,28; **27** 156,8; **30** 162,2.3.5.7; 163,6
metekhein, share in, **30** 162,4
methê, drunkenness, **29** 158,27.29; 159,1.3
methuein, be drunk, **29** 158,28; 159,3
metienai, pursue, **27** 155,20
metrein, moderate, **24** 146,16.20
metron, measure, assess, **23** 145,5; **26** 151,24; moderation, **24** 146,19
miktos, mixed, **23** 146,7a
mimeisthai, imitate, **25** 148,15
mimnêskein, mention, **23** 144,35a
misein, hate, **9** 130,3; **11** 132,8.9.10
misêtos, hateful, **21** 142,11-12
Mitulênaios, of Mytilene (on the spelling cf. *Oxford Classical Dictionary*), **29** 158,30
mixis, mixture, **27** 155, 30.34; 156,3.7; **28** 157,30.33
moikheia, adultery, **27** 156,29
moikheuein, commit adultery, **27** 156,33
mokhthêria, wickedness, **29** 159,9
mokhthêros, bad, wicked, **5** 124,6.9.20. 25.27; 125,6.23; **9** 129,31; **13** 134,24; **16** 137,4.15
monimos, stable, **3** 122,9.11.12; **30** 163,4
monoeidês, of a single kind, **16** 137,1
monos, isolated, **24** 147,30
morion, part, **12** 133,6; **27** 153,2
muthologein, tell stories, **2** 121,3

naus, ship, **12** 133,13
neos, young, **9** 129,19; **21** 141,17; 142,21
neuein, incline, **9** 129,12
Nikomakheios, Nicomachean (Ethics), 117,20; 118,5.19; **12** 132,18; **14** 134,30; **18** 138,7; **21** 141,14; **29** 158,3
noein, observe, **27** 154,22; 155,21
noêma, thought, **24** 147,29
noêtikos, intellectual, **25** 149,13
nomê, distribution, **24** 147,23
nomos, law, **9** 129,16; **29** 159,6
nomothetês, lawgiver, **18** 138,24
nosein, be diseased, **9** 128,28
nosêmatôdês, diseased, **7** 127,29
nosos, disease, **16** 137,19
nous, intellect, **25** 151,8

odunê, pain, **6** 126,16
oiesthai, think, **29** 158,11; 161,12

oikeios, proper, appropriate, having
affinity, 117,22; **1** 119,8; **2** 120,23.29;
5 125,13.17.29; 126,1.2; **6** 126,31; **7**
127,9; **13** 133,20.24; 134,19; **14**
136,11; **16** 137,12-13; **17** 137,34;
138,2; **19** 139,23; **20** 140,30; **22**
143,3; **23** 143,<22>.24.29-30; **25**
148,13.16.22.23.24.25; 149,8.9.31;
150,7; 151,6; **27** 153,7.14.18
oikeiotês, affinity, **2** 120,12; **5** 124,29; **13**
133,27; **17** 137,27
oikeioun, endear, **1** 119,24.26.27
oikia, house, **10** 131,12; **24** 147,1.5
oikodomein, build, **25** 148,21
oikodomikê, building, art of (house-)
building, **24** 146,25-6; 147,1.5; **27**
153,9-10
oikodomos, builder, **25** 148,20
oikonomikos, economic, **24** 147,17
oknein, shrink from, **23** 144,29
ombros, rainstorm, **29** 160,9
omma, eye, **18** 139,9; **29** 161,17.28
onomazein, name, **27** 156,27
onta, beings, **25** 148,12-13
ontôs, really, **16** 137,17
ôphelimos, beneficial, 118,3; **9** 129,29-
30; **17** 137,23
ophthalmos, eye, **27** 152,36; 153,1
opsis, sight, act of seeing, **14** 135,25;
136,1; **29** 158,13; 161,24.26
oregesthai, have appetite, **29** 159,32
orektikos, appetitive, **22** 143,5; **25**
149,6.9.17-18; 150,10
orektos, object of appetite, **25** 150,32
orexis, appetition, appetite, **2** 120,5; **25**
150,32.33; **29** 160,23.24.25
organikos, bodily, **9** 129,22; **12** 133,5.12
organon, instrument, 117,8.9; **4** 122,30.
31-2.33.34; 123,1.4.5.6.9.10.11.13.14.
16.18.27.29.33; **25** 148,32
orgê, anger, **24** 146,23
orgizesthai, be angry, **29** 159,33
orthos, right, **22** 142,24.26.30; 143,7; **25**
150,31.33.34; *orthos logos*, right
reasoning, **7** 127,36; **8** 128,9.10; **16**
137,8; **22** 143,2; **25** 150,9.22; **27**
153,31; 154,1.9-10; 155,12.15;
156,13.15
orthotês, rightness, **25** 150,36
osmasthai, smell, have sense of smell,
14 136,7
osmê, smell, odour, **27** 155,31
osphrantos, object of smell, **14** 136,7
osphrêsis, act of smelling, sense of
smell, **14** 135,25; 136,6
osphrêtos, object of smell, **14** 136,6
ousia, essence, substance, **4** 123,5.6.10.

14.21; **25** 149,14; **30** 162,12;
163,10.12
oxus, sharp, sharpness, **4** 123,25.26

paidagôgein, educate, **25** 150,18
paidagôgos, tutor, **9** 129,17
paidia, amusement, **20** 141,1.4.6.11
paidion, child, **29** 159,29
pais, child, **1** 119,27; **3** 121,33;
122,1.18.27; **9** 129,14; **18** 139,13-14
palaiein, wrestle, **24** 146,27
palaistikê, art of wrestling, **24** 146,26
pantapasin, completely, **9** 129,10-11
parabasis, deviation, transgression, **14** 135,22; **27** 154,30; 155,2
parainein, advise, **9** 129,18
parakalein, attract, **14** 135,31-2
parakolouthein, attend on, accompany, **2** 120,20; **23** 143,33; 144,1
paramelein, neglect, be negligent, **14**
136,2.3
paramutheisthai, excuse, **23** 144,25
parapempein, lead on, **23** 144,29
paraskeuazein, provide, **23** 145,10; **26**
151,29-30; *paraskeuazesthai*, adopt
a contrivance, **23** 145,27; **26** 152,14
paraspeirein, introduce, **23** 144,28
par' autois, in their hands, **29** 161,13
pareinai, be present, **23** 143,28; 144,23
par' hautôn, by our own efforts, **29**
161,27
paroran, pass over, **9** 130,28
parousia, presence, **10** 131,16; **23** 144,1
pas, whole, **8** 128,19; **11** 132,9.12; **18**
157,30
paskhein, be acted on, be affected,
suffer, experience (a feeling), **11**
132,4; **12** 132,21.24.25.26.30;
133,1.2; **18** 139,13; **27** 156,15
pathos, affection, feeling, **4** 123,22; **20**
141,4; **21** 141,14.15.17; 142,6.15.16;
24 146,15.19; 147,8.29; **25** 149,9.28.
32; 150,6.11.15.17.22; **27** 153,26.29.
33; 154,13.19.31; 155,10.17.21;
156,12.14.26
pauesthai, cease, stop, **9** 129,2; **13**
134,17
peirasthai, try, **29** 161,27
peithein, convince, persuade, **9** 128,26;
129,6; **21** 142,19; *peithesthai*, obey,
25 149,5
penia, poverty, 117,9; **4** 122,31; 123,28;
13 134,23; **16** 137,19
perainein, peperasmenos, limit,
limited, **4** 123,8; **15** 136,22
peras, limit, **27** 155,3
periginesthai, come about, result, **13**

productive, create, act, have effect, be efficient (cause), perform, commit, 9 130,14.15.16; **11** 131,34; 132,4.6; **12** 133,10.15.16.17.18; **13** 134,13.17. 18; **18** 138,19; **19** 139,21.22; **20** 139,31; 140,16.31; **21** 141,30.31; 142,4; **22** 142,31; **25** 148,20.23; **27** 153,1.3.21.23; 154,27; 155,2; 156,33; **28** 157,30; **29** 158,10; 159,14.24.30; 160,15; 161,2 (per emend.)

poiêteos, to be done, **15** 136,16.19.20. 21

poiêtikos, producing, produce, create, productive; **13** 133,22.23; 134,4.14; **18** 138,12.13; **20** 140,4.5.9. 13; **23** 145,2.3.4.11.24.30.33; **24** 146,27; **25** 149,22.25.27.30; 150,21; **26** 151,21.23.31; 152,10-11.17.19; efficient (cause), **12** 132,27; 133,1

poiotês, quality, **4** 123,22.24

polemioi, enemy, **27** 153,4

politeuesthai, govern selves, **29** 160,11

politikos, political, inclined to live in a city-state, **24** 146,25; 147,17.23; 148,1.2

pollakhôs (legesthai), have several senses, be said in many ways, 117,(19); **8** 128,14-15; **11** 131,(18).19. (21).(23).(24).(25).26; 132,7.8.9.12.13. 14.17

ponein, make effort, **9** 129,8

ponos, pain, 117,12; **5** 125,33; **6** 126,6.7.9.11.13.14.16.18; **7** 127,9.10. 17; **16** 137,10; **18** 138,10.13.23; **23** 144,11

pornoboskia, living off immoral learnings, **13** 134,23

posos, quantity, quantitative aspect, **27** 153,15; 155,17

posotês, quantity, **27** 155,34

pragma, thing, **27** 154,24

praktikos, doing, capable of doing, performing actions, practical, **21** 141,23; **22** 143,2; **25** 150,35; 151,1

praktos, able to be done, can be done, **29** 160,13.14.18.26.28

praotês, mildness, **24** 146,22-3

prattein, do, deed, act, be agent, perform action, enact, 117,17; **9** 128,24.<26>.28; 129,2.5.20.21.28; 130,5.11; **11** 132,1; **12** 132,21.23.25. 28.29.30.32; **21** 141,32-142,1; 142,18; **22** 142,31; **25** 148,6.8.11; **27** 153,31; 155,15; 156,15; 157,5; **29** 158,11.25. 18; 159,22.24.27.31; 161,10.11.13.14

praxis, action, doing, deed, 118,7; **9** 129,22; 130,4; **12** 133,13; **20** 139,30;

21 142,5; **23** 145,5-6.9; **24** 146,19.20; 147,8.16; **25** 148,10; 149,9.18.28.32; 150,6.11.15.18.22.35.36; 151,2; **26** 156,25.28; **27** 153,26.30; 154,1.13.19. 31; 155,11.17.22; 156,12.15.26.28; **29** 159,21.23; 160,22.24

priein, to saw, **1** 118,31; 119,1

priôn, saw, **4** 123,19

proaireisthai, choose, **9** 129,23; **12** 133,16

proairesis, choice, **22** 142,23.24.25.30; **29** 160,1.2.3.4.24.25.27

proairetikos, choosing, choose, **27** 153,33

proairetos, object of choice, **29** 160,1.20.22

probainein, advance, **21** 141,20.22-3; 142,7.16

probouleuesthai, deliberate beforehand, **29** 160,3

prodêlos, quite clear, **23** 146,8; **26** 152,30

proêgoumenos, prime, primary, **1** 119,13; **25** 148,31.32; *proêgoumenôs* primarily, **1** 119,4.11; **30** 162,26

proelthein, persevere in, **9** 129,30

proienai, go on, extend, proceed, **20** 140,15; **27** 154,20; 156,11

proistasthai, defend, **23** 145,28; **26** 152,14

prokeisthai, be set before, be a goal, be proposed or in question, **12** 132,31. 32-3; **13** 133,30; 134,9; **29** 160,21.34

prokheirizesthai, examine, **27** 154,3

prokheiros, easy, easily, **24** 147,25

prokoptein, be on the way to virtue, **27** 156,9

prokrinein, prefer, **29** 160,20.22

prolêpsis, conception, preconception, **9** 129,9.15; **18** 138,16; 139,6

pros hen legesthai, be said in relation to one thing, **8** 128,15

prosêkein, be fitting, **22** 142,29

prosekhein, attend to, **17** 137,32

proskeisthai, be added, **25** 148,30; **27** 154,22

prosodos, approach, **27** 155,2

prosthêkê, addition, being added to, **6** 126,30

prosthesis, addition, **27** 153,16.26-7

protasis, premiss, **4** 123,3.16

prothesis, purpose, **12** 133,9

prôtos, first, primary, **8** 128,13; **24** 147,24; **25** 151,6.7.8; *prôtos ... deuteros*, first ... second, **19** 139,28

proxenoun, recommend, **23** 145,8a

pseudesthai, be in error, **15** 136,18

pseudos, false, falsehood, **18** 139,1; **23** 145,18; **25** 151,4; **26** 152,5

psogos, blame, **29** 159,9

psukhê, soul, **4** 123,30; **6** 126,9.12.16; **8** 128,19; **18** 139,10; **23** 144,8; **25** 148,26.27.28; 149,2.3.6; 150,10.24. 29; 151,13.15; **27** 155,25; Aristotelian book-title, **14** 136,5

psukhikos, of the soul, **5** 125,34.35.36; **6** 126,7-8

pur, fire, **4** 123,20.23

rhâidios, easy, easily, **3** 122,10; **21** 141,23; **29** 161,28; **30** 163,4

rhêteon, one should say, should be called, **5** 125,19.22; **8** 128,17

rhuthmizesthai, be ordered, **25** 149,5-6

saphôs, clearly, **27** 154,23

Sardanapalos, Sardanapulus (a byword for luxury), **23** 144,7

sêmainein, indicate, mean, **5** 125,35; **11** 132,12.15

sêmeion, sign, **5** 124,31; **23** 143,27; 144,1; **24** 147,26

semnos, respected, **21** 142,9

sitia, food, **25** 149,26; **27** 153,22

skelos, leg, **12** 133,8.11

skeparnon, adze, **4** 123,24

skepê, shelter, **24** 147,6

skhêma, shape, **15** 136,21

skopos, goal, **1** 118,27; 119,6; **12** 133,18; **22** 142,26.27; 143,4.7; **25** 148,6.9a. 9b.10.33; 150,34

Skuthai, Scythians, **29** 160,11

sôzein, preserve, preservation, retain, maintain, 117,23; **9** 129,11; **14** 134,28; **24** 148,2; **25** 150,1; **27** 153,21.22; *sôzesthai*, survive, be preserved, **23** 144,21.26

sôma, body, bodily, **4** 123,30; **6** 126,10.13.14.15.24; **18** 157,25; **25** 149,24; **27** 153,2.6.8.18.19

sômatikos, bodily, of the body, **5** 125,33.35.36; **6** 126,7.8.14.23; **7** 127,25; **18** 138,8; **23** 144,5; **27** 154,7

sophia, understanding, **25** 151,8

sôphrôn, temperate, **2** 120,27; **13** 134,20.23.24; **19** 139,26.27

sôphronikos, temperate, **2** 121,10; **13** 134,21

sôphrosunê, temperance, **18** 157,23.24; **24** 146,17; 147,9; **25** 149,33.34; **27** 154,7; 157,3

sôstikos, preserving, preserve, **24** 146,24; **25** 149,22

sôtêria, preservation, **1** 119,24-5; **24** 147,17.19.21.23

speudein, be eager, **9** 129,5

spoudaios, good, good man, virtuous man, **1** 120,1; **4** 123,13; **7** 127,9; **10** 131,6.7; **14** 135,11; **16** 137,13.19; **27** 153,1.3; serious, **20** 141,5

spoudazein, be eager, pursue eagerly, **19** 139,19; **23** 144,10; **29** 160,32; take seriously, **20** 140,24-5.26

spoudê, seriousness, take seriously, be concerned, **1** 119,27; **20** 141,1

sterêsis, privation, absence, **1** 119,15; **4** 123,29.31.33; **14** 136,11; **30** 162,8.9. 10.11.14.15.20.21.26.27; 163,3.5

stokhastikos, aiming at, **7** 127,8-9

sullambanein, combine, **27** 156,27

sullogizesthai, argue syllogistically, **4** 123,2-3

sumbainein, come about, happen, turn out, happen to, apply to, **4** 123,7; **18** 139,2; **21** 141,16; 142,11; **23** 144,30; **25** 149,31; **27** 156,16; *sumbebêkos*, accident, accidental, **4** 123,7.15

sumballein, contribute, **12** 132,19-20.21.23; 133,2.6-7

summetria, due measure, **25** 149,22.25. 27.30.32; 150,2.3; **27** 155,13.15

summetros, *–ôs*, proportionate, due proportion, due measure, **6** 126,23. 27; **24** 146,22.23; **27** 153,17.21.23.30; 154,29; 155,1.4-5.23; 156,2

sumpherein, be fitting, advantageous, **18** 138,31; **29** 159,8

sumprattein, co-operate, **12** 133,2

sunairesthai, give assistance, **20** 140,28

sunaitios, contributory cause, **29** 158,22

sunallagma, contract, **24** 147,23

sunamphoteros, concrete, total, totality, **4** 123,18.20-1

sunanairein, remove, remove along with, **8** 128,4.5.7; **28** 157,14

sunauxein, encourage, **18** 133,24.25.29

sundiairein, differentiate in a corresponding way, correspondingly, **2** 120,14.21.22.29; **5** 124,7.19.22-3.29; **16** 137,2; **17** 137,35.36; **23** 145,33a

sunduasmos, mating, **23** 144,29

sunêmmenon, conditional, **29** 161,3

sunêthês, normal, **12** 133,10

sunêtheia, familiarity, **21** 142,17

suneidenai, be conscious, **21** 141,26.32

suneinai, associate, be associated, accompany, **2** 120,18.20

sunekhôs, continuously, continuous, **14** 135,28.29

sungignôskein, pardon, **9** 130,6

sungnômê, pardon, **9** 130,5.9
sunistanai, construct, constitute, establish, **14** 135,13; **25** 148,14; 149,32; 150,1.2-3; **29** 161,1-2
sunkeisthai, be composed, combined, combination, **27** 155,29-30; 156,9
sunkhôrein, accept, agree to, concede, **4** 123,1; **23** 145,26; **26** 152,13
sunônumôs, synonymously, in a single sense, **8** 128,17; **28** 157,16.18.19.22; 158,1
sunteleia, contribution, contribute, **25** 149,16; 151,12.14-15
suntelein, contribute, **11** 132,6; **12** 133,6.8.10; **15** 136,25; **20** 140,19; **22** 142,27; **23** 143,19; 145,23; **25** 148,8.9b; 150,32.34-5.36; **26** 152,9; **29** 159,17; 160,21
sunthesis, combination, **27** 156,2
suntithenai, combine, **27** 156,6
sunuparkhein, exist together, **11** 132,3-4; **23** 144,33; 145,15; **26** 152,1
sustasis, establishment, constitution, constituted, 118,14; **25** 148,5; 150,23; **27** 155,31.35
sustolê, contraction, **6** 126,8

taxis, ordering, **29** 160,7
têrêtikos, preserving, preserve, **25** 149,25.27-8.30
tekhnê, art, skill, **1** 118,29; 119,5; **25** 148,15; **27** 153,5.10.29; 154,28.29; 156,1; **29** 160,29.33.34.37; 161,22.29
tekhnitês, craftsman, **29** 161,23
teknopoiia, production of offspring, **23** 144,28
tektôn, carpenter, **29** 160,32
tektonikê, art of carpentry, **1** 118,31-119,1; **27** 153,10
tektonikos, of a carpenter, **29** 160,32
teleios, –ôs, perfect, perfectly, complete, **1** 119,9.20; **8** 128,21; **14** 135,4.5.8-9.10.11; **24** 147,32; **25** 148,31; **28** 157,20.22; **29** 158,17; *teleos*, perfect, perfection, **23** 144,4 (per emend.)
teleiôsis, completion, **18** 157,29
teleiotês, perfection, **1** 119,8
teleutaios, last, **23** 143,26
telikos, final (cause), **12** 132,27
telos, end, final (cause), 118,4; **1** 119,2.22; **2** 128,13; **5** 124,7.30; **7** 127,11; **10** 131,1.2.3.5.14.15.16; **12** 132,30.31.32; 133,18; **18** 138,6; **19** 139,24; **20** 140,29; 141,4.5.8; **22** 142,31; **23** 143,14; 145,1; **25** 148,7. 20.<21>.23.24.29; 151,3; **26** 151,21;

29 158,8.11.12.21; 160,16.17.21; 161,10.13
terpein, give enjoyment, **14** 135,30; **23** 145,31; **26** 152,18
thalassa, sea, **12** 133,14
thanatos, death, **1** 119,29
tharrein, be bold, boldness, **27** 154,20
tharros, boldness, **24** 146,17; 147,9.14; **25** 150,3; **27** 154,4
theatron, theatre, **19** 139,20
theôrein, consider, **25** 150,30
theôrêtikos, theoretical, **25** 151,1
theôria, speculative thought, contemplation, **7** 127,28; **14** 135,10.15-16.17; **15** 136,25
theos, god, **9** 128,30; **20** 141,2
thêran, hunt, **25** 148,18
therapeuesthai, be treated (medically), **2** 121,7-8
thêriôdês, bestial, **7** 127,29
thermos, hot, **19** 139,17.18
thermotês, hotness, **4** 123,23
theros, summer, **24** 147,6
thlipsis, affliction, **5** 125,33.35; **6** 126,7.11.15
thrasutês, boldness, **27** 154,6; 156,20
thumos, anger, passion, **9** 130,15.17.18; **29** 159,27
timê, honour, **21** 141,29; **24** 146,22
timios, honourable, 118,2; **17** 137,22
tithenai, tithesthai, locate, place, 118,4; **18** 138,6-7.8; **20** 141,4; **23** 144,5; **29** 158,30; suppose, **5** 124,35; **23** 143,21
tode ti, see hode
topos, place, **30** 163,8; commonplace, **11** 131,23; 132,7.10.11
tragêmatizein, eat sweetmeats, **19** 139,21
trekhein, run, **25** 148,17; **27** 153,3
trepein, turn, **9** 130,21.23
trephein, trephesthai, nourish, take nourishment, **23** 144,22.25
tropê, turning, **29** 160,8
trophê, nourishment, **17** 138,4; **23** 144,22.23; **25** 149,23
tukhê, chance, **5** 124,36; **23** 143,20; **29** 160,10
tunkhanein, chance, happen to be, achieve, reach, arrive at, receive, **1** 119,2; **9** 130,5; **17** 137,30; **22** 143,4; **25** 148,9a; 150,8; **27** 154,2.5.8; **29** 160,19; 161,12; *tukhôn*, just any, **22** 143,8

xêrotês, dryness, **4** 123,23

zêmia, penalty, **18** 138,24.26

Index of Passages Cited

Numbers in **bold** type refer to the works cited; numbers in ordinary type refer to the pages of this book.

Subject Index

See also English-Greek Glossary and Index of Passages Cited. The Appendix (pp. 91-101) has been indexed here selectively, with emphasis on topics that concern Alexander and the *Ethical Problems*. References are to the pages of this book.

above and below, 47
absence: *see* privation
accident, opposed to essence, 24
acquittal, applies to voluntary rather than involuntary, 78
action: and choice, 36, 80; and compulsion, 42-3; and goal, 63, 68; and pleasure, 59; and utility, 52; and virtue, 61-2, 64-8, 70-5; voluntary and involuntary action, responsibility for actions, 8, 34-8, 42-3, 78; wrong actions, 34-8, 41, 54, 77-8; *see also* activity
activity: and character development, 77-8, 80; healthy activities, 70; and pleasure, 5 n.22, 19-20, 26-31, 43-6, 48-50, 52, 57-60; relation to utility, 54; and virtue, 61, 63, 76
actuality: and potentiality, 17-18, 23; actuality the basis for judgement, 17-18, 23
addition and subtraction, 70
Adrastus of Aphrodisias, 6-7 n.28, 93
adultery, never right, 74
advantage, advantageous: chosen even if unpleasant, 51; *see also* beneficial, usefulness
adze, how its being is determined, 24
affection, feeling: and quality, relation to opposition, 24; whether shame is an affection, 54-6; virtue and feelings, 61-2, 66-7, 69 n.240, 70-4; *see also* passion
affinity, between pleasures and activities, 27, 43, 49-50

affliction, pain defined as, 28-30
age, time of life: and shame, 54-6; *see also* children, young
agent, agency: *see* action
Alexander of Aphrodisias: life, 2; relation to Aristotle, 1-6, 10, 11, 99; school, 1-2, 4, *see also* school-discussions; style of writings, 7, 44 nn.133, 134, 136, 48 n.151, 84-5; techniques of argument, 2, 6, 21 n.22, 37 n.106, 46 n.142; treatment of predecessors 2, 99; use of Stoic terminology, 25 n.49, 36 n.100, 73 n.253; of Stoic definitions, of pleasure and distress, 29 n.67; of Stoic argument forms, 52 n.170, 81 n.283; his writings as evidence for Stoic arguments, 2, 21 n.22, 22 n.29, 99 n.37; commentary on Aristotle's *Ethics*?, 4 and n.20; *Ethical Problems*, title and nature of collection, 2-5, 15 and n.1; minor works, and their relation to commentaries, 2-4, 24 n.43, 56 n.181, 76 n.268; *see also* Index of Passages Cited
alienation: distress a sign of, 27; whether shame is alien for those who are older, 54-5
alteration, 83
ambiguity, what is said in many ways or in several senses, 28, 33-4 and n.89, 39-41 and nn.111,112; *see also* synonymous predication
ambition, 61; in argument, 71

133

optative with *an*, *see* potential optative

origin, principle, in compulsory and in voluntary action, 41-2, 78-9; *see also* principle

ousia, translation of, 9; *see also* being, essence

Owen, G.E.L., 34 n.89

pain: physical, and one type of distress, 25 n.48, 28-30; but distress a type of pain, 31; opposite to bodily pleasure, 30; taking pains, 30; pain for sake of what is noble, 48; pain produced by what is noble or virtuous, 50, 58; whether pain is to be avoided on own account, 50-1

pardon, for what is involuntary, 37

part, parts: relation to whole, 33-4, 75; parts or species, 40; mean not part of excess, 74

passion, 79; *see also* affection

pastime: *see* amusement

Pears, D., 61 n.203

Pembroke, S.G., 18 n.10

penalty, of refraining from pleasure for conventional reasons, 51; for misdeeds as a result of drunkenness, 78

perception of truth, 54; *see also* senses

perfection, not present at birth, 17-18; of best activity, 45; and virtue or excellence, 69-70; falling short of perfection in virtuous activity, 58; to be born with moral insight would be most perfect natural endowment, 77; *see also* completion

philosophy, moral, knowledge of happiness its starting point, 63

physics, relation to ethics, 5 n.22

pipe, pleasure from listening to, 20, 49

Pittacus of Mytilene, 77

place, change in, 83

Plato, 8 n.31, 24, 45 n.138; *see also* Index of Passages Cited

Platonists, 34 n.90; *see also* Neoplatonists

pleasure: (I) defined as unimpeded activity of natural state, 45, 57; as relaxation of the soul, 29-30; supervenes on activity, 19-20, 26-8, 30-2, 43-4, 48-9, 52, 57, 59-60; is as it were the end of activity, 19, 26-7, 31; but pleasure for sake of activity, 5 n.22, 58-9; pleasure and happiness, 57-8; pleasures derive value from activities, 19, 26, 31, 48-9, 60. (II)

differences among pleasures, 19-20, 26-32, 43- 4, 48-9, 52, 60; according to activities, 19-20, 26-8, 30-2, 43-4, 48-50, 52, 60; one pleasure hinders another, 20, 44, 49, 52; some to be chosen, some avoided 19, 30-2, 48, 50-1, 58-60; some good, some evil 25-33, 48, 50-2; what type of good pleasure is, 49-50; excess or moderation in pleasure, 30, 32-3, 61-2, 67, 71; natural and unnatural pleasures, 27- 9, 32; pleasure and nobility or shame, 31, 44, 45, 50-1, 58-60, 69. (III) pleasure and distress or pain, how opposed, 26- 33, 47-8, 60; pleasure distinct from absence of distress, 45- 7; pleasures mixed with distress, 60. (IV) pleasure and appetitive faculty, 67; pleasure only one among motives for choice, 51; bodily pleasure, 29-30, 32, 50, 58; and temperance, 61-2, 67, 71; pleasure in thought, 32, 45-6; in sense-perception, 46-7; in touch, 61-2, 71; in virtues, 30-1; yielding to pleasure as cause of wrong-doing, 35; actions done through pleasure not due to compulsion, 43, 78

political community, 1, 61-3

Posidonius, 29 n.67

possession, coming from privation, 25; possessions, acquisition of, 44

potential optative, 9, 21 n.23

potentiality, 16-18

poverty, not opposite to wealth, 25, cf. 23; not related to one's character in the same way as distress, 44; distressing for good man, 48

power, 42; in one's power, *see* responsibility

practical action, place in human happiness, 69 n.238

practical virtue, wisdom described as, 68

Praechter, K., 92 n.2

praise, praiseworthy: praiseworthy, class of goods, including virtuous activities, 49-50; even wrongdoers praise those who act rightly, 39; shame praiseworthy, 54; praiseworthy class of behaviour, 78

prayer, by mentally diseased, 35

preconceptions: *see* common notions

predication, of genus, 26, 34, 75; in relation to whole and part, 33-4, 75; of definition of virtue, 33-4, 75-6

preferred, to be, Stoic term, 16 n.5, 25 n.49; preference and choice, 80

words, *see* ambiguity

separability, of matter from form, denied, 82-3

Septuagint, *thlipsis* in, 29 n.67

series, 33, 34 n.90

several senses, said in: *see* ambiguity

sex, pleasure in: good as a faculty, 50; for preservation of species, 58-9

shame: whether a feeling or a disposition, 54-6; at which time of life it is appropriate, 54-6; whether the shameful is to be avoided in itself, 50-1; whether anything is shameful in its own right, 50-2; the shameful is recognised naturally, 52; knowledge of what is shameful, 78; those who begin to do wrong ashamed, 35; those who have developed the habit are not, 36; shameful pleasures, 51, 58-60; shameful activities bring distress to temperate, pleasure to profligate, 44; distress at shameful activities desirable, 31-2 and n.78

shamelessness, does not admit of a mean, 74

shape of world, 47

sharpness, of adze, opposite of bluntness, 24

shelter, makes art of building valuable, 62

skills, how acquired, 80-2

slackening of activities, 46

slave, how acquired, 39; place happiness in bodily enjoyments, 50, 58; not concerned with serious activities, 54

sleep, no sensation in, 46

smell, man's weak sense of, 46-7

softness, causes lack of self-control, 35

solstice, not object of deliberation, 79

Sorabji, R., 4 n.16, 11, 29 n.67, 30 n.71, 33 n.85, 34 n.89, 36 n.100, 37 n.106, 61 n.203, 62 n.207, 63 nn.210,212,214, 65 n.223, 66 n.227, 69 n.240, 81 n.284,92 n.1

soul: man composed of body and soul, 25; appetitive soul, 65-6; rational soul, its faculties and their virtues, 67-9; activities of soul, 58; soul and distress, 28-30; and pleasure, 29-30, 45 n.138; and happiness, 64-5; and virtue, 34, 65-9, 73; 'eye of the soul', moral insight, 52

sound bodily condition, and pleasure, 30; preserved by moderation in exercise, 66, 70, 73; *see also* health

spear, ignorance of its sharpness makes action involuntary, 78 n.276

species: relation of species to genus, 33, 75; genus to species as matter to form, 24 n.42; species of the involuntary, 40; of goods, 49-50; eternity of living creatures in species, 58-9

speculative thought, theory, theoretical enquiry: pleasure in, 32, 45-6; its objects, 47, 68; place in happy life, 69 n.238

speech, special to man, 10-11, 62-3

Spengel, L., 16 n.4, 19 n.16, 21 n.27, 29 n.64, 31 n.71, 35 n.96, 50 n.161, 58 n.190, 64 n.216, 65 n.221, 78 n.275, 83 n.288, 84-7

Speusippus, on pleasure, 45 n.138

spirit, greatness of, a virtue, 61

stability, of what is not easily changed, 22, 83

stars, number of, 47

state, contrasted with disposition, 56 n.180; *see also* in Greek-English Index under '*hexis*'

statue, and its parts, 75

Stobaeus, 5 n.24

Stoics, Stoicism: Alexander and Stoic theses, 2; his use of Stoic terminology, 25 n.49, 36 n.100, 73 n.253; of Stoic definitions, of pleasure and distress, 29 n.67; of Stoic argument forms, 52 n.170, 81 n.283; his writings as evidence for Stoic arguments, 2, 21 n.22, 22 n.29, 99 n.37; Stoics on absence of intermediate state between virtue and wickedness, 20-1 n.22, 22 nn.28,29, 25 n.49; on whether virtue can be lost, 21 nn.22; denying that virtue can be increased, 30 n.71; on progress to virtue, 73 n.253; on whether life is a good, 16 n.5; on endearment or affinity (*oikeiôsis*), 27 n.55; on pleasure and distress, 29 n.67; on whether pain is evil, 48 n.152; on elimination of passions, 69 n.240; on states and dispositions, 56 n.180; on common notions, 36 n.100; *see also* Arius Didymus

style of Alexander's writings, 7, 44 n.134; *see also* pronouns

substance, whether it has an opposite, 24 and n.43; coming-to-be of, 82-3

subtraction: *see* addition

sum: *see* totality

summaries (*epidromai*), 4, 6

survival of individual, 58; of species, 58-9

suspicion, 55